# Revitalising Leadership

T0384153

*Revitalising Leadership* connects leadership theory and practice with context. It argues that the universal prescriptions favoured by most leadership scholars ignore the reality that context always matters in leadership practice—and so it should matter in leadership theorising, too. Addressing this gap, the book offers a novel framework that enables the development of context-sensitive leadership theory and practice. This framework directs theoretical and practical attention to the key challenges for leadership in different organizational contexts. It involves developing a specific purpose for leadership in a given context, as well as formulating the values, norms and domains of action which should guide leadership efforts in that context. Determining these various matters then informs the role, responsibilities, rights, behaviours and attributes especially relevant to leaders and followers for that context and the focus, purpose and boundaries of the leader-follower relationship. Deploying this framework, six in-depth illustrative theorisations are provided, showing how leadership practice might best take shape in the contexts of supervisory management; HR management; innovation and entrepreneurship; strategy; governance; and leadership studies itself.

*Revitalising Leadership* will appeal to diverse audiences, due to its theoretical novelty, its diversity of illustrative examples, its practice-focussed orientation and its clear, engaging style. These include leadership scholars concerned with the lack of attention being paid to context in leadership theorising; organizational scholars wanting to learn how leadership thinking can be brought to bear on the different management functions the book explores; practitioners seeking leadership ideas that are tailored to the context they lead and follow in; and those involved in MBA or leadership development programmes who are looking to combine the personal reflection sought by such programmes with a thoughtful analysis of the context in which their leadership practice takes place.

**Suze Wilson is** a Senior Lecturer at the School of Management, Massey University, Palmerston North, New Zealand.

**Stephen Cummings** is a Professor of Strategic Management at Victoria University of Wellington, New Zealand.

**Brad Jackson** is Professor of Public and Community Leadership in the School of Government Victoria University of Wellington, New Zealand.

**Sarah Proctor-Thomson** is a Senior Lecturer in the School of Management at Victoria University of Wellington, New Zealand.

# Routledge Studies in Leadership Research

# Revitalising Leadership
Putting Theory and Practice
into Context

Suze Wilson
Stephen Cummings
Brad Jackson
Sarah Proctor-Thomson

Routledge
Taylor & Francis Group

LONDON AND NEW YORK

First published 2018 by Routledge

2 Park Square, Milton Park, Abingdon, Oxfordshire OX14 4RN

52 Vanderbilt Avenue, New York, NY 10017

*Routledge is an imprint of the Taylor & Francis Group, an informa business*

First issued in paperback 2019

*Library of Congress Cataloging-in-Publication Data*
Names: Wilson, Suze, author. | Cummings, Stephen, author. |
    Jackson, Brad, 1960– editor.
Title: Revitalising leadership : putting theory and practice
    into context / by Suze Wilson, Stephen Cummings,
    Brad Jackson, Sarah, Proctor-Thomson.
Description: New York : Routledge, [2017] | Includes index.
Identifiers: LCCN 2017013941| ISBN 9781138920040
    (hardback) | ISBN 9781315687438 (ebook)
Subjects: LCSH: Leadership.
Classification: LCC HD57.7 .W5465 2017 | DDC 658.4/092—dc23
LC record available at https://lccn.loc.gov/2017013941

ISBN: 978-1-138-92004-0 (hbk)
ISBN: 978-0-367-87264-9 (pbk)

Typeset in Sabon
by Apex CoVantage, LLC

# Contents

# Tables, Boxes, Diagrams, Figures and Images

## Tables

## Boxes

## Diagrams

## Figures

## Images

# Acknowledgements

Thanks go to my co-authors for their enthusiasm for this thought experiment into how we might revitalise leadership theory and practice and to my partner, Steve Harris, Mum and Dad and wider family for their unwavering support. *(Suze Wilson)*

To my Mum and Dad. *(Stephen Cummings)*

I'd like to acknowledge the special love and the moral support of my partner, Cristina Almeida Schumacher, as well as the inspiration provided by Leicester City Football Club in finally winning the English Premiership after 51 years of tireless support. It's amazing what 'Revitalised Leadership' can do! *(Brad Jackson)*

I would like to acknowledge and thank Ken Parry, who started me musing on leadership almost 20 years ago. I also want to express my love and thanks to my family: Alan, Scout and Trix. *(Sarah Proctor-Thomson)*

# 1 Why Revitalise Leadership?

## Introduction

> [T]he leadership field over the past decade has made tremendous progress in uncovering some of the enduring mysteries associated with leadership. . . . The period that leadership theory and research will enter over the next decade is indeed one of the most exciting in the history of this planet.
>
> (Avolio, Walumbwa & Weber, 2009, p. 442)

> Researchers seem content to ask smaller and smaller questions about fewer and fewer issues of genuine significance, producing statements of the blindingly obvious, the completely irrelevant or the palpably absurd.
>
> (Tourish, 2015, p. 137)

Our proposition is that the time has come to revitalise leadership, to radically rethink what should constitute its purpose, focus and the role it plays in our organizations. Far too often, those holding formal leadership positions, those who make the strategy, policy and resource allocation decisions, are leading in ways which frustrate or disappoint, or are pursuing objectives unlikely to provide a sustainably better life for those they claim to lead. Self-interest, not service to others, along with a focus on short-term results without regard to their longer-term consequences, takes precedence far too frequently.

We see these problems as being deeply systemic in nature, shaped in part by particular ways of thinking about and practicing leadership in organizations which have come to the fore in recent decades, and not simply the result of a few 'bad apples' in leadership roles. Convention now has it that organizational leadership takes for granted the primacy of a managerialist lens on organizational life and the capitalist imperative for endless growth (Alvesson, 1996; Parker, 2002). Often, only an *individual* leader's personal 'style' and the *short-term* results achieved on their watch are given detailed attention, thereby reinforcing ways of thinking and behaving which are 'functional' but also fundamentally 'stupid', given the *collective* effort needed for *long-term* organizational (and planetary) sustainability

(Alvesson & Spicer, 2012). Indeed, much of the focus of organizational leadership practice these days appears fundamentally directed toward enhancing profitability and preserving managerial status for the immediate future, whilst offering sufficient psycho-social support and developmental challenge to worker-followers to sustain their active involvement in this state of affairs. However, a questioning of the larger purposes and longer-term ends which organizational leaders pursue is increasingly necessary, given the problems posed to the capitalist 'logic' of never-ending growth and accumulation by climate change and the reality that ever-improving material wealth does not guarantee greater human happiness (Diener, Harter & Arora, 2010; Koch, 2015).

Simultaneously, though, in communities (and some organizations) all over the world, we are witnessing the growing incidence and impact of leadership which is not reliant on formal authority, rank and status, which speaks to shared concerns and often seeks to brings people together to advance otherwise forgotten or marginalised issues and interests (Kellerman, 2012). This kind of leadership effort is often focussed on achieving goals which reflect deeply held, value-based concerns. It is often grounded in a concern for larger purposes, such as securing justice, peace, democracy, freedom and empowerment of those whose interests are otherwise neglected, or the protection of the natural environment, and aims to mobilise and promote change for the betterment of all on a sustained basis (Eslen-Ziya & Erhart, 2015; Raelin, 2011, 2016). These developments, too, we understand as a systemic response to a changing world, one where many have grasped that 'the centre cannot hold' and that local initiative is both needed and can bring about real change. At the level of practice, then, we see both the best and worst of what leadership can offer all around us.

Meanwhile, if we look to the scholarly and popular literature on organizational leadership, it seems as if we are drowning in a sea of leadership theories, be they formal or more anecdotal in nature. While substantively new and different ways of thinking about leadership have emerged in recent years (e.g., Grint, 2000, 2005a, 2005b; Ladkin, 2010; Raelin, 2003, 2016; Sinclair, 2007, 2015), the mainstream of scholarly effort largely comprises competing recipes prescribing how manager-leaders should craft their selves in bold and heroic terms in order to advance their careers (Alvesson & Kärreman, 2016; Wilson, 2016). This excessive and often exclusive focus on the personal characteristics or style of the leader both reflects and feeds a recognised leader-centric bias in our thinking (Meindl, Ehrlich & Dukerich, 1985). Simultaneously, it encourages a grandiose, narcissistic mindset amongst leaders (Alvesson & Gabriel, 2016; Tourish, 2013), crowds out a proper appreciation of the crucial influence of followers (Kelley, 1992) and pays scant heed to the varying contexts in which leadership work takes place (Osborn, Hunt & Jauch, 2002). Yet if 'leadership' is constituted as nothing more than a project of rendering the self more perfect so as to enable career advancement, shaping the self in ways that align to whatever approach or style constitutes the latest leadership fad, then something so self-absorbed in its focus likely offers little in terms of advancing collective well-being.

To respond to these various concerns, our argument is that we must revitalise leadership. We believe we must develop new and different ways of thinking about the purpose, focus and role of leadership in organizations, in order to help inform changes in leadership practice. We want to explore here how leadership can be crafted in a *variety* of ways that directly address the key challenges which arise in different contexts. This implies a re-appraisal of the expectations we have of leaders and followers, including the powers, rights and responsibilities we give to them. It means thinking, too, about the limits of leadership, resisting the temptation to romanticise its powers and potential or to treat it as the magic bullet that can solve every problem.

With this book, our goal is to demonstrate why we must and how we can revitalise leadership theory and practice. Our focus is on offering a new way of theorising leadership, theorising that can genuinely inform practice though paying attention to the particular matters which are of salience to leadership in different settings. Rather than another generic recipe intended to shape the self of the leader, what we set out here is a flexible suite of ingredients that addresses multiple dimensions of leadership, such as its purpose, underpinning values and norms, role and responsibilities, and demonstrating how these matters can be configured variably to meet the needs of particular organizational contexts. We formulate approaches to leadership shaped by the diverse range of challenges and needs which arise in the context of different organizational roles and functions. Our approach derives from what we call *leadership-practice-in-context*, the idea that leadership is only of value if it is shaped by, and responds to, the needs of a particular context.

For over a century, leadership scholars have, by and large, directed their efforts at producing theories which they claim to have universal applicability. They have assumed leadership is something 'natural', something that has an enduring 'essence'—even though they also keep changing their minds about what that 'essence' might be (Kelly, 2013; Wilson, 2016). The predominant focus has been on the psychology of the leader—their behaviours, personality, cognitive habits, influencing and communicative style and such like. And, the concern has routinely been that of leader effectiveness considered narrowly in terms of its impact on worker productivity, morale and organizational commitment (Sinclair, 2007; Wilson, 2016).

All these matters have been examined extensively, but much less attention has gone to addressing the contextual dimensions which are salient to and shape leadership practice. The larger purpose and substantive results that leadership in a given context might be called on to achieve, beyond an effect on followers' perceptions and feelings, has largely been ignored (Kempster, Jackson & Conroy, 2011; Porter & McLaughlin, 2006). Here, we reject the universalist, essentialist, a-contextual paradigm which has dominated leadership studies over the last century and instead offer a theoretical framework and exemplar theorisations which are grounded in a new approach—a *contextualised theorising* of leadership, where 'leadership' is understood as something that can be *constructed or invented* in an endless variety of ways (see also Wilson, 2016). We seek to build on and extend leadership research which has taken contextual issues seriously, resulting in formulations that have a direct and deep connection with specific settings (e.g., Faris & Parry, 2011; Hannah, Uhl-Bien, Avolio & Cavarretta, 2009; Quick & Wright, 2011).

When we speak of *contextualised theorising*, we mean theorising which hones in on, and is tailored to, particular contexts and issues. We are taking leadership theory local, you might say, enabling us to pay attention to the challenges of *leadership-practice-in-context* in different organizational settings, using this to craft a leadership approach designed for the particular demands of various roles and functions within organizations. For us, the context is the stage, the setting in which leadership occurs, so we therefore take it as the starting point for our thinking about what approach to leadership is likely to be of value. The salient aspects for leadership of a given context are, of course, contestable, as is what is constituted as leadership (Grint, 2000), so recognising the futility of prescriptive precision our theorising is deliberately heuristic in tenor.

When we say we understand leadership as something *constructed or invented*, we connect to the philosophical stance of nominalism and to postmodernist, post-structuralist perspectives more generally, in two key ways. Firstly, we understand social reality as itself being (constantly) constructed or invented, rather than the inevitable consequence of natural causes. For us, social reality has an historically specific yet fluid form and is open to competing interpretations (Blaikie, 2000, 2007; Dickens, 2013; Potter, 2013). Arising from this, 'leadership' is likewise something that is (constantly) constructed rather than derived from nature and is historically specific, fluid and open to competing interpretations.

Secondly, we treat what is commonly said and believed to be true—discursive regimes—as influential forces shaping how social reality gets constructed, irrespective of whether a given discourse is empirically correct or not (Foucault, 1977, 1978). This means ideas about leadership matter regardless of their veracity, for discursive regimes shape what is accepted as constituting leadership. As a consequence of these understandings, it becomes possible to conceive of 'leadership' as something that has already been constructed and invented in many different ways, ways that can be found in the various discursive regimes which speak of leadership—and to which we now add our efforts.

In our approach, rather than simply maintain the conventional focus on the self of the leader, we seek to be more expansive in the factors our theorising addresses. Consequently, we consider the kinds of *challenges* thrown up by different organizational contexts, to which leadership may be constructed to offer some response. Specifically, we examine leadership in the context of operational-level supervision, the HRM function, innovation and entrepreneurship, strategy, governance, and leadership studies itself, arguing each of these settings offers specific challenges and possibilities for how leadership can be conceived and practiced. We explore the *purpose* of leadership in these different contexts and the *values and norms* that we argue, normatively, ought to inform it, as well as the *domains* of action within that context where it might usefully contribute. We identify personal *attributes and behaviours* that, given the preceding points of analysis, we see as especially salient to those engaging in leadership work in each of these different contexts, whilst recognising that someone's identity as 'leader' or 'follower' is fluid and contestable. We also look at the *roles, rights and responsibilities* of both leaders and followers in these different contexts and the nature of the *relationship* to be forged between them.

We are concerned, then, about the substantive results to which leadership efforts may contribute and how those results are to be achieved. In this approach a concern with psychological issues of individual behaviour has a role to play, but does not dominate the scene. Instead, we bring in sociological, political, ethical and philosophical concerns about what leadership does for and to us. However, what emerges as salient is not presumed universal in nature but, rather, varies in the different contexts of leadership practice that we will explore.

Our approach is informed, also, by our commitment to the constructive value of critical thinking—thinking which questions what is normally taken-for-granted. This critical orientation is not about being hostile to leaders or leadership, but it does mean we question the faith which many now seem to have that leadership is the answer to every problem (Alvesson & Kärreman, 2016; Wilson, 2016). Consistent with the broader tradition of critical social science, it also means we are attentive to issues of power in its many and various forms, as well as issues of justice, equality, freedom and democratic participation (Alvesson & Deetz, 2000; Alvesson, Bridgman & Willmott, 2009). These are issues which any serious effort to examine leadership cannot avoid, in our view, as to hold a leadership role is to be in a position of power relative to others, while participating in leadership work which advances a particular outcome carries with it the ethical duty to consider what means may legitimately be used and whose or what interests are served through that (Ciulla, 1995; Price, 2003). Unfortunately, in our opinion, much of the scholarly and popular leadership literature has adopted a much narrower, functionalist orientation, in which the primary concern is essentially about how 'leadership' results in greater productivity (Alvesson, 1996; Sinclair, 2007). We are not opposed to productive workplaces: clearly, un-productive workplaces are an exercise in frustration and wastefulness. However, we join with others who argue that thinking seriously about leadership demands sustained attention to its social, political and ethical dimensions (e.g., Ciulla, 2004; Gosling & Mintzberg, 2003; Ladkin, 2010; Sinclair, 2007), and so we unapologetically bring these matters into our approach.

Having thus far offered you a very brief precis of what this book is about, then, in the balance of this chapter, we explore aspects of the leadership literature which have informed the focus and approach taken. We begin by offering a broad historical review which highlights how the wider context has, in fact, always played a key part in shaping leadership thought and practice, and how contextual issues have traditionally been treated in leadership knowledge. This, we hope, will sow seeds of doubt on the common belief that modern leadership knowledge develops via the production and accumulation of objective evidence and the elimination of error, by highlighting wider contextual forces that inform where, how and on what issues leadership scholars focus their efforts (Trethewey & Goodall, 2007; Wilson, 2016). We then examine major trends in the leadership studies field as of today, offering a critique of the dominant 'leadership science' approach before honing in on the emerging new paradigm in leadership studies which informs our approach. To demonstrate the potential of heuristic theorising, we explore some key texts from this paradigm which adopt this approach, before turning to examine how an engagement with contextual issues has been addressed in some recent studies. We conclude this chapter by explaining how the book is organized and identifying who may find it relevant.

## Issues of Context in Leadership Knowledge

The Western study of leadership has a long history in which what is claimed to be the truth about leadership has undergone continuous revision, at each stage reflecting particular values, norms and concerns which were influential at that point in time (for an extended analysis of this history, see Wilson, 2016). In ancient and medieval times, leadership knowledge was produced via the holistic combining of what we would today conceptualise as philosophy, ethics, religion, political science, sociology and psychology (e.g., Erasmus, 2010; Lipsius, 2004; Plato, 1995, 2007; Xenophon, 1997, 2006). Moreover, leadership scholars in these times produced knowledge that did not abstract the leader from their context: the concern was not simply the desired personal attributes of leaders and issues of leadership technique but, also, the provision of advice and insights that directly addressed the substantive issues leaders faced and the particular goals they ought to pursue. Heads of state were the main point of interest at this time, with some limited attention also going to military leadership, while connections were sometimes drawn to those with expertise or authority to lead in other settings, such as ships' captains, doctors, farmers, priests and heads of household estates.

## Classical Greek Knowledge

Aristotle, Plato and Xenophon provide advice for heads of state in relation to a wide variety of substantive issues involved in governing a city state, as well as addressing the personal qualities of leaders and how they ought to conduct themselves to best effect (Aristotle, 2009; Plato, 1995, 2007;

Xenophon, 1997, 2006). For these scholars, leadership is understood to be a rare and exclusively male quality which is a gift of the gods; hence leaders are imbued with the spark of the divine. The philosopher-king-warrior is constituted as the ideal, one who knows, loves and pursues the truth, governs decisively without pandering to popular opinion and possesses a soldier's strength, discipline and tolerance for hardship (Plato, 1995, 2007; Xenophon, 2006). Followers, however, are said to be lacking in such qualities to varying degrees and, therefore, are expected to act in accordance with the leader's directives, without scope for debate: deference to a superior being is, thus, the proposition being advanced.

The leader's role here, as the one who knows best, was to determine all matters which could affect the well-being of the people and the state. This, in turn, required extensive knowledge by leaders of such diverse matters as statecraft, agriculture, town planning, warfare, religious practices to keep the gods happy and child-rearing, these all being matters on which leadership scholars could be expected to formulate advice. To fulfil this demanding set of duties, leaders were expected to live an ascetic existence in which personal pleasure was effectively prohibited: the demand was that every waking hour should be directed toward protecting and advancing the interests of the people and the state. While leadership here entailed complete and absolute power over others, this was simultaneously paired with the expectation that a leader's exclusive focus be on serving the interests of those he led. Consequently, leaders were positioned as both master and servant, and perhaps even slave, to those they led (Wilson, 2013, 2016).

The wider context shaping the formation of these ways of thinking about leadership and its practice was the continuous political and military upheavals which plagued the ancient Greek world, along with its epistemological, ontological and cultural assumptions and religious beliefs (Grant, 1991; Morris & Powell, 2006; Wilson, 2013, 2016). Emerging from these influences, 'leadership' is positioned as offering truth, morality and the answer to every problem for a world racked by conflict and uncertainty. The nature of leadership as constructed here is an approach that comprehensively reflects the values, norms and issues that were seen as salient to this particular context. These truths about leadership were inventions, designed to address concerns which their inventors held dear. This, we argue, remains fundamentally the case even unto today.

Politically, the legitimacy of the Athenian democracy was undermined by claims that leaders are divinely gifted beings incapable of wrong doing, for its ideal of equality (amongst wealthy men of the aristocracy, at least) is thereby reconstituted as something contrary to the natural, divine, truth and morality which is leadership (Wilson, 2013, 2016). The death of Socrates, mentor to Plato and Xenophon, in response to sedition charges laid by the Athenian democracy offers a personal motivation for such a move, one that is supplemented by a general concern by these scholars to advance the interests of the aristocratic class (Grant, 1991; Morris & Powell, 2006; Wilson, 2013, 2016). From the ancient Greeks, then, we learn that it is possible to produce an account of leadership which is deeply informed by one's socio-cultural, intellectual and political context and which provides substantive and personal guidance for leaders on how to navigate in this context. This knowledge, of course, is not free of political value, intent or effect, nor will it have universal applicability. Instead, its relevance and credibility derives from the connections it makes to values and issues of high salience to the context to which it seeks to respond.

## Medieval Knowledge

In the medieval era, scholars such as Calvin (2010), Erasmus (2010), Lipsius (2004), Luther (2010) and Machiavelli (2005) likewise directed their attention to the substantive issues faced by leaders who were heads of state, as well as to analysis of the desirable personal qualities of such leaders and issues of leadership technique. Monarchy was then the most common form of governance in Europe, and the truth about leadership could be found in a genre of books known as 'mirrors for princes' (Gilbert, 1938; Morrow, 2005; Skinner, 2002). An estimated 1,000 such texts were written between 800 and 1700 AD, and they were widely read amongst the elite classes (Gilbert, 1938; Lambertini, 2011). The general purpose of these texts was to issue guidance to princes on how best to lead, knowledge which, in turn, also helped to inform those with whom princes regularly engaged as to their needs and what might be expected of them. The particular texts our analysis focusses on originate from the 16th century, when the Renaissance and the Reformation gave rise to significant social, political, religious and intellectual change (Craigie, 1950; Gilbert, 1938; Skinner, 2002).

At this time leadership was again tied to the masculine and the divine, as kings and princes were understood to be an instrument of God's will, indeed their special standing in God's eyes was central to the legitimacy of their status and role. (e.g., Erasmus, 2010; James VI, 1950; Lipsius, 2004). As with the ancient Greek approach, leadership knowledge here addressed the whole of the leader's life from cradle to grave and included both their official, public efforts and their personal conduct. The scrutiny of the leader implied by this holistic view extended to include God himself, with the warning being issued that "the judgement after death is not the same for all: none are treated more sternly . . . than those who were powerful. No other achievement will better enable you to win God's favour than if you show yourself to be a beneficial prince to your people" (Erasmus, 2010, pp. 18–19). In contemporary terms, a kind of multi-rater feedback process is thus envisaged, in which God and the people judge the leader for how well he has served their interests.

Defining the 'virtues' of leaders was a key focus at this time, with scholars offering various prescriptions. Table 1.1 below summarises three such models, offered by Calvin (2010), Erasmus (2010) and Lipsius (2004). What is notable is how these virtues speak to an underlying concern to

*Table 1.1* 16th-century European leadership virtues

| Calvin's model | Erasmus's model | Lipsius's model |
| --- | --- | --- |
| Integrity | Wisdom | Virtue |
| Prudence | A sense of justice | • Modesty |
| Clemency | Personal restraint | • Majesty |
| Moderation | Foresight | • Ensure justice |
| Innocence | Concern for the public well-being | • Prefer clemency |
| | | Prudence (force + virtue) |
| | | • Military prudence |
| | | • Civil prudence |

Source: Calvin, 2010; Erasmus, 2010; Lipsius, 2004

ensure leaders exercised their extensive powers in a considered, just manner. One key purpose of leadership knowledge here, then, is to seek to constrain what leaders can legitimately do.

Beyond the focus on the self of the leader, though, substantive issues of statecraft, warfare, religious doctrine and public policy were also key concerns for leadership knowledge and practice (e.g., Erasmus, 2010; James VI, 1950; Lipsius, 2004). Issues of *realpolitik*, concerned with the maintenance of the leader's position through the exercise of techniques such as inciting fear, being deceitful and acting with cunning were also addressed (Lipsius, 2004; Machiavelli, 2015). To develop this broad and diverse capability, considerable focus is given over to the leader's education from their birth onwards. This education is not only to ensure the leader is equipped to perform his duties, but also to prevent him being wrongly swayed by poor advice or polluted by bad influences, such as are said to be posed by the great majority of people. Distance from followers is considered important in order to maintain the leader's majesty, focus and purity (Erasmus, 2010; James VI, 1950).

Medieval leadership scholars needed to tread carefully, given the powers of their key audience routinely extended to issues of life and death decided according to their personal judgement (Allen, 1951; Cameron, 2001; Skinner, 2002). Yet the growing tensions between Church and state arising from the Reformation, and within and between states, often due to competing dynastic ambitions, were such as to make this a dangerous time for leaders (Cameron, 2001; Gunn, 2001; Jardine, 2010). In this context, scholars went to considerable effort to connect their ideas about leadership to the moral, ethical and religious code of their day. They commonly sought to promote an approach which constituted a considered, stabilising response to the varying substantive issues and threats that leaders were facing, although boldness was also sanctioned in regard to some issues (Erasmus, 2010; Lipsius, 2004; Machiavelli, 2015). Politically, an acceptance of the monarchical system of governance was assumed, thereby helping to sustain its legitimacy. As part of this, accepting or promoting a divine foundation for kingly leadership and advocating the importance for leaders to work in the interests of the people, aided in justifying the limitations that were placed on the political rights of the population.

From our review thus far what we see, then, is that the nature of leadership knowledge in both the ancient and medieval world entailed a detailed consideration of the context in which leaders were situated as a central concern for scholars seeking to explain the nature of leadership and offer advice to leadership practitioners. Questions of both the means and the ends of leadership were considered. Both leaders and their particular context were analysed. Normative considerations were not separated out when addressing these matters. This holistic basis for theorising leadership reflected the epistemological norms of these times, in which the modern separation of fact and value simply made no sense.

## The Emergence of 'Leadership Science'

It is not until Carlyle's influential work, first published in 1840, that we see the beginning of the turning away by leadership scholars from the substantive issues which arise in the context of actual practice and a narrowing in on leader psychology (Carlyle, 1993; Wilson, 2016). This development, of course, coincides with the general splintering of disciplines one from another as modern social science first emerges, bringing with it the adoption of a 'natural science' epistemology, in which leadership is understood as something which can be accounted for in objective ways, free from researcher bias (Gordon, 1981; Spoelstra, Butler & Delaney, 2016; Winch, 1967). In leadership studies, this development finds its first full expression in Galton's Social Darwinian and statistical approach to the identification of the traits of exceptional men (yes, men), an orientation and methodology which heavily influenced the subsequent five decades of focus on leader traits (Galton, 1892, 1970; Smith & Krueger, 1932; Stogdill, 1948; Wilson, 2016).

Subsequent major developments in the field, such as emergence of behavioural theories, contingency/situational theories and 'new leadership' approaches, which emphasise notions of vision, charisma, transformation and, more recently, authenticity, have also developed primarily via a 'natural sciences' epistemology (Alvesson, 1996; Jackson & Parry, 2011; Wilson, 2016). Hence, the conventional narrative has it that modern leadership studies progresses via the careful and objective accumulation of evidence which enables the elimination of ignorance and error and brings us ever close to the truth about leadership (e.g., Avolio et al., 2009; Huczynski & Buchanan, 2006). The concern with precision and measurement, which is a key feature of this epistemological paradigm, is a major reason why grappling with complex, dynamic contexts has proved problematic for contemporary leadership scholars. However, wider contextual influences, not simply the accumulation of evidence, have continued to be crucial influences shaping major developments in the field.

The shift from trait to behavioural theory around the end of WWII, for example, is commonly credited to Stogdill's (1948) review of the trait literature (Bass, 2008; Huczynski & Buchanan, 2006). Yet a careful reading of Stogdill's review shows he is not as damning of trait theory as is now commonly assumed, for he identifies a number of traits which he reports multiple studies had shown as having a strong association with leadership. In fact, the project leader of the team where Stogdill then worked, Shartle, reports that a shift in focus onto leader behaviour was one he identified as important by war's end, some three years prior to the publication of Stogdill's review (see Shartle, 1979; also Bowers & Seashore, 1966, confirm this same timing). This decision, we suggest, constitutes an astute and pragmatic reading by Shartle of the post-war political context, in which claims of natural superiority *a là* trait theory likely sounded suspiciously close to Nazi ideology. Moving the focus onto leader behaviour thus provided a politically acceptable way forward for leadership scholars at this time, rather than this development emerging simply in response to clear evidence of the problems with trait theory (Wilson, 2016).

The later shift from trait to contingency/situational approaches was partly informed by evidence (see, in particular, Korman's damning 1966 review of the Ohio State leader behaviour model). However, the intellectually fashionable status of contingency thinking at that time was also an important influence (Reed, 2006; Wilson, 2016; Wren, 2005). Notably, a number of contingency/situational theories continued the focus on tasks and relationships, which were the core elements of behavioural theories, despite Korman's findings, again indicating issues other than evidence were shaping the research agenda (e.g. Fiedler, 1967; Hersey & Blanchard, 1974; House, 1971). Meanwhile, the assumptions made about followers in contingency/situational theories, whereby they are now seen as potentially difficult to manage, reflects a response to the growing challenge to authority which emerged as part of the counter-culture at that same time (Ackerman, 1975; Cornuelle, 1975; Roos, 1972; Wilson, 2016). Wider contextual influences, then, rather than simply the accumulation of evidence, are again influential here in how leadership is understood and what we expect from it.

In a similar vein, the emphasis of 'new leadership' approaches, which focus on 'vision', 'transformation', 'charisma' and 'authenticity', also reflects challenges and concerns that go well beyond matters of evidence (Bass, 1985; Burns, 1978; Bennis & Nanus, 1985; House, 1977; Luthans & Avolio, 2003). These ideas first emerged at a time when America was facing a series of political, military and business challenges which threw into doubt its ability to sustain its world dominating position (Ackerman, 1975; Hodgson, 2005; Magaziner & Reich, 1982). Dramatic changes were thought to be needed and 'new leadership' approaches are strongly oriented toward the achievement of change. They also often drew on by-then widely accepted cultural assumptions about human potential for growth and change, promising to foster this amongst followers (Burns, 1978; Gitlin,

1993; Hall, 2005). This focus on change and personal development likely helps to sustain the continued popularity of these approaches through to the present day, aligning as they do with the requirements of capitalism and the focus of contemporary culture on self-development (Alvesson & Kärreman, 2016; Wilson, 2016).

In the era of 'leadership science', then, the focus of theorising continues to be shaped by issues of wider social salience, even at the same time as such issues are not overtly acknowledged or addressed in such theorisations. Indeed, we now have the paradoxical situation whereby theories that claim a basis in science and to offer universally applicable prescriptions, are, in their basic orientation, derived from non-scientific and historically specific contextual influences. This occurs at the same time as such theories routinely ignore contextual considerations in their prescriptions for leadership practice, due to their epistemological and methodological commitments. A key problem is the lack of attention to basic assumptions (Alvesson & Kärreman, 2016; Spoelstra et al., 2016; Wilson, 2016). The desire for precise 'scientific' findings has led to a situation whereby "sterile preoccupations dominate the literature" and "the identification of ever more mediating processes and moderating factors takes precedence over interrogating fundamental assumptions" (Tourish, 2015, citing Van Knippenberg and Sitkin, p. 137). The end result is a field of studies where its mainstream of effort now suffers from "unrelenting triviality" (Tourish, 2015, p. 138).

## Leadership Studies Today and the Problem With 'Leadership Science'

Focussing now on the current state of play, three key trends are evident in the field of organizational leadership studies today and thus warrant discussion. The first key trend is the sustained, incremental development of a range of now well-established theories, theoretical perspectives or approaches to the study of leadership. This Kuhnian 'normal science' is continuously expanding and refining established theories, mostly by seeking out further dependent, mediating and moderating variables via empirical methods and hypothetico-deductive logics of inquiry (Alvesson, 1996; Hunter, Bedell-Avers & Mumford, 2007). Within this, neo-charismatic (i.e. 'new leadership') theories were identified in an influential review of *The Leadership Quarterly* as the single largest category used in studies published in that key journal for the period 2000–2009 (Gardner, Lowe, Moss, Mahoney & Cogliser, 2010). Other long-established approaches also attracted continued attention, such as trait, behavioural, cognitive and multi-level perspectives (Gardner et al., 2010).

The second key trend is the rapid proliferation of new avenues of research and theorisation which, simultaneously, remain committed to the epistemological and methodological expectations of 'leadership science'. This development has seen attention shifting to studying leadership in conjunction with some other related phenomenon, such as emotions, strategy, change, creativity and innovation, or to studying leadership in particular settings, such as in teams or in political and public service roles (Gardner et al., 2010). Ethical, servant, spiritual and authentic leadership theories have also garnered growing attention by 'leadership science' (Gardner et al., 2010).

Despite these two trends, however, the assumptions and limitations of 'leadership science' which inform both of them have come under increasing challenge. The scientific approach is fundamentally concerned to identify 'fact not opinion' (Atwater, Mumford, Schriesheim & Yammarino, 2014, p. 1174), thus relying on the problematic understanding that phenomena deemed 'facts' are somehow beyond legitimately variable interpretations and not subject to the arbitrary influence of social construction as to their very existence (Hacking, 1999; Foucault, 1970; Spoelstra et al., 2016). It typically regards the appropriate domain and focus of social science to be concerned with what is empirically 'true', while philosophy, politics and religion are left to deal with the murky issue of determining what is (morally) 'good' or acceptable (Gordon, 1981; Saul,1983; Winch, 1967). At the same time, of course, what is on offer from 'leadership science' is not actually value free but, rather, has typically served organizational interests in the post-WWII era by way of its concern to improve worker performance (Sinclair, 2007; Trethewey & Goodall, 2007; Wilson, 2016). This effort to serve the interests of capitalism and managerialism is partisan, even ideological, in orientation, yet these matters are readily camouflaged behind a wall of statistics (Alvesson & Kärreman, 2016; Wilson, 2016).

The focus of 'leadership science' goes to identifying correlations between precisely defined and de-contextualised features of social reality, which are rendered into constructs and variables for quantitative analysis. Parsimony in theorising is *de rigour*, from which precise propositions and hypotheses emerge for testing, validation and, eventually, conversion into a psychometric or some other instrument intended to offer standardised application in manager assessment and development (Alvesson, 1996; Spoelstra et al., 2016; Wilson, 2016). This approach, which is broadly consistent with the mainstream approach of the wider field of management and organization studies, thus suffers from the "ongoing fetishization of positivist methodologies and functionalist perspectives", a state of affairs which has become "institutionalized by a deference to supposedly leading US journals" (Tourish, citing Wilkinson and Durden, 2015, p 138).

In 'leadership science', considerable effort goes to claiming impartiality and objectivity as regards data and its analysis (Atwater et al., 2014). Yet, the credibility of the epistemological underpinnings of all this effort have long been in contention. Gordon (1981), for example, identifies that while the natural sciences provide the reference point by which the social sciences are conventionally judged, "there is no agreement concerning the epistemic foundations of the natural sciences" (p. 635). The ready confidence that 'leadership science' constitutes a viable, credible approach to a phenomenon that is so open to varying interpretation, and is so imbued with the problem of power, has attracted sustained critique, yet the scientific project nonetheless continues to dominate the field (Alvesson & Kärreman, 2016; Wilson, 2016).

The pervasive assumption in 'leadership science' that its object of inquiry is part of 'human nature' and thus possesses timeless and universal qualities routinely obscures a proper appreciation of the socially constructed nature of how our ideas about leadership come to pass (Alvesson, 1996; Wilson, 2016). The alternative viewpoint that we adopt here is, we think, the most plausible explanation for why leadership theories have kept changing over the last 2,500 years: not because we are steadily progressing toward understanding "The Truth" about leadership but, rather, because 'leadership', whatever that term is taken to mean, is something continuously re-invented to meet the needs of a changing society.

None of this, of course, should be taken to imply we think 'anything goes' when it comes to theorising and practising leadership, or that careful, logical reasoning and the accumulation of evidence to inform our thinking ought to be abandoned. However, these efforts will not bring us to the kind of certainty which 'leadership science' desires or claims to offer. Norms and values, while being fundamentally historically and culturally contingent in nature (Foucault, 1970), also provide anchor points to enable a given community of interest to assess whether a particular approach to leadership theory or practice is to be considered legitimate and helpful or otherwise. Indeed, ensuring the ethical and normative basis of leadership theory and practice is rendered visible, and hence readily open to challenge, is something we hope our framework (which we examine in Chapter 2) facilitates.

However, with the splintering of disciplines one from another in the modern era and the adoption by most modern leadership scholars of a 'natural science' epistemology, a narrow focus on leader psychology has been dominant: the question of what ends leaders might pursue is simply not territory into which most leadership scholars now venture (Kempster, Jackson & Conroy, 2011; Wilson, 2016). This has resulted in much contemporary leadership knowledge being concerned with issues of technique, with addressing questions of 'how to lead', or on assessing the immediate effects of leader attributes and actions on followers. Difficult and unavoidably normative and political questions about purpose, values and the appropriate limits of leadership are largely ignored, as such matters cannot be so readily reduced to survey questions for statistical analysis (Alvesson, 1996; Wilson, 2016).

Reflecting these kind of concerns with the 'leadership science' project, then, the third trend now apparent in the leadership studies field is the emergence of approaches which, in part or in full, reject its epistemological and methodological demands and constraints. These new lines of research are interpretive, social constructionist and/or critical in orientation (Bryman, 2004; 2011; Collinson, 2011; Tourish, 2015). We turn now to consider these developments in more detail.

## A New Paradigm in Leadership Studies

Over the last two decades, more and more leadership scholars, including ourselves, have come to reject, in part or in full, the assumptions and commitments entailed by the 'leadership science' approach discussed above. Epistemologically and methodologically this has seen a much greater openness to using different, typically qualitative, approaches, along with the development of theory and research that is often critical of the constraints of parsimony, precision, replicability and generalisability demanded by 'leadership science' (Bryman, 2004; 2011; Collinson, 2011). A willingness to forego a degree of precision in favour of ideas and findings that resonate as offering real insight for understanding and action is an important feature of these developments, helping to pave the way for approaches such as we adopt here.

A move away from a leader-centric focus is also a marked feature of this trend, resulting in a new, loosely aligned paradigm where leadership is conceptualised in processual, practice, relational, emergent, discursive, pluralistic or distributed terms, all of which de-centre the leader as the primary source of leadership (e.g., Crevani, Lindgren & Packendorff, 2010; Denis, Langley & Sergi, 2012; Fairhurst, 2007, 2009; Gronn, 2000; Hosking, 2007; Raelin, 2011; Uhl-Bien & Ospina, 2012). Indeterminacy, contestation and complexity are seen here as central characteristics of both leadership research and practice, meaning no 'one best way' or definitive 'truth' about leadership is deemed possible (Gosling & Mintzberg, 2003; Grint, 2000, 2005a, 2005b; Sinclair, 2007; Uhl-Bien, Russ & McKelvey, 2007). Leader and follower selves and identities are understood as fluid, multi-faceted and always in a state of construction: from moment to moment, the question of who is the leader and who is the follower is no longer seen as certain or fixed (Ford, Harding & Learmonth, 2008; Ladkin, 2010; Nicholson & Carroll, 2013). The rejection of heroic, leader-centric and, hence, white, masculinist thought and practice is accepted as critical, too, to help reduce the barriers to women's leadership or that of people from minority cultures (Liu & Baker, 2016; Stead & Elliott, 2009). Sensitivity to context as something which shapes leadership practice is a further feature of this paradigm: we consider this aspect in more depth later in the chapter.

Broadly speaking, we see this book as being part of this new paradigm, and we are supportive of its desire to 'open up' leadership thought and practice in more nuanced, variable and inclusive ways. Where we think our distinctive contribution lies is that while these different approaches provide a variety of ways to conceptualise the basic character of leadership (as a process, as a practice, as a relationship, as an emergent quality of groups, as discursive, for example), thereby enabling close and precise study of its enactment using such viewpoints, efforts to formulate broader, multi-dimensional theories of leadership which are philosophically consistent with these kinds of basically inclusive assumptions have been rather less common. Mostly, effort goes to theorising the specific empirical material uncovered by a given study, focussing on the micro-level of the enactment of leadership, in order to contribute to the incremental, inductive development of the perspective being deployed (e.g., Fisher & Robbins, 2015; Mailhot, Gagnon, Langley & Binette, 2016).

We support the value of these efforts to contribute to knowledge, accepting they constitute a form of Kuhnian 'normal science', albeit without the quantitative, functionalist, epistemological and methodological straight-jackets of 'leadership science'. However, to generate broader, multi-dimensional theories and perspectives as guides for understanding, Keith Grint (2000, 2005a, 2005b), Amanda Sinclair (2007) and Donna Ladkin (2010) have provided heuristic models which we highlight here, as they serve as inspiration for the kind of approach to theorising which we offer in the next chapter. Each is concerned with establishing ways of theorising the leadership phenomena that can powerfully frame our way of understanding it and offer a non-prescriptive, but still informative, guide to practice and research.

In terms of the key conceptual categories that have salience to understanding the character of leadership, Grint has put forward several approaches. Framing leadership as something socially constructed and a site of ongoing contestation, Grint argues that issues of identity, strategic vision and tactics are central to leaders' engagement with followers, which, in turn, relies on persuasive communication (2000). Conceptually, he argues that productive responses to these demands can be developed through an appreciation of philosophy, the fine arts, the martial arts and the performing arts respectively. Another approach offered by Grint addresses the kinds of problems faced in the exercise of leadership and whether these are constructed as 'wicked', 'tame' or 'critical' in nature (2005a). The interpretation taken of a problem informs whether 'leadership', 'management' or 'command' constitutes the 'appropriate' response, all the while accepting that indeterminacy as to the nature of the problem and what constitutes a useful response to it is an immanent feature of the leadership landscape. In a further effort to overcome the limiting tendency to locate leadership in individual leaders, results, positions or processes, Grint turns the focus to the paradoxes involved in leadership, its hybridity in connecting people, processes and technologies and the problem of assessing cause and effect in relation to leadership (2005b). These dimensions reveal the critical need to focus on leader ethics, how leaders learn from followers and leader-follower interaction as key considerations.

Ladkin, meanwhile, has drawn from Husserl's phenomenology to highlight 'context', 'purpose', 'leader' and 'follower' as the central, but dynamic and indeterminate, dimensions of leadership (2010). Here, the criticality of varying perceptions, which are themselves grounded in the rich and complex 'lifeworld' of perceivers, means that trying to understand leadership means being attentive to the context in which it arises, in order to try to grasp the meaning it has for the people involved in that context (2010). The contributions of both leaders and followers become central to this framing;

however, because individual perceptions vary, no definitive or exhaustive account of leadership is considered possible. Despite this, where collective mobilisation toward a shared goal occurs, then a leadership 'moment' is said to have occurred (Ladkin, 2010).

Sinclair has sought to deconstruct the gendered expectations and experience of leadership, in order to open up space for leadership that is not narrowly masculinist in orientation, but which instead draws on feminine/feminist approaches to relationships and self-care (1998). Drawing on humanistic values, psychoanalysis, critical theory and yoga to identify the kinds of intra-personal, interpersonal and socio-political forces at play in leadership, Sinclair has also highlighted a range of critical factors which are implicated in leadership. These include the vital role of values, the influence of fears and desires, the problem of power and the embodied nature of leadership. Emerging from a sensitivity to these matters, self-awareness and a sensitivity to others' fears and desires are factors requiring attention. To grapple with power relations entails advocating change, covert subversion, critique, collaboration and experimentation with new ways of working that get beyond traditional usages of power and the protection of privileged interests. The embodied nature of leadership, meanwhile, requires attention to breath, to being mindful, to being open to the spiritual dimensions of life and a willingness to let go of ego-based concerns.

Each of these approaches, then, has something important to say about the what, the why, the where, the who and the how of leadership. Each theorises heuristically rather than with prescriptive precision, offering a wider view of the complex and multi-faceted dimensions of leadership. To our way of thinking, worrying less about precise details enables scholars to say more about the big things they think really matter. It is an approach we think needs to be encouraged in the leadership studies field, where fine points of statistical methods or micro-level theorising have come to dominate many scholarly conversations (Alvesson, 1996; Tourish, 2015). The heuristic model for theorising contextually which we introduce in the next chapter, then, takes inspiration from these examples at the same time as it offers a new framework for understanding leadership and informing leadership practice. Before doing this, however, we want to conclude our review of the contemporary leadership literature by considering its treatment of context.

## Contextual Issues in Contemporary Leadership Research

Scholars have been calling for greater attention to context in leadership research for quite some time (e.g., Osborn, Hunt & Jauch, 2002; Shamir & Howell, 1999; Tosi, 1991). In 2006, Porter and McLaughlin's review suggested limited progress had been made in making contextual issues a more central consideration. However, since that time, consistent with the greater diversification within the field generally, more effort has gone to engagement with contextual issues in leadership studies.

Very precisely defined and delimited contexts, such as leadership in face-to-face vs virtual teams (Purvanova & Bono, 2009), recruitment processes (Ogunfowora, 2014) or creative tasks (Serban & Roberts, 2016), are now quite regularly incorporated as variables in studies or as the setting for a study. 'Context' is also at times constituted as a set of fictional criteria or scenarios given to participants in experimental designs (e.g., Little, 2014; Rule & Tskhay, 2014). Contingency and situational theories have also for some decades sought to formulate prescribed leader responses to specified contextual features (e.g., Fiedler, 1967; Hersey & Blanchard, 1974; House, 1971; Vroom & Yetton, 1977). Where contextual issues are factored into the design of a study or a theory, then, this kind of tightly defined notion of context or abstraction from a real-world setting appears to be the dominant approach, in order to fit or render 'context' amenable to a study or theorisation which is concerned with precise measurement. This approach to dealing with context is what we find in the domain of 'leadership science'. A tightly defined, atomised approach to issues of context remains too limited, however, for it fails to engage broadly and deeply with the multiple, dynamic, indeterminate and contestable dimensions of a real-world context, such as is actually experienced by a work group, organization or community.

Ospina and Foldy (2009) propose the contextually rich approach found in education, communication and black studies has much to offer, but is routinely neglected by leadership studies. The new paradigm in leadership studies discussed earlier also places considerable emphasis on the contextualised character of leadership. Our focus thus turns to examine a sample of studies that engage with matters of context in a serious, holistic and interpretive fashion, to highlight how doing so can open up new insights into leadership theory and practice. In conceptualising the role and influence of context, it is argued that effective leadership practice is informed and shaped by an understanding of the context in which the leader is located, requiring attention and adaptation to its demands and constraints, features from which the leader must learn in order to become and remain effective (Grint, 2000; 2005a; Ladkin, 2010; Quick & Wright, 2011). Such a stance poses a profound challenge to the universalist theoretical prescriptions offered by 'leadership science': if context is seen to really matter for what constitutes effective leadership, then claiming universal relevance for a prescribed set of leader behaviours cannot be sustained.

The first example offers one approach for how we might theorise leadership in relation to a particular context. To do this, Hannah et al. (2009) offer a 'conceptual toolbox' (p. 898) for exploring leadership in extreme contexts, such as those regularly involving the risk of severe physical or psychological harm or damage to material and equipment. These include contexts such as those faced by military personnel or other 'first response' organizations (police, fire, rescue etc.). This 'conceptual toolbox' is intended to guide further research into leadership in such contexts and is thus more heuristic than prescriptive in orientation. It identifies various dimensions of extreme contexts, varying types of organizational preparedness for dealing with extreme contexts, factors that may attenuate or intensify the extreme context and the need for an adaptive leadership response to these factors. Notably, this framework is itself drawn out of earlier research on extreme contexts, meaning the theory-building process begins not with abstracted, generalised ideas about leadership, but with particularised issues of a given context. As explained in Chapter 2, we adopt a similar approach with the model we provide.

The second example we consider examines leadership in the context of Islamic organizations in Australia. In this study, Faris and Parry (2011) identify that the varying national and cultural background of Australian Muslims, the teachings people take from the Qur'an, the currently marginalised, even vilified, status of Muslims in mainstream Australian society and the influential role of Imams and Islamic scholars within the Muslim community all contribute to shaping the focus and approach taken to Islamic organizational leadership. They found that hostility toward Muslims by the wider community has a key role in limiting and directing the focus of Islamic leaders' attention, while fear constrains their ability and confidence to such an extent that these contextual problems "have the potential to nullify the leadership of individuals" (p. 143).

This explicit emphasis on what, in sociological terms, we recognise as 'structure' and how it shapes individual leader 'agency' (Faris & Parry, 2011) thus results in a provocative re-appraisal of how leadership is normally portrayed. In a hostile context, such as that faced by Australian Muslim organizations, leadership can form a defensive, limited orientation, primarily focussed on trying to protect a community from external pressure, but unable to form a proactive agenda for the positive advancement of that community. To reduce this state of affairs to individual failings would be to ignore the powerful structuring influences of the context which shapes the potential for individual agency to arise.

Our next example comes from the context of our own country, Aotearoa/New Zealand. In this case, researchers investigating leadership by Māori, the indigenous people of Aotearoa/New Zealand, provide accounts that foreground the criticality of one's cultural worldview, and of one's identity in terms of both gender and ethnicity, and how these contextual factors profoundly shape the leadership experience of Māori women (Forster, Palmer & Barnett, 2016). Māori women's leadership is informed by 'mana wahine', this being a Māori cultural concept which "acknowledges the importance of Māori women in society and advocates for the continued empowerment and expression of power and authority of women" (2016, p. 327). In other words, the cultural framework of Māori society offers its women a resource from which to claim a legitimate and powerful stake in leadership work. Māori cosmogeny also includes a range of powerful female archetypes which constitute a further cultural resource, providing Māori women leaders guidance on questions of purpose, ethics, relationships, values and the kinds of issues to which they ought to be attentive. These resources help to shape the aims pursued by Māori women leaders and how they enact leadership (Forster et al, 2016), meaning their approach to leadership is deeply informed by their cultural context.

Our final example, also from Aotearoa/New Zealand, is Henry and Wolfgramm's (2015) study of Māori leadership, which has a particular focus on its connections with relational leadership theory (Uhl-Bien, 2006). They highlight the spiritual/divine (mana atua), terrestrial/geographic (mana whenua), ancestral (mana tupuna), social (mana tangata) and feminine (mana wahine) dimensions of Māori ontology and identity as key considerations which inform how Māori leadership is embodied and enacted, along with an appreciation of the macro-dimensions facing Māori, such as the effects of colonisation and institutionalised racism. The practice of genealogical recitation (whakapapa), particularly at the beginning of important meetings (hui), as a way of forming relational connections across time and space is identified as one specific method for embodying and enacting relational leadership in the context of a Māori worldview. Through analysis of Māori "cultural, identity and macro-contextual dimensions", then, that "influence ways of being and doing leadership", Henry and Wolfgramm bring to light a context-specific form of leadership, whilst also showing its connection with the wider literature on relational perspectives on leadership (2015, p. 13).

The above examples point to how a deep and sustained engagement with questions of context reveals multiple forms of—and truths about—leadership, as it takes different shape and focus in response to varying challenges, purposes, values and norms. What we learn is that leadership practice can be, and is, enormously variable and inventive. Productive ways of engaging theoretically with this variability, however, warrant further development, as conventional concerns with parsimony, statistical analysis, deductive methods of inquiry to test pre-set hypotheses and generalisability cannot embrace contextual issues in responsive or holistic ways. The model which we introduce in Chapter 2 is intended to help guide people in building their own leadership approaches by paying need to issues of salience to their context, just as these examples advocate and exemplify.

In summary, then, through our review of the leadership literature, we have highlighted that contextual influences have consistently played a vital role, since the Classical Greek times onwards, in how leadership is understood and practiced, even though such influences are now, paradoxically, ignored in most leadership studies and theories. We have identified some important limitations with the 'leadership science' approach, which help to explain why we favour a newly emergent paradigm in leadership studies, one that is deeply informed by social constructionist, interpretive and critical thought. We have highlighted key new approaches to leadership research which have emerged in recent years as part of this and, in particular, considered examples which help point to the value of heuristic approaches to theorising leadership. We have also specifically highlighted a sample of studies that examine contextual issues to offer an indication of just now rich, interesting and practical leadership theorising can become when it really takes context seriously.

## How the Book Is Organized—and Who It Is For

In the next chapter, we introduce our approach to *contextualised theorising*. We start by examining some broader trends in the contemporary context which we see as being of particular salience to leadership today, before introducing our model and explaining its componentry. Chapters 3 through 7 then illustrate the potential of this model in a variety of different organizational contexts where leadership is commonly expected to make a significant contribution: in supervisory roles (Chapter 3); in the HRM function (Chapter 4); in enabling innovation and entrepreneurship within organizations (Chapter 5); in organizational strategy (Chapter 6); and, in the governance function of organizations (Chapter 7). Finally, in Chapter 8, we turn the tables back on ourselves, applying our model to explore what leadership might look like in the field of leadership studies itself.

Given the focus of the book, we believe a diverse range of readers will find it of use for a variety of purposes. Leadership scholars, whether adherents or critics of the 'leadership science' tradition, can use our model empirically to inform their own studies of leadership in particular contexts and/or to further develop its use for leadership theorising and knowledge production. The illustrative examples we develop (Chapters 3 to 8) offer inspiration and guidance for empirical investigations and/or the further development of leadership theorising which directly addresses these sites of action. Meanwhile, the influence which post-heroic, relational, practice, process, distributed, plural, shared, complexity, discursive and emergent approaches to leadership have had on our thinking are infused within our illustrative examples. They offer insights as to how these important new perspectives give rise to new ways of understanding and practising leadership which are not centred on the qualities of the individual leader. As a consequence, leadership scholars working in these new traditions will likely find ideas here which will support their research agenda.

For scholars involved in leadership education and development efforts, which are often focussed on self-development, our model for contextualised theorising can be used to guide participants in conducting a wide-ranging analysis that looks at factors 'outside of me' as well as those 'inside of me', to help avoid the risk that self-reflection turns to narcissistic navel gazing. The illustrative examples we provide can, moreover, serve as provocations for debate as to their relevance and suitability for participants' contexts, further supporting critical self-reflection as they encounter and react to our proposals.

MBA or other executive education (ExecEd) programmes, in contrast, tend to be less focussed on introspective self-reflection and development and more applied in orientation. This book is also concerned with issues of practical application, yet it is simultaneously an accessible prompter of introspective self-reflection and development, thereby extending the reach of the typical MBA/ExecEd experience. Specifically, by working through the elements of our model and our illustrative examples, MBA/ExecEd students will be required to think critically about both the contextual demands facing the different parts of their organization and what this means for the kind of leadership needed, thereby exploring and connecting both what is 'outside of me' and what is 'inside of me'. In particular, we believe the book can be useful as part of a 'leadership cap-stone' course within an MBA/ExecEd programme, where participants are needing to think through the leadership approach that each element of their organization's management entails, thereby avoiding a 'one size fits all' view of organizational leadership.

Management and organizational scholars working in the areas of supervisory management, HRM, innovation and entrepreneurship, strategy and governance, and who are interested in leadership will find our illustrative examples helpful in forging connections with leadership scholarship and in conceptualising what leadership entails in these different roles and functions. Fostering dialogue between what are often separate literatures is something we believe this book supports. Indeed, other organizational scholars focussed on different functional areas, such as IT, marketing, sales and finance, will find our model for contextualised theorising helpful in formulating leadership approaches relevant to those contexts. Going further, we believe our model focusses attention on elements that are central to leadership, even if their precise formation legitimately varies from context to context. We believe the model is therefore usefully focussed yet sufficiently flexible to have relevance to many different contexts where leadership is sought far beyond those that we illustrate here, such as community groups, political bodies, not-for-profits and even online communities that are organizing in relation to shared goals.

For students, the book offers a wide-ranging basis for engaging with both the leadership literature and the literatures that pertain to the various organizational roles and functions which our illustrative examples address. This kind of breadth, coupled with the deep diving we do into particular roles and functions, can, we believe, animate a sensitive and rich understanding of the complexity involved in organizational leadership, something which more conventional leadership textbooks routinely underplay. Our engagement with the newer paradigm of interpretive, social constructionist and critical approaches to leadership studies also stands in contrast with the 'leadership science' approach which most leadership textbooks offer, thereby connecting students with important new developments in leadership studies.

Last but certainly not least, practitioners will, we believe, value our interest in connecting with the complexity and variability of the various contexts in which they may engage, supported by a narrative style that is accessible and engaging. We believe practitioners can use our model and relevant illustrative examples in formulating a leadership approach suited to their own unique context. This kind of inventiveness, grounded in a careful analysis of the situation at hand, as prompted by our model, is in many ways the best outcome the book could give rise to, as doing so would surely support our core aim of revitalising leadership. In the next chapter, then, we set out that model, preceded by a wide-ranging discussion of some major trends in contemporary society that influence the context for leadership today and which help further build the case for the necessity of its revitalisation.

## References

Ackerman, R. W. (1975). *The social challenge to business.* Cambridge, MA: Harvard University Press.

Allen, J. W. (1951). *A history of political thought in the sixteenth century.* London: Methuen and Co.

Alvesson, M. (1996). Leadership studies: From procedure and abstraction to reflexivity and situation. *The Leadership Quarterly,* 7(4), 455–485.

Alvesson, M., Bridgman, T., & Willmott, H. (2009). *The Oxford handbook of critical management studies.* Oxford: Oxford University Press.

Alvesson, M., & Deetz, S. A. (2000). *Doing critical management research.* London: Sage.

Alvesson, M., & Gabriel, Y. (2016). Grandiosity in contemporary management and education. *Management Learning,* 47(4), 464–473.

Alvesson, M., & Kärreman, D. (2016). Intellectual failure and ideological success in organization studies: The case of transformational leadership. *Journal of Management Inquiry,* 25(2), 139–152.

Alvesson, M., & Spicer, A. (2012). A stupidity based theory of organizations. *Journal of Management Studies,* 49(7), 1194–1220.

Aristotle (2009). In S. Everson (Ed.), *The politics and the constitution of Athens.* Cambridge: Cambridge University Press.

Atwater, L., Mumford, M. D., Schriesheim, C. A., & Yammarino, F. J. (2014). Retraction of leadership articles: Causes and prevention. *The Leadership Quarterly,* 25, 1174–1180.

Avolio, B. J., Walumbwa, F. O., & Weber, T. J. (2009). Leadership: Current theories, research, and future directions. *Annual Review of Psychology,* 60, 421–449.

Bass, B. M. (1985). *Leadership and performance beyond expectations.* New York: Free Press.

Bass, B. M. (2008). *The Bass handbook of leadership: Theory, research and managerial applications* (4th ed.). New York: Free Press.

Bennis, W. G., & Nanus, B. (1985). *Leaders: The strategies for taking charge.* New York: Harper & Row.

Blaikie, N. (2000). *Designing social research: The logic of anticipation.* Cambridge, UK: Polity Press.

Blaikie, N. (2007). *Approaches to social enquiry: Advancing knowledge* (2nd ed.). Cambridge, UK: Polity Press.

Bowers, D. G., & Seashore, S. E. (1966). Predicting organizational effectiveness with a four-factor theory of leadership. *Administrative Science Quarterly,* 11(2), 238–263.

Bryman, A. (2004). Qualitative research on leadership: A critical but appreciative review. *The Leadership Quarterly,* 15(6), 729–769.

Bryman, A. (2011). Mission accomplished?: Research methods in the first five years of Leadership. *Leadership,* 7(1), 73–83.

Burns, J. M. (1978). *Leadership.* New York: Harper & Row.

Calvin, J. (2010 (1559)). On civil government (H. Hopfl, Trans.). In H. Hopfl (Ed.), *Luther and Calvin on secular authority* (pp. 87–95). Cambridge: Cambridge University Press.

Cameron, E. (2001). The power of the word: Renaissance and reformation. In E. Cameron (Ed.), *Early modern Europe: An Oxford history* (pp. 63–101). Oxford: Oxford University Press.

Carlyle, T. (1993 (1840)). In M. Goldberg (Ed.), *On heroes, hero-worship, and the heroic in history*. Berkeley, CA: University of California Press.

Ciulla, J. B. (1995). Leadership ethics: Mapping the terrain. *Business Ethics Quarterly, 5*(1), 5–28.

Ciulla, J. B. (Ed.). (2004). *Ethics, the heart of leadership* (2nd ed.). Westport, CT: Praeger.

Collinson, D. (2011). Critical leadership studies. In A. Bryman, D. Collinson, K. Grint, B. Jackson, & M. Uhl-Bien (Eds.), *The Sage handbook of leadership* (pp. 181–194). London: Sage.

Cornuelle, R. (1975). *De-managing America: The final revolution*. New York: Random House.

Craigie, J. (1950). Introduction. In *Basilicon Doron of King James VI* (pp. 3–48). Edinburgh: William Blackwell and Sons.

Crevani, L., Lindgren, M., & Packendorff, J. (2010). Leadership, not leaders: On the study of leadership as practices and interactions. *Scandinavian Journal of Management, 26*(1), 77–87.

Denis, J.-L., Langley, A., & Sergi, V. (2012). Leadership in the plural. *The Academy of Management Annals, 6*(1), 211–283.

Dickens, D. R. (2013). Post-modernism. In B. Kaldis (Ed.), *Encyclopedia of philosophy and the social sciences* (pp. 746–748). Thousand Oaks, CA: Sage.

Diener, E., Ng, W., Harter, J., & Arora, R. (2010). Wealth and happiness across the world: Material prosperity predicts life evaluation, whereas psychosocial prosperity predicts positive feeling. *Journal of Personality and Social Psychology, 99*(1), 52–61.

Erasmus (2010 (1516)). (N. M. Cheshire & M. J. Heath, Trans.). In L. Jardine (Ed.), *The education of a Christian Prince*. Cambridge: Cambridge University Press.

Eslen-Ziya, H., & Erhart, I. (2015). Toward post-heroic leadership: A case study of Gezi's collaborating multiple leaders. *Leadership, 11*(4), 471–488.

Fairhurst, G. (2007). *Discursive leadership: In conversation with leadership psychology*. Thousand Oaks, CA: Sage.

Fairhurst, G. (2009). Considering context in discursive leadership research. *Human Relations, 62*(11), 1607–1633.

Faris, N., & Parry, K. (2011). Islamic organizational leadership within a Western society: The problematic role of external context. *The Leadership Quarterly, 22*(1), 132–151.

Fiedler, F. E. (1967). *A theory of leadership effectiveness*. New York: McGraw-Hill.

Fisher, K., & Robbins, C. R. (2015). Embodied leadership: Moving from leader competencies to leaderful practices. *Leadership, 11*(3), 281–299. doi:10.1177/1742715014522680

Ford, J., Harding, N., & Learmonth, M. (2008). *Leadership as identity: Constructions and deconstructions*. Basingstoke: Palgrave Macmillan.

Forster, M. E., Palmer, F., & Barnett, S. (2016). Karanga mai ra: Stories of Māori women as leaders. *Leadership, 12*(3), 324–345.

Foucault, M. (1970). The order of things: An archaeology of the human sciences. London: Tavistock.

Foucault, M. (1977). (A. Sheridan, Trans.). *Discipline and punish: The birth of the prison*. London: Penguin Books.

Foucault, M. (1978). (R. Hurley, Trans.). *The history of sexuality: The will to knowledge* (Vol. 1). New York: Random House.

Galton, F. (1892). *Hereditary genius: An inquiry into its law and consequences* (2nd ed.). London: MacMillan.

Galton, F. (1970). *English men of science: Their nature and nurture* (Vol. 2). London: Frank Cass & Co.

Gardner, W. L., Lowe, K. B., Moss, T. W., Mahoney, K. T., & Cogliser, C. C. (2010). Scholarly leadership of the study of leadership: A review of The Leadership Quarterly's second decade, 2000–2009. *The Leadership Quarterly, 21*(6), 922–958.

Gilbert, A. H. (1938). *Machiavelli's Prince and its forerunners: The Prince as a typical book de regimine principum.* Durham, NC: Duke University Press.

Gitlin, T. (1993). *The sixties: Years of hope, days of rage.* New York: Bantam.

Gordon, S. (1981). *The history and philosophy of social science.* London: Routledge.

Gosling, J., & Mintzberg, H. (2003). The five minds of a manager. *Harvard Business Review, 81*(11), 54–63.

Grant, M. (1991). *A short history of classical civilization.* London: Weidenfeld & Nicolson.

Grint, K. (2000). *The arts of leadership.* Oxford: Oxford University Press.

Grint, K. (2005a). Problems, problems, problems: The social construction of 'leadership'. *Human Relations, 58*(11), 1467–1494.

Grint, K. (2005b). *Leadership: Limits and possibilities.* London: Palgrave Macmillan.

Gronn, P. (2000). Distributed properties: A new architecture for leadership. *Educational Management Administration and Leadership, 28*, 317–338.

Gunn, S. (2001). War, religion, and the state. In E. Cameron (Ed.), *Early modern Europe: An Oxford history* (pp. 102–134). Oxford: Oxford University Press.

Hacking, I. (1999). *The social construction of what?* Cambridge, MA: Harvard University Press.

Hall, S. (2005). *Peace and freedom: The civil rights and anti-war movements in the 1960s.* Philadelphia: University of Pennsylvania Press.

Hannah, S. T., Uhl-Bien, M., Avolio, B. J., & Cavarretta, F. L. (2009). A framework for examining leadership in extreme contexts. *The Leadership Quarterly, 20*(6), 897–919.

Henry, E., & Wolfgramm, R. (2015). Relational leadership – An indigenous Māori perspective. *Leadership.* doi:10.1177/1742715015616282

Hersey, P., & Blanchard, K. H. (1974). So you want to know your leadership style? *Training & Development Journal, 28*(2), 22–37.

Hodgson, G. (2005). *America in our time: From World War II to Nixon: What happened and why.* Princeton, NJ: Princeton University Press.

Hosking, D. M. (2007). Not leaders, not followers: A postmodern discourse of leadership processes. In B. Shamir, R. Pillai, M. C. Bligh, & M. Uhl-Bien (Eds.), *Follower-centred perspectives on leadership* (pp. 243–264). Greenwich, CT: Information Age Publishing.

House, R. J. (1971). A path goal theory of leader effectiveness. *Administrative Science Quarterly, 16*(3), 321–339.

House, R. J. (1977). A 1976 theory of charismatic leadership. In J. G. Hunt & L. L. Larson (Eds.), *Leadership: The cutting edge* (pp. 189–207). Carbondale, IL: Southern Illinois University Press

Huczynski, A., & Buchanan, D. (2006). *Organizational behaviour.* New York: Prentice-Hall.

Hunter, S. T., Bedell-Avers, K. E., & Mumford, M. D. (2007). The typical leadership study: Assumptions, implications, and potential remedies. *The Leadership Quarterly, 18*(5), 435–446.

Jackson, B., & Parry, K. (2008). *A very short, fairly interesting and reasonably cheap book about studying leadership.* London, UK: Sage.

Jackson, B., & Parry, K. (2011). A very short, fairly interesting and reasonably cheap book about studying leadership. (2 ed.). London: Sage.

James VI (1950 (1599)). *Basilicon doron.* Edinburgh: William Blackwell and Sons.

Jardine, L. (2010). Introduction (N. M. Cheshire & J. F. Heath, Trans.). In L. Jardine (Ed.), *Erasmus: The education of a Christian Prince* (pp. vi–xxiv). Cambridge: Cambridge University Press.

Kellerman, B. (2012). *The end of leadership.* New York: Harper Business.

Kelley, R. (1992). *The power of followership.* New York, NY: Currency Doubleday.

Kelly, S. (2013). Towards a negative ontology of leadership. *Human Relations,* 67(8), 905–922.

Kempster, S., Jackson, B., & Conroy, M. (2011). Leadership as purpose: Exploring the role of purpose in leadership practice. *Leadership,* 7(3), 317–334.

Koch, M. (2015). Climate change, capitalism and degrowth trajectories to a global steady-state economy. *International Critical Thought,* 5(4), 439–452.

Korman, A. K. (1966). "Consideration", "Initiating structure" and organizational criteria: A Review. *Personnel Psychology, 19*(4), 349-361.

Ladkin, D. (2010). *Rethinking leadership: A new look at old leadership questions.* Cheltenham, UK: Edward Elgar.

Lambertini, R. (2011). Mirrors for princes. In H. Lagerlund (Ed.), *Encyclopedia of medieval philosophy* (pp. 791–797). Dordrecht, Netherlands: Springer.

Lipsius, J. (2004 (1589)). (J. Waszink, Trans.). In J. Waszink (Ed.), *Justus Lipsius' politica: Six books of politics or political instruction.* Assen, The Netherlands: Royal Van Gorcum.

Little, A. C. (2014). Facial appearance and leader choice in different contexts: Evidence for task contingent selection based on implicit and learned face-behaviour/face-ability associations. *The Leadership Quarterly,* 25(5), 865–874.

Liu, H., & Baker, C. (2016). White knights: Leadership as the heroicisation of whiteness. *Leadership,* 12(4), 420–448.

Luthans, F., & Avolio, B. J. (2003). Authentic leadership: A positive developmental approach. In K. S. Cameron, J. E. Dutton, & R. E. Quinn (Eds.), *Positive organizational scholarship: Foundations for a new discipline* (pp. 241–258). San Francisco: Berrett-Koehler.

Luther, M. (2010 (1523)). On secular authority (H. Hopfl, Trans.). In H. Hopfl (Ed.), *Luther and Calvin on secular authority* (pp. 47–86). Cambridge: Cambridge University Press.

Machiavelli, N. (2005). The prince (W. J. Connell, Trans.). In W. J. Connell (Ed.), *The prince by Niccolo Machiavelli, with related documents.* Boston: Bedford/St Martins.

Magaziner, I. C., & Reich, R. B. (1982). *Minding America's business: The decline and rise of the American economy.* New York: Harcourt Brace Jovanovich.

Mailhot, C., Gagnon, S., Langley, A., & Binette, L.-F. (2016). Distributing leadership across people and objects in a collaborative research project. *Leadership,* 12(1), 53–85.

Meindl, J. R., Ehrlich, S. B., & Dukerich, J. M. (1985). The romance of leadership. *Administrative Science Quarterly,* 30(1), 78–102.

Morris, I., & Powell, B. P. (2006). *The Greeks: History, culture and society.* Upper Saddle River, NJ: Pearson Prentice Hall.

Morrow, J. (2005). *History of Western political thought: A thematic introduction* (2nd ed.). Basingstoke, UK: Palgrave Macmillan.

Nicholson, H., & Carroll, B. (2013). Identity undoing and power relations in leadership development. *Human Relations,* 66(9), 1225–1248.

Ogunfowora, B. (2014). The impact of ethical leadership within the recruitment context: The roles of organizational reputation, applicant personality, and value congruence. *The Leadership Quarterly,* 25(3), 528–543.

Osborn, R. N., Hunt, J. G., & Jauch, L. R. (2002). Toward a contextual theory of leadership. *The Leadership Quarterly,* 13(6), 797.

Ospina, S., & Foldy, E. (2009). A critical review of race and ethnicity in the leadership literature: Surfacing context, power and the collective dimensions of leadership. *The Leadership Quarterly*, 20(6), 876–896.

Parker, M. (2002). *Against management: Organization in the age of managerialism.* Oxford: Polity Press.

Plato (1995). (R. Waterfield, Trans.). In J. Annas & R. Waterfield (Eds.), *Statesman.* Cambridge: Cambridge University Press.

Plato (2007). (D. Lee, Trans.). In M. Lane (Ed.), *The Republic* (2nd ed.). London: Penguin Books.

Porter, L. W., & McLaughlin, G. B. (2006). Leadership and the organizational context: Like the weather? *The Leadership Quarterly*, 17(6), 559.

Porter, L., W. , & McLaughlin, G., B. (2006). Leadership and the organizational context: Like the weather?*. *The Leadership Quarterly,* 17(6), 559–576.

Potter, G. (2013). Structuralism and poststructuralism. In B. Kaldis (Ed.), *Encyclopedia of philosophy and the social sciences* (pp. 966–969). Thousand Oaks, CA: Sage.

Price, T. L. (2003). The ethics of authentic transformational leadership. *The Leadership Quarterly*, 14(1), 67–81.

Purvanova, R. K., & Bono, J. E. (2009). Transformational leadership in context: Face-to-face and virtual teams. *The Leadership Quarterly*, 20(3), 343–357.

Quick, J. C., & Wright, T. A. (2011). Character-based leadership, context and consequences. *The Leadership Quarterly*, 22(5), 984–988.

Raelin, J. A. (2003). *Creating leaderful organizations: How to bring out leadership in everyone.* San Francisco, CA: Berrett-Koehler Publishers.

Raelin, J. A. (2011). From leadership-as-practice to leaderful practice. *Leadership*, 7(2), 195–211.

Raelin, J. A. (2016). Imagine there are no leaders: Reframing leadership as collaborative agency. *Leadership*, 12(2), 131–158.

Reed, M. (2006). Organizational theorizing: A historically contested terrain. In S. R. Clegg, C. Hardy, T. B. Lawrence, & W. R. Nord (Eds.), *The Sage handbook of organization studies* (2nd ed., pp. 19–54). London: Sage.

Roos, J. (1972). American political life in the 60's: Change, recurrence and revolution. In R. Weber (Ed.), *America in change: Reflections on the 60's and 70's.* Notre Dame: University of Notre Dame Press.

Rule, N. O., & Tskhay, K. O. (2014). The influence of economic context on the relationship between chief executive officer facial appearance and company profits. *The Leadership Quarterly*, 25(5), 846–854.

Saul, J. R. (1983). *Voltaire's bastards: The dictatorship of reason in the West.* New York: Vintage Books.

Serban, A., & Roberts, A. J. B. (2016). Exploring antecedents and outcomes of shared leadership in a creative context: A mixed-methods approach. *The Leadership Quarterly*, 27(2), 181–199.

Shamir, B., & Howell, J. M. (1999). Organizational and contextual influences on the emergence and effectiveness of charismatic leadership. *The Leadership Quarterly*, 10(2), 257–283.

Shartle, C. L. (1979). Early years of the Ohio State University Leadership Studies. *Journal of Management*, 5(2), 127–134.

Sinclair, A. (1998). Doing leadership differently: Gender, power and sexuality in a changing business culture. Carlton South, VIC: Melbourne University Press.

Sinclair, A. (2007). *Leadership for the disillusioned: Moving beyond myths and heroes to leading that liberates.* Crows Nest, NSW: Allen & Unwin.

Sinclair, A. (2015). Possibilities, purpose and pitfalls: Insights from introducing mindfulness to leaders. *Journal of Spirituality, Leadership and Management*, 8(1), 3–11.

Skinner, Q. (2002). *Visions of politics volume 2: Renaissance virtues.* Cambridge: Cambridge University Press.

Smith, H. L., & Krueger, L. M. (1933). A brief summary of the literature on leadership. *Bulletin of the School of Education, Indiana University*, 9(4), 3–80.

Spoelstra, S., Butler, N., & Delaney, H. (2016). Never let an academic crisis go to waste: Leadership studies in the wake of journal retractions. *Leadership*, 12(4), 383–397.

Stead, V., & Elliott, C. (2009). *Women's leadership.* Basingstoke, UK: Palgrave Macmillan.

Stogdill, R. (1948). Personal factors associated with leadership: A survey of the literature. *Journal of Psychology*, 25, 35–71.

Tosi, H. L. (1991). The organization as a context for leadership theory: A multilevel approach. *The Leadership Quarterly*, 2, 205–228.

Tourish, D. (2013). *The dark side of transformational leadership: A critical perspective.* London: Routledge.

Tourish, D. (2015). Some announcements, reaffirming the critical ethos of leadership, and what we look for in submissions. *Leadership*, 11(2), 135–141.

Trethewey, A., & Goodall, Jr., H. L. (2007). Leadership reconsidered as historical subject: Sketches from the cold war to post-9/11. *Leadership*, 3(4), 457–477.

Uhl-Bien, M. (2006). Relational leadership theory: Exploring the social processes of leadership and organizing. *The Leadership Quarterly*, 17(6), 654–676.

Uhl-Bien, M., Russ, M., & McKelvey , B. (2007). Complexity Leadership Theory: Shifting leadership from the industrial age to the knowledge era. *The Leadership Quarterly,* 18(4), 298–318

Uhl-Bien, M., & Ospina, S. (Eds.). (2012). *Advancing relational leadership research: A dialogue among perspectives.* Charlotte, NC: Information Age Publishing.

Vroom, V. H., & Yetton, P. W. (1977). *Leadership and decision-making.* London: University of Pittsburgh Press.

Wilson, S. (2013). Situated knowledge: A foucauldian analysis of ancient and modern classics of leadership thought. *Leadership*, 9(1), 43–61.

Wilson, S. (2016). *Thinking differently about leadership: A critical history of leadership studies.* Cheltenham, UK: Edward Elgar.

Winch, P. (1967). *The idea of a social science and its relation to philosophy.* London: Routledge & Kegan Paul.

Wren, D. A. (2005). *The history of management thought* (5th ed.). Hoboken, NJ: Wiley.

Xenophon (1997). (E. C. Marchant & O. J. Todd, Trans.). *Xenophon: Memorabilia, oeconomicus, symposium, apology.* Cambridge, MA: Harvard University Press.

Xenophon (2006). (R. Waterfield, Trans.). In P. Cartledge (Ed.), *Hiero the Tyrant and other treatises.* London: Penguin Books.

# 2 A Framework for Revitalising Leadership

## Introduction

The focus of this chapter is two-fold. In the first part, we discuss six major trends which are key features of the contemporary landscape. These trends inform our argument that we need to revitalise leadership and, substantively, provide the macro-level context for leadership practice today. Then, in the second part of the chapter, we lay out the conceptual framework that provides the approach we propose for revitalising leadership, that of *contextualised theorising*. It is this framework, we argue, which enables us to build leadership theorisations—models, if you prefer—attuned to the need of different contexts. The illustrative examples we develop in Chapters 3 to 7 will put this framework to use, illustrating its potential for guiding *practice-in-context* by formulating contextually specific theorisations of leadership.

## Leadership Practice Today: A Changing Landscape of Priorities, Possibilities and Limitations

There are six major developments which, over the last half century or so, have become central to how our world now functions, developments which we think fundamentally re-shape the wider landscape in which organizational leadership practice occurs, giving rise to different priorities, possibilities and limitations than were previously the case. In no ranked order of importance, these developments are globalisation; the greater influence of financial markets on business practices; the decline of 'authority' as a source of power; the increased status and influence of women in business and politics; the dispersion of information and knowledge (often enabled by technology); and climate change.

No doubt there are other developments in contemporary society that also have relevance to leadership practice, so we make no claim that this list is exhaustive. We also accept that our decision to focus on these particular developments is based on subjective judgement, albeit we think it would be difficult to argue that any of them is not of great significance to contemporary society and, consequently, organizational leadership. As each of these developments has been very widely discussed elsewhere, our particular interest is to explore what they each imply for the practice of leadership. Consequently, after introducing key features of each of these developments, we seek to sketch here their implications for leadership, cognisant that these are often ambiguous or contradictory and, moreover, often in tension with the implications generated by other developments.

## Globalisation

The complex nature of globalisation comprises, most tangibly, the increased flow of goods, services, information, capital and people across national borders (Michie, 2011; Scholte, 2005). Arising from this, many countries are now increasingly reliant on importing for their basic needs, exporting for their income and employment levels and global financial markets for the value of their currency, share market and access to capital (OECD, 2010). High degrees of volatility, complexity and uncertainty are marked characteristics arising out of this globalised (and financialised) form of capitalism (Hodgson, 2011; Radice, 2015; Scholte, 2005).

These shifts in trading practices have both caused and been enabled by significant changes to the laws, regulations and policies of nation states. Governments have entered into trade agreements, established 'export/free trade' zones in which foreign-owned businesses are encouraged to set up operations, changed their import/export duties and tariffs regimes and revised their commercial, consumer, property and labour laws and regulations, for example, in an effort to secure increases in the flow of goods, services, information, capital and labour (Higgins & Hallström, 2007; Peet, 2003; WTO, 2003, 2007). Globalisation has been promoted and enabled by influential organizations such as the World Bank, the Organization for Economic Co-operation and Development, the World Trade Organization and the International Monetary Fund, which routinely depict the continued growth in the global flows of goods, services, capital, information and people as necessary, desirable and entirely unstoppable (Murphy, 2007; Peet, 2003; Spicer & Fleming, 2007).

The missionary zeal of these particular organizations highlights, moreover, how the flow of ideas and the transmission of values, norms, ideologies and practices from one cultural context through to others is also a central disciplining strategy which facilitates the process of globalisation (Banerjee & Linstead, 2001; Murphy, 2007). The internet now enables the immediate transmittal and exchange of 'free trade' discourse and practice: as we shop online to secure goods or services from foreign suppliers, we become individually linked into the processes of globalisation, and our sense of the world and our identity are changed in subtle but still powerful ways (Bauman, 2007). Cultural and symbolic goods, such as movies, music and fashionable products like smartphones and 'designer' clothes, likewise have an important role to play in spreading a shared understanding across different cultures of how we should think and act, as we are increasingly encouraged to view ourselves as global citizens (Mayo, 2005; Paulicelli & Clark, 2009).

Nation states and corporations have become engaged in globalisation processes from varying positions of strength and influence, seeking to advance their position further through engaging in the practices and techniques of globalised trade (OECD, 2010; WTO, 2007). Thus, for all that it brings together people from diverse backgrounds, with all the potential joys and conflicts that can bring, simultaneously, globalisation has also had some homogenising effects, as more and more people in different countries consume the same set of goods and services and are influenced by the particular values and norms which these symbolise (Frenkel, 2005; Scholte, 2005). Neoliberal ideas have also been especially influential in shaping the particular form that the process of globalisation has taken in recent decades, encouraging self-responsibility and self-disciplining practices that serve to sustain consumer demand and create selves that are docile to the requirements of ever-changing market conditions (Foucault, 2010; Sennett, 2006; Cerny, Menz & Soederberg, 2005).

Multi-national corporations have become very powerful agents of influence, with globalisation providing the opportunity for companies to grow to previously unseen dimensions. Consider the following, drawn from Forbes' 2015 ranking of the world's biggest publicly listed companies (see Table 2.1 below). These are enormously large and influential organizations. They employ, on average, 338,000 people each and have an average market value of $267.9 billion. To put these numbers in some kind of perspective, the GDP of New Zealand, a nation of around 4.5 million people, was US$174 billion in 2015 (The World Bank, 2016). Our largest employer, Fonterra, a co-operative which is also the world's largest dairy exporter, employs 16,000 people (Fonterra, n.d.). Many of these 'top ten' companies operate directly in multiple countries, while the effects of their actions extend even more broadly (Schaefer, 2016). Yet they come from just two of the world's nations, the US and China, the latter having adopted many managerial and business practices that originated in the US. The particular character of contemporary globalisation is, then, one where American business practices and values are, to date, especially dominant.

Businesses have sought to exploit the opportunities to grow sales and decrease costs which have come with the increased capacity to trade and operate across national borders (Coucke & Sleuwaegen, 2008; Doh, 2005). Competitive pressures are intensified through this, as even small local businesses now find themselves competing against goods and services sourced from throughout the globe (Lewin & Peeters, 2006). Thus while consumers experience more choice, producers find themselves facing a much bigger competitive field, making the task of survival much more challenging. Moreover, when a crisis of demand, supply, currency, share prices and/or

*Table 2.1* Forbes' top ten publicly listed companies, 2015

| Forbes Ranking | Company | Country | Industry | Number of employees | Market capitalisation |
|---|---|---|---|---|---|
| 1 | Industrial and Commercial Bank of China | China | banking | 462,282 | $278b |
| 2 | China Construction Bank | China | banking | 372,321 | $212b |
| 3 | Agricultural Bank of China | China | banking | 493,583 | $189b |
| 4 | Bank of China | China | banking | 308,128 | $199b |
| 5 | Berkshire Hathaway | USA | investment services | 316,000 | $354b |
| 6 | JP Morgan Chase | USA | banking | 241,359 | $225b |
| 7 | Exxon Mobil | USA | oil & gas operations | 83,700 | $357b |
| 8 | PetroChina | China | oil & gas operations | 534,652 | $334b |
| 9 | General Electric | USA | conglomerate | 305,000 | $253b |
| 10 | Wells Fargo | USA | banking | 264,500 | $278b |

Source: Schaefer, 2016

credit occurs in one location, the vast and complex interdependencies that now exist across national borders means such crises are more rapidly and extensively spread (Chossudovsky, 1997; Crotty, 2009).

The 'offshoring' of production or service functions from high-wage to low-wage countries has been a common business strategy to enhance competitiveness, such that many of the products and services consumed in the so-called developed world (or, if you prefer, the Global North) now come from the efforts of workers in developing countries (or, if you prefer, the Global South), who are paid but a fraction of what they would receive for doing that same work if it were done in a developed country (Arnold & Hewison, 2005; Doh, 2005). The working conditions these employees contend with are frequently onerous and unsafe, even though their employers are often well-resourced and profitable multi-nationals (Harrison & Scorse, 2006; Locke, Qin & Brause, 2007). Massive layoffs of workers in developed nations is a further dimension of this equation (Brown & Slegel, 2005). And arising from all this is the ready access to cheap products and services, something often presented as a key benefit of globalisation (Michie, 2011;

Scholte, 2005). Businesses, then, have greater potential to increase sales and profits through the advancement of globalisation and for consumers there is greater choice, often at a lower cost. However, these results routinely depend upon low paid, onerous and unsafe working conditions in developing countries and the loss of employment in developed countries.

The flow of people across national borders means workforces (and communities) are often now much more diverse than in earlier times. This has significant implications for employment and people ('human resource') management practices (Shen, Chanda, D'netto & Monga, 2009). Communication between management and the workforce is just one such issue. It may mean that newly migrated workers quite literally speak different languages from that of their managers. Beyond this, however, differences in values, norms, cultural practices and communication styles affect how people from different cultures interact, creating new problems for the long-standing managerial focus on issues of motivation, morale, team work and commitment to the organization's mission, purpose and values (Prasad, Mills, Elmes & Prasad, 1997). At a minimum, manager-employee communication becomes more complex as a consequence of this increased diversity in the workforce.

For multi-national corporations, decisions arise about how best to function in different countries in respect of their commercial, operational and managerial practices. A key question is deciding what matters shall be set at a head office level and then applied consistently, irrespective of location, and what matters shall be delegated to country level and be permitted to flex to meet local custom and practice (Morgan & Kristensen, 2006). What is readily apparent is that products and services, along with their mechanised or routinised processes of production, are often highly standardised by multi-national corporations across their multiple locations in order to manage the 'brand' itself: the particular point of interest here is how this constitutes an homogenising strategy which acts to constrain diversity and overrule local customs and practices.

As these various processes and practices of globalisation have expanded their reach and intensity of impact, their implications for leadership practices are many and contradictory. A large, geographically distributed workforce is suggestive of significant physical and psychic distance between those at the top and those at the bottom of the organization: perhaps leadership practice in this context is frequently impersonal and expressed via strategies, plans and processes rather than human interaction. Physical, social, cultural and power distance, where head office is located in the affluent North but actual production or customer service is undertaken by those located in an impoverished South, means that any sense of an organization as a shared community with a common purpose will be challenging to develop and sustain. Whether leadership, in terms of communicative practice, can or should offer rhetoric with sufficient meaning and impact to overcome this division is debatable if inequalities are not also challenged as part of this.

The ethical question for leaders as to what constitute a 'fair wage' and 'proper working conditions' in such situations is starkly evident, yet this is apparently answered in many instances by recourse to economic rationalism to legitimate the practices adopted (Pfeffer, 2016). However, relying on economic rationalism as the framework for leaders to address the ethical issues of globalisation seems entirely inadequate, as it is this very way of thinking that is the source of the ethical issues that concern us. Meanwhile, a diverse workforce means that finding ways to lead that takes account of these differences would seem to be important (Prasad et al., 1997). Yet, as we have also noted, the dominance of American business practices and the tendency to standardise organizational practices in the name of 'efficiency' and protecting 'the brand' suggests leading in multi-national corporations may routinely be akin to an exercise in colonisation (Banerjee & Linstead, 2001; Morgan & Kristensen, 2006).

The sheer complexity of operating in diverse and dynamic markets, often dominated by large organizations operating in multiple jurisdictions, is also a significant influence on leadership practice. Even with some regularisation of trade policies, local legislation, issues and customs remain matters to be considered, creating a situation where leaders have to contend with different 'rules of the game' for different parts of the organization (Newlands & Hooper, 2016). There is, moreover, a clear need to focus attention outwards, to try to make sense of wider trends and identify opportunities and threats to the organization, as well as to focus inwards on the practical realities of day-to-day operations, building future capability in products, systems and people and sustaining the organization's culture and values (Bryson, 2010; Buckley, Burton & Mirza, 2008).

Realistically, these efforts need to be both distributed within an organization of any size, so that different people can focus attention outwards or inwards, and coordinated, so that the insights obtained in relation to each area of focus can be compared and combined to inform decision making and organizational learning (Senge, 2006). Leadership has a role to play, then, in process terms, in organizing for these points of focus to be addressed and facilitating their coming together, and in substantive terms, in the strategy and operational decisions which arise from the insights which those with these varying points of focus can bring to the debate. Notice, for a moment, how this way of accounting for leadership highlights matters such as institutional arrangements and decision-making processes as key, not simply the leader's personal attributes and style, in order to understand the nature of leadership in the context of globalisation.

It is also important to recognise that globalisation, despite its aforementioned tendency toward standardisation and homogenisation, simultaneously facilitates rapid shifts in the competitive landscape: top-down approaches to leadership are thus likely to miss important local issues which affect organizational success, unable to keep up with the sheer variety and pace of what is happening in diverse local markets where a multi-national corporation operates. This means that the letting go of power at the top, enabling the delegation of decision making to greater numbers of people, may be an appropriate approach to dealing with the effects of globalisation, a move which again puts the focus squarely on coordination and facilitation of debate as central issues for leadership if some consistency of strategy, product, service or organization culture is still deemed important.

At a local level, the existence of a diverse workforce implies that knowledge of different cultural norms, values and practices becomes more important if those in leadership roles are to have an understanding of the identities and values of those they claim to lead (Johnson, Lenartowicz & Apud, 2006). For ex-patriate leaders, this need is even greater if they are to engage with the local population in something other than a colonialist manner. Local/global tensions constitute a further challenge, requiring skill in working across and within different cultural contexts, in negotiation and in conflict resolution (Dörrenbächer & Geppert, 2011).

What all this can be read to imply is that the heavy focus given by leadership scholars in recent decade to issues of vision, charisma and transformation is, when we contemplate the challenges of leading in the context of globalisation, a far too narrow agenda, one, moreover, that is redolent of a kind of conquest, where leaders from head office direct a strategic vision that does not reflect local concerns. Our reading of globalisation implies that a different and more diverse range of challenges exist for leadership, including issues of organizational design to enable a diversity of views to be considered in decision making and to enable organizational learning, and where the inequalities that form part of the globalising project are challenged.

## The Influence of Financial Markets on Business Practices

From around the 1980s onward, financial markets have grown in influence and impact as capitalism has become increasingly financialised (Foster, 2007; Magdoff & Sweezy, 1987). Particularly in the case of publicly listed companies, this has given rise to a focus on quarterly earnings reports, as companies strive to curry favour with market commentators in order to sustain or increase their share price (Yang & Krishnan, 2005). The increasing use of executive remuneration practices which link rewards to stock prices has aided in ensuring this focus, which, in turn, has been shown to increase the misreporting of results (Burns & Kedia, 2006; Efendi, Srivastava, & Swanson, 2007; Harris, 2008). This focus on quarterly earnings reports is assuredly a short-term and highly restricted lens for assessing organizational performance. The interests of other stakeholders, such as employees, suppliers, customers and the local communities in which businesses operate, are undermined when share price becomes the primary focus of managerial effort (Banerjee, 2008; Pfeffer, 2009). However, this approach to business, which fails to build capability for the longer term and encourages unethical practice, has become increasingly normalised in recent decades.

The implications of this development for leadership are, we believe, troubling. Executives are encouraged to look for both short-term and personal gains, these being potentially at the expense of other stakeholders and longer-term interests. The glossing over of challenges and ambiguities in organizational capability and results is incentivised via the pressure to keep market analysts, who focus on metrics, happy. Bold promises of dramatic change are also encouraged, especially in respect of cost reductions which flow directly to the bottom line. While there is much research to show us that organizations are complex, dynamic entities operating in contexts that are frequently unpredictable and unstable (e.g., Kunda, 2006; Mintzberg, 2009), the culture of 'the market' encourages leaders to pretend this is not so and instead speak with (false) certainty of plans, goals and projections. Effectively, then, what leaders can *safely* say when talking to 'the market' is strictly prescribed by expectations of control, certainty and predictability which, we argue, are at best serious distortions of organizational realities and at worst complete fantasies. Needless to say, we think it problematic that business leaders are encouraged to offer up fantasies because the accepted narrative of the market expects as much from them.

## The Decline of 'Authority' as a Source of Power

Emerging from around the early 1960s onwards, 'authority' in its various guises has generally been in a state of decline, while 'elite-challenging' activities have been rising (Inglehart, 1977, p. 3; see also Gitlin, 1993). This has changed the landscape for leadership in profound but also subtle and ambiguous ways. Given the often close connection between 'leadership' and 'authority', we explore this trend in some depth, examining the case of both formal leadership positions (leadership-with-authority, be that legal or institutional) and leadership-without-authority.

Those in leadership positions or those possessing expertise, these being the traditional grounds for exercising or possessing 'authority', can now no longer simply count on others less powerful or qualified to comply with their instructions or advice, in the West at any rate (Collinson, 1992; Kellerman, 2012). The traditional expectation of deference to 'authority' or 'status' is no longer widely accepted here as a legitimate or useful way of ordering social relations (Inglehart, 1977). Respect and compliance with directives thus now often have to be 'worked for' by those in positions of authority; they are matters which can no longer be taken for granted. Rules and laws, too, have increasingly been regarded as matters automatically, legitimately and reasonably open to question and challenge by those subject to them (Hall, 2005; Inglehart, 1977). Simultaneously, greater legal protections of human and civil rights in many jurisdictions serve as constraints on the use of authority, albeit that many post-9/11 security laws are a notable exception to this (Hafner-Burton & Tsutsui, 2005; Levi & Wall, 2004; Webb, 2007).

For those in *formal leadership positions*, this general erosion of 'authority' has potentially profound implications. One of these is the significant importance now attached to leaders being seen to be 'in touch with' and visible to their followers (Gabriel, 1997; Wilson, 2016). Leaders now prioritise being 'friendly' and 'approachable' as important elements of their practice (Alvesson & Sveningsson, 2003), whereas in earlier times, a rather more reserved and sober demeanour was expected, reflecting and reinforcing the status of leadership (Gowin, 1915; Wilson, 2016). Our former Prime Minister's response to this trend, for example, seemed to involve going to considerable effort to be seen as an 'ordinary kiwi',[1] even though, with a personal wealth estimated at $60 million (Read, 2016), his situation was far from ordinary. His successful execution of this strategy appeared central to his sustained popularity, separating out the leader's 'likeability' from assessment of the government's policy goals or their achievement.

In the past, the power of 'authority' meant that 'command' and 'control' were central features of what effective organizational leadership and management was expected to involve (Fayol, 1930). Nowadays, it is commonplace that organizational leaders are expected to have a 'vision' and be 'transformational', 'charismatic' and 'authentic', approaches intended to motivate followers to give of their best based on the understanding that 'command' and 'control' techniques no longer exert the hold they once did (Bass, 1985; Conger, 1989; Luthans & Avolio, 2003). One obvious implication is that those who are shy or reserved may struggle to gain credibility as a 'leader' in a milieu where being highly visible and extroverted in interactions with others are seen as key indicators of the leader identity. Yet leadership as a staged performance, where focus goes on being seen to do the right thing, rather than on achieving substantive results, is incentivised when it is conceived in such grandiose terms (Alvesson, 2013; Tourish, 2013; Wilson, 2016).

Persuasion, coalition building and negotiation emerge as key leadership practices when mere assertion of authority is an inadequate basis for securing compliance (Kellerman, 2012). With 'authority' a weakened source of power, the importance for leadership of listening, bargaining and forging relationships grounded in mutual trust and understanding of others' perspectives seem greater. Despite this, it is the construction of leadership in heroic terms, approaches in which the leader is cast as the one who knows best, that have been the most influential responses offered by leadership scholars to the decline in authority, ideas that function to re-stabilise leader power to a considerable extent (Wilson, 2016).

With the decline of 'authority', a key consequence is that followers' power to exert influence rises: their support has to be more routinely sought through persuasive efforts, dissent and resistance are enabled, and seeking compliance via instruction or enforcement is less effective (Collinson, 1992, 2006; Kellerman, 2008, 2012). All these matters point to followers having greater scope to argue their own case and to have it heard and considered. Arguably, however, efforts by those in authority positions to gain control over the 'management of meaning' (Smircich & Morgan, 1982), something commonly embraced as a legitimate practice (Pearce & Pearce, 2000), can function to nullify, neutralise or constrain follower power relative to that of the leader, and while authority may have declined, it has not simply disappeared. The decline in authority, then, does not simply remove the power imbalance between designated leaders and followers, rather, these relations of power become more fluid and reliant on other, less certain sources of influence (Collinson, 2005, 2006; Wilson, 2016).

The tensions that may arise between those engaged in leading (with authority) and their ostensible followers seem to be intensified with the decline in the power of authority. Leaders nowadays have to work hard to garner followers' compliance and support (Collinson, 2005; 2006, 2009). Their wishes are more likely to be frustrated by followers challenging what is asked of them. Followers now expecting leaders to take heed of their needs and views, meanwhile, are more likely to be frustrated rather than simply resigned to disappointment if those matters are not addressed, and to act upon these frustrations in both overt and covert ways (Collinson, 1992, 2005, 2006; Kellerman, 2008, 2012). With 'authority' no longer keeping followers in their traditional, subservient state, then, tensions and competing interests and perspectives are unleashed and intensified, systemic challenges which help explain why we are so often disappointed by leaders. Arguably, this contested environment is such as to shape not only the dynamics of leadership work today but also to reconfigure its purpose. Rather than its purpose being to achieve the strategies and plans developed by (expert, authoritative) leaders, perhaps its primary purpose becomes (more modestly) to facilitate the development of strategies and plans to which people will choose to commit.

Having argued that the power of authority has been in a general state of decline, and that this is re-shaping leadership practice, we do want to note that this general trend is attenuated in many workplaces. The authority of manager-leaders to hire and fire typically remains intact. The decline of trade union power in many countries, along with the rise of precarious work as against stable employment, further aid in ensuring manager-leaders' authority is still highly potent in many cases (Dyer, Humphries, Fitzgibbons & Hurd, 2014; Standing, 2011). The pervasive influence of neoliberalism and managerialism, through which reality is framed from the perspective of market relations and managerial interests whilst appearing to cater for a wider set of concerns, also serves to stabilise organizational leaders' power (Parker, 2002; Springer, Birch & MacLeavy, 2016). The hierarchical nature of most workplaces, in which formal power flows from the top down, is, then, arguably a domain only somewhat affected by the general decline in the power of 'authority'. However, it is also a context which we believe could benefit from the greater use of the kinds of leadership practices identified above, something which this book explores further.

In the case of *leadership-without-authority*, the decline in the power of authority offers greater scope for leadership to emerge from across the social spectrum, and indeed, this has been precisely what has occurred (Kellerman, 2008, 2012). This is because a social context is enabled where those who do not hold formal positions of authority have greater freedom and legitimacy to lead and to be accepted as leading, be that undertaken *individually or collectively*. We may say, then, that the decline in the power of authority appears to be productive of more leadership emerging from amongst the community as a whole, enabling more people to develop relevant skills and experiences and generating more collective, distributed efforts to address issues of common concern.

Leaders acting without formal authority require a strong focus on shared concerns to secure follower support (Johnson, Safad & Faraj, 2015; Schweigert, 2007). Given the enormous variety of topics and values that may inform communities of interest who are not conventional organizations, leadership in this context may also be given expression in diverse ways, reflecting the values and concerns of the group in question. Leading in the context of an animal rights community, for instance, may emphasise caring as a key uniting value, while leading in the context of reading group may emphasise bringing forth diverse views. Leading without authority, however may be reasonably well placed to ensure substance trumps style, because in assessing the leader's actions there arises "a kind of sober pragmatism that sifts rhetoric for truth and authenticity" (Schweigert, 2007, p. 327). This contrasts with leading-with-authority, where heroic, grandiose theories create incentives for organizational leaders to focus on issues of image. In collective form, leading-without-authority also implies a focus on substantive issues, insofar as through collective effort the aim is to provide leadership to advance a particular set of shared interests. To achieve this, a focus on deploying processes which enable debate and decision making likely become central issues. Leading-without-authority, due to its voluntaristic basis, is likely less prone to the particular tensions and conflicts associated with leading-with-authority, yet it generates its own complications: sustaining follower support relies on a constant recalibration between leader effort and follower response, while collective decision making relies on effective processes that will allow this to happen.

Overall, the decline in the power of authority gives rise to a complex and diverse set of implications for leadership. It renders persuasive practices an important feature of the contemporary landscape for those in formal leadership positions, in response to followers' increased power to have their say and to resist. These persuasive efforts may serve to nullify the desire to resist, while the positioning of leaders as visionary, charismatic and transformational beings functions to sustain leader power. Issuing instructions based on expertise or authority has become a less viable means of ensuring compliance, and more effort and time must go to dialogical, relational efforts. This, in turn, means leaders must be more visible and accessible to followers; however, this carries with it the risk that the public performance of 'being the leader' takes priority over actually achieving results: style could trump substance. Tensions and contestation abound, such that perhaps the purpose of leadership might be usefully constrained to that of facilitating shared commitment of the priorities for action. Leadership-without-authority, meanwhile, flowers in diverse ways but with a clear focus on the advancement of shared interests, while its collective expression requires close attention to issues of process.

## The Increased Status and Influence of Women in Business and Politics

In many countries, women have, ever so slowly, come to secure some greater say in business and politics and to have their needs, concerns and views treated with greater respect and consideration by decision makers (Inglehart & Norris, 2003). Women's legal rights and social status have been improved in many places, although gender inequality persists, and is frequently compounded by racial/ethnic inequality (United Nations Women, 2016). The proportion of MPs, CEOs, board members and managers who are women has grown over time in many countries and, while equal representation is a long way from being been achieved in most countries and industries, it is becoming more common for women to comprise at least a significant minority of those in decision-making roles (Terjesen & Singh, 2008). Their under-representation in such roles is, moreover, now more commonly accepted as a matter of valid concern, creating pressure for continued improvement in the number of women in these roles.

In terms of organizational leadership, the rising influence of women has a number of implications. One is that issues of common concern to women workers are now less easily ignored by those in leadership positions. Access to child care facilities, maternity leave and the development of flexible working arrangements to fit around child-care responsibilities, for example, are now much more commonplace in organizations (Christensen & Schneider, 2010). Demands from women that organizational attention be paid to their particular needs and opinions has resulted in manager-leaders rethinking policies and practices that were designed with men in mind (Acker, 1990; Moghadam, 2015). Although the gender pay gap remains a problem, legislative bans on direct gender-based pay discrimination have been secured in many jurisdictions (United Nations Women, 2016). As a consequence, those in leadership roles can increasingly expect to be called on to demonstrate that equal employment opportunity practices inform their hiring, promotion and remuneration decisions. How women are treated interpersonally by men, during the course of their employment, has also been subjected to challenge. While sexual harassment and sexist language that excludes and/or denigrates women remain common workplace problems, organizational policies prohibiting such behaviours have spread, providing some kind of platform for challenge (Douglas & Sutton, 2014; McDonald, 2012).

The egalitarian principle, that all persons deserve equal respect and consideration, places a clear and specific moral duty on male leaders vis-à-vis women: to ensure that the leader himself leads in ways that respects, values and enables women, and to demand the same of the men they lead. As part of the increased influence of women in business and politics, male leaders have been openly challenged to change their sexist, misogynistic attitudes and behaviours and to show greater respect in how they interact with women and respond to issues of concern to women (Wright & Holland, 2014). While women who make such demands are likely to encounter harsh criticism and misrepresentation of their messages, addressing these matters may help to broaden men's skills, scope of attention and reduce the risk of decisions that are adverse for women (Wright & Holland, 2014). Other men, too, likely benefit from male leaders who have learned to pay greater heed to relationship issues and demonstrate greater interpersonal sensitivity.

The women who do manage to get hold of organizational leadership positions also create effects: research has shown that women leaders tend to deploy democratic, participatory approaches more frequently than men and rely on autocratic approaches less often than men (Eagly & Carli, 2003; Stead & Elliott, 2009). Women have been shown to be more likely than men to adopt transformational leadership approaches and to offer rewards based on performance (Eagly, Johannesen-Schmidt & van Engen, 2003). In considering a range of contradictory findings as regards 'women's leadership style', Psychogios reports that "major findings show an integrative women's leadership model characterized by task commitment, personal sacrifice, goal orientation, commitment to personal relationships with employees and an emphasis on teamwork" (2007, p, 169). These inclusive and empowering approaches provide a greater scope for followers to express their views and to influence decisions, thereby opening up organizational decision making to a wider variety of ideas and heightening employee motivation and creativity (Sinclair, 1998; Zhang & Bartol, 2010).

The rising status and influence of women, then, means women's needs, concerns and views demand new organizational practices and policies, widening the scope of issues to which leaders must attend and creating pressure on male leaders (and their male followers) to behave in ways respectful to, and inclusive of, women. Simultaneously, leadership by women is changing the experience of followers through typically placing greater priority than their male counterparts on attending to follower concerns, ideas and rewards. Combined, these developments extend the leadership agenda in both substantive and behavioural terms, adding a further layer of complexity as leaders are expected to navigate gender relations with care and skill. Looking ahead, closing the gender (and racial) equality gap suggests further changes in leadership are still needed to provide the opportunity for those currently under-represented in leadership ranks to gain entry on terms acceptable to them.

## The Dispersion of Information and Knowledge (Often Enabled by Technology)

Knowledge, by which we mean insights about some phenomena gained through research and/or experience, and information, by which we mean facts and data, have long been understood as potent sources of power and prestige (Plato, 1995; Machiavelli, 2005). Having access to specialist, valued knowledge or information can create an advantage over one's competitors, be that at an organizational or national level (Dosi, Faillo & Marengo, 2008; Porter, 1990). Those who are 'in the know', who have entry to the 'inner sanctum', who have been granted 'clearance' to access that which is otherwise deemed secret, all have power relative to those excluded from such knowledge and information (Costas & Grey, 2014).

With the advent of the printing press in 1440, access to formal knowledge slowly spread to more and more of the population until, eventually, universal access to tertiary levels of knowledge and education became the norm, at least in the West (Cameron, 2001; Trow, 2007). Over the last couple of decades, the internet has further heightened expectations that both knowledge and information be readily accessible to lay audiences (Porter & Donthu, 2006; Ross et al., 2005). More and more people have become engaged in 'online research' and 'online communities', using the internet to obtain information and knowledge needed for professional and personal interests and to build connections with others with similar interests (Porter & Donthu, 2006; Sum, Mathews, Pourghasem & Hughes, 2009). Rising expectations of government and corporate transparency have also intensified demands for access to information, albeit that the institutional response to such demands has been often fallen short of community aspirations (Bonsón, Torres, Royo & Flores, 2012; Chadwick & May, 2003; Vaccaro & Madsen, 2009).

This mass dispersion has not rendered knowledge and information any less powerful, in that it can still be used in analysis, establishing expertise and legitimacy, formulating arguments and informing decision making. In practical terms, knowledge and information are perhaps more powerful than ever before, because of our heavy reliance upon them (Castells, 2010). However, knowledge and information located in the now vast 'public domain' do have limited prestige value, because of their sheer accessibility.

Technology, meanwhile, has played an ever-increasing role in changing our lives in diverse but profound ways since the Industrial Revolution, such that even those living in poverty will now often have access to sophisticated technology such as smartphones (Aker & Mbiti, 2010; Hudson, 2005). These days, knowledge and information are routinely embedded in technology or transmitted through technology. More and more data are gathered by both public and private organizations, and both these data and the technological ability to gather them constitute a source of power, often of significant military, political and economic importance (Bauman, 2007; Lyon, 2014). Thanks to the internet, the transmission of information and knowledge can now be instantaneous and global in character, hence information and knowledge security has become a major issue for governments and corporations alike (Schatz & Bashroush, 2016; Smith & Jamieson, 2006).

The implications of these developments for leadership are many and various. A directive leadership approach founded upon privileged access to knowledge and information is less viable when access is democratised. More effort must go to persuade by means of dialogue and debate. Fostering these skills becomes an important dimension of leadership development. Followers' ability to access knowledge and information gives them material with which to question and challenge leader's propositions, suggesting a more inclusive, consultative approach to decision making will also be expected. The knowledge and information used to inform leadership decisions may have its reliability and validity scrutinised to a much greater extent. Technology may enable the automation or delegation of some decisions previously made by leaders, as well as providing mechanisms for fast feedback to be gathered from followers. Leaders are increasingly dependent on those with specialist knowledge, unable to be experts themselves in all activities for which they may have responsibility (Gosling & Mintzberg, 2003). Information security and individual privacy, in the era of mass surveillance and WikiLeaks, are hotly contested matters, requiring ethical and policy responses by leaders as regards the practices of their organizations (Vaccaro & Madsen, 2009)

What emerges, then, is that mass access to knowledge and information changes the landscape for leaders. Their hold on power and authority is rendered more open to scrutiny and challenge when followers understand and know what is going on. Technology spreads information rapidly, enables fast and mass follower responses and can also result in the devolution or automation of decision making. Leaders increasingly depend on experts to guide (i.e. lead, in some sense) their efforts, while followers with knowledge and information at their disposal are likely more inclined to demand reasoned debate and dialogue rather than just decree. That which was previously the exclusive or restricted domain of leaders is, thus, now commonly open to the gaze and the action of followers. These developments change both the 'how' and the 'what' of leadership practice.

## Climate Change

We take it as read, here, that the science on climate change is sufficiently clear and credible such that the effects of human activity upon planetary systems are indeed unsustainable, and that dramatic changes to natural resource usage and activities that emit $CO_2$ are therefore urgently needed (see, for example, IPCC, 2014). Given, then, that we face a challenge of quite literally planetary proportions which threatens our current way of life, we think the implications for organizational leadership practices are very significant.

The transition to a low or no carbon-emitting society will require leaders to identify, support and secure fundamental changes to many well-established organizational practices (Koch, 2015). This transition will demand often radical changes to the methods of sourcing raw materials and producing and distributing goods and services which constitute the very value chain that presently renders many organizations profitable (Linton, Klassen & Jayaraman, 2007; UNEP, 2013). In some industries, the scale and scope of change needed is nothing short of revolutionary in nature (Barbier, 2012; UNEP, 2013). Garnering support for such momentous changes and ensuring they are effectively designed and implemented will not be easy, as the effects of changes on suppliers, employees, customers and shareholders will frequently be unwelcome and hotly contested (Meadowcroft, 2009). Some products and services will simply stop being produced altogether, potentially spelling the end of the organizations which produce them (Borel-Saladin & Turok, 2013; UNEP, 2013). In all this, the focus for leadership efforts will be challenging the status quo and advancing the new and different, even in the face of resistance. The temptation for leaders to resort to autocratic approaches in response to such pressures is, however, worryingly high; therefore, more collectivist approaches will be vital features of the transition process (Meadowcroft, 2007).

Developing an environmentally sustainable organization means that the criteria for what constitutes success cannot be a singular, bottom-line focus, but must instead also address the wider effects of the organization's activities on the environment (Kolk, 2008). Gauging the short-, medium- and long-term consequences of various change options in terms of both profitability *and* environmental considerations will, thus, become central to leader decision making. Planning time horizons and the timeframe over which investment 'paybacks' are calculated will need to be extended. Attention will need to go to reviewing all existing business practices, to understand their environmental impact and, to the greatest extent possible, eliminating or minimising the harm they create. Choices will exist in the extent to which an organization responds minimally to public policy requirements around environmental matters, or seeks to go beyond what is required of it by regulators: the ethics of such choices must be weighed up by leaders. In changing how an organization carries out its activities with a view to minimising or eliminating environmental harm, competing views on issues of science and technology will need to be confronted by organizational leaders. In all of this, practical, commercial and eco-ethical concerns will often sit in acute tension with each other.

A general implication of these matters is that decision making by leaders will be complex, requiring consideration of competing interests and a weighing up of diverse concerns. A tolerance amongst leaders for complexity and ambiguity therefore seems crucial, along with the ability to foster that tolerance in others, through what and how they communicate with followers. More than just the technical deployment of scientific, commercial and ethical criteria, what is also implied is that leadership practice must strive to bring about decisions that are wise, knowing that at times this may involve choosing the lesser of many evils. To achieve this suggests leaders will need to listen carefully to competing advice and views, meaning followers will need to speak up to ensure their advice and views get taken into account. Dealing with conflict, forging coalitions and negotiating compromises that secure the support of stakeholders are also implied as crucial leadership practices in the context of the transition to sustainability.

As the transition to a low or no carbon society appears, of all the developments we have considered here, to be the one that implies the most radical scope of change, so too does it seem to imply the most radical change for leadership. Whilst complexity and increased contestation of leader power/ authority have repeatedly been identified as issues for leadership practice throughout the whole of the preceding discussion, the complexity of decision making in responding to climate change seems likely, for many organizations, to far exceed the capability of any one individual leader, no matter how visionary, charismatic, authentic, moral or transformational they may be. If this is so, then this serves as further encouragement to shift the focus from leaders onto leadership practice, this being understood in a more holistic, inclusive and systemic manner than a focus on individual psychology alone provides. In the next section, then, we lay out our conceptual framework which seeks to do just this.

## Contextualised Theorising: A Framework

Earlier research (see Wilson, 2016) has identified a handful of key ideas or topics of interest which have been of long-standing and repeated relevance to scholarly efforts to theorise leadership. The specific form these key elements for theory-building take has varied at different times and in different paradigms; however, they are nonetheless core matters to which leadership scholars have repeatedly paid attention, from the Ancient Greeks through to the present day. Seeking to learn from this history of scholarly effort, our aim here is to demonstrate how these elements can be flexibly deployed in developing leadership theorisations tailored to particular contexts. In what follows, we will be introducing what this core componentry for leadership theory-building entails and the kinds of questions and issues it requires theorists to consider. In later chapters, we deploy this model to formulate specific contextualised theorisations of leadership, in order to illustrate its potential in depth.

Our aim here is both adventurous and cautious. We are adventurous in that we are aiming to demonstrate a new approach to leadership theory-building, one which pulls out key ideas found in the (Western) history of leadership thought and proposes these can be both flexed to meet contemporary conditions and deployed in varying configurations to meet the needs of different contexts. However, the approach is also cautious in that we are seeking to build localist, not universalist, theories designed to focus on specific, limited contexts. We also see leadership as only ever being one amongst a number of potentially useful responses to meet our needs. Laws, rules, policies, collective effort, science and technology are potentially just as, if not more, relevant to address some matters than is 'leadership', in whatever form it may take. In aiming to invent new forms of leadership, then, we will both draw from and learn from the past whilst also seeking to formulate useful responses to the challenges we encounter in different organizational settings today.

Our approach to theorising is not in the nature of formulating precise hypotheses such as one commonly finds in positivist leadership research, but is instead heuristic in its tenor. Those familiar and comfortable with more prescriptive approaches may therefore wish to treat our efforts as 'model-building' rather than theorising. Regardless of the terminology you prefer, what we are attempting to do here is to describe and define a means of developing tailored approaches to leadership for different contexts. We propose this can be done by systematic consideration of a set of elements which the history of leadership thought shows have been of recurring concern in leadership scholarship. What we offer can thus be understood as a meta-theoretical methodology for theorising leadership.

In our approach, the empirical question of what correlations exist between phenomena is initially bracketed off, positioned as an operational issue and not a matter of the first order for theory-building. Instead, theory-building develops through attending to the different elements of our framework and the questions they invoke a theorist to address. These elements often entail normative considerations, meaning their ethical and political dimensions must be consciously considered, ensuring that leadership theorising pays attention to the concerns and interests of those to whom it directs its efforts. They also entail pragmatic considerations, taking account of what may be possible within a reformist rather than revolutionary approach. Taking these questions seriously also means universalist propositions are unlikely to emerge; hence, the framework itself drives the theorist toward the production of a contextualised theorisation.

The elements of our framework are the *challenges* deemed of salience to leadership in a given context; the *purpose* intended for leadership in that context; the *values and norms* to guide and constrain leadership in that context; and the *domains of life* to which leadership is directed in that context and how it may act in those domains. These matters, cumulatively, lay out the scope, nature, focus, boundaries and ethical and normative requirements of a theorisation of leadership, all of which are oriented around consideration of a particular context, or site, where leadership is sought. The outcome of theorising these matters informs the other dimension of the framework, namely the expectations placed on *the leader* and the *follower* in terms of their *personal attributes, behaviours, rights, responsibilities and roles.*

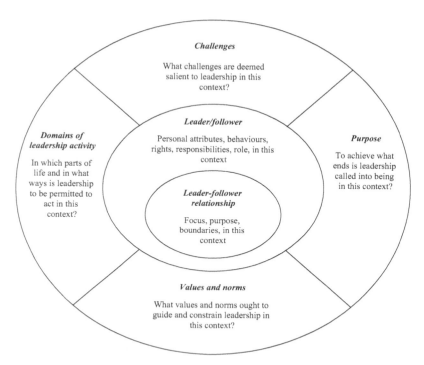

*Diagram 2.1* A meta-theoretical methodology for theorising leadership

These matters in turn shape the approach to be taken to the *leader-follower relationship* in terms of its *focus, purpose and the boundaries* which govern it. In the process of theory-building, we believe each of these elements demands consideration; however, a specific theorisation developed for a particular context need not, of necessity, end up actually incorporating every element. We can, for example, envisage a contextualised theorisation of leadership which conceptualises it in collective or distributed forms, such that no account of a 'leader' or 'follower' role is required.

Diagram 2.1 above represents this framework in visual form. The subsequent discussion explains each element, followed by a brief summation of how we apply it throughout the course of the book.

## What Challenges Are Deemed Salient to Leadership in This Context?

As we highlighted in our earlier review of the leadership literature (see Chapter 1) the social, political, economic, ethical and intellectual context in which a given leadership theory emerges has repeatedly, over many centuries, profoundly shaped what was then claimed as the truth about leadership. Varying models of leadership have emerged in response to particular issues being understood as challenges which are of direct salience to leadership, these being either matters which constrain leadership, matters which constitute systemic dynamics to be grappled with or needs and opportunities to which leadership effort is to be directed. The positive lesson we take from the history of our field, then, is that the challenges which are deemed as being salient to leadership in a given context are a core aspect of theorising leadership. Conscious attention to these matters is needed to craft a form of leadership that will be relevant and meaningful to a given context. The 'deeming' of something as being salient to leadership is a process of construction, not something given by nature, and hence requires careful assessment as to why certain features of the context are selected as being of salience to leadership. Prior research which examines the nature of the tasks, issues, opportunities and difficulties that a particular context involves provides a key source of information in this process.

Our approach has it that leadership theory-building requires, then, a detailed grasp of the challenges which constrain the focus and scope of leadership in a given context, as well as the issues needing resolution, development or sustenance to which 'leadership' is expected to make some useful contribution. Rather than starting by asking, 'what are the characteristics of the leader and how do these affect followers?', as is so often the case in leadership theorising today, we start by asking *what challenges are deemed salient to leadership in this context?* By asking this question, we believe we are better placed to generate theorisations of leadership consciously shaped by the very context in which leadership action will take place.

To develop the kind of contextualised theorisations that we believe offer a useful way forward for leadership studies, we suggest focussing leadership theories on quite tightly specified 'challenges' and contexts. "Fostering of creativity in knowledge-intensive workplaces" or "leadership in a start-up business context" could be potential challenges and contexts warranting customised theorisations of leadership, for example. Assuming that the actions or attributes of 'the leader' can only ever provide a partial solution to the challenges at hand is also recommended. This helps to ensure that other sources of influence conducive to the context and the challenges it entails, influences such as policy, legislation, procedures, systems, rules and shared values, norms and behaviours can be factored in to how we theorise leadership. Through starting with the context and positioning leadership as only part of the solution, our theories become targeted and modest, not universal and grandiose.

## The Purpose of Leadership

*For what purpose, to achieve what ends, is leadership called into being?* This element of our framework is considered far too infrequently in leadership theorising (although for a notable exception, see Kempster, Jackson & Conroy, 2011). However, this is a powerful question to explore, the answers to which help direct the focus of effort and generate boundaries for leadership action. We suggest here two different ways in which the purpose of leadership can be conceptualised as part of the theory-building process. The first is our formulation below of a generalised, but nonetheless constraining, statement of the purpose of leadership. The second is to form context-specific, localised notions of purpose.

Repeatedly in the history of leadership studies *"ensuring community and follower well-being"* has been understood as the purpose of leadership (Wilson, 2016). At first glance such a purpose for leadership may seem appealing, as it seems to imply leaders ought to serve the interests of followers. However, there is also a distinctly paternalistic dimension to this framing and, indeed, assumptions of follower inadequacy have often been central to theorisations of leadership which adopt this understanding of its purpose (for more, see Wilson, 2016). Rejecting such assumptions is important to us when we think about the purpose of leadership.

Doing so directs us toward a more modest, inclusive, process- and values-oriented view, in which *"enabling the achievement of shared goals, via means that are consistent with shared values"* is constituted as the core purpose of leadership. This purpose statement is one which implies that attention should go not only to *what* results are to be achieved, but also to *how* those results are achieved, moves which seek to centre ethical considerations, as advocated by Ciulla (1995), in what is constituted as the purpose of leadership. Moreover, the emphasis placed here on *shared* goals and *shared* values orients leadership to be that which serves and sustains the common interests that bind a community together, rather than simply the interests advocated by those in leadership roles. Reaching some tenable level of agreement on the nature of those shared goals and values necessitates, in our view, a working through and response to inevitably competing or conflicting goals and values, meaning there is a pluralist, not unitarist, assumption underpinning this purpose statement. This framing, then, functions to constrain leader action to that for which they can garner support and which adheres to accepted group or community values, constraints which, in the absence of democratic processes, provides some greater protection for worker-followers than the common presumption that manager-leaders know best what ought to be done in the name of leadership.

This is also a subtle but profound shift with this statement of purpose which moves us away from positioning the leader as one who saves others from their own inadequacies to one who, more modestly, helps others in achieving shared goals. Note, too, how in this framing there is no automatic requirement that the purpose of leadership implies the existence of a leader as such: where the purpose of leadership is "enabling the achievement of shared goals, via means that are consistent with shared values", then its enactment can readily be constituted as something that is shared amongst many. To further flesh out this generalised framing of the purpose of leadership, behavioural, functional or procedural matters could all be considered in the theorising process.

Alternatively, a more localised, specific notion of the purpose of leadership could be formulated, directly related to the contextual issues upon which a given theorisation is focussed. A theorisation of 'sustainable workplace leadership', for example, could have as its purpose 'achieving the long-term viability of the organization'. Adopting a more localised conception of the purpose of leadership also implies that both substantive knowledge and other sources of influence (e.g., policies, procedures, rules etc.) again appear as part of how we can theorise leadership in a more holistic yet context-sensitive manner.

Beyond these two approaches, we also suggest that concerns of a philosophical and political nature, such as personal autonomy or the care and respect we might propose we owe to others, could be used to inform our thinking about the purpose of leadership. Testing any proposed statement of purpose for its potential to foster an ethic of care for others or for its effect on individual autonomy is a means of checking the value-based assumptions that may reside in any proposed statement of purpose.

## Value and Norms to Guide and Constrain Leadership

While today positivist leadership theorising favours empiricist methods and likes to claim value neutrality, our earlier analysis of the literature highlighted how values and norms nonetheless remain implicit or implied in leadership theorisations. From this, then, the lesson we take is that theory-building should directly address the question of *what values and norms ought to guide and constrain leadership in this context?* Clearly this is a normative question and, thus, requires a reflexive accounting of these matters by those in engaged in theory building. It requires direct attention to issues of ethics in theorising leadership, a further feature of our approach which is consistent with Ciulla's demand that such matters have a central place in leadership (1995).

Attending to values and norms as an explicit feature of the theory-building process demands attention to both the ethical and political basis of a contextualised leadership theory, so as to gauge its potential effects upon the stakeholders involved in leadership in that context. Specifically, a focus on values requires articulation of what is to be considered desirable by way of means or ends, while a focus on norms requires articulation of what behaviours are to be considered acceptable or appropriate in a given situation (Marini, 2000; Rich, 1995). In combination, attention to values and norms provide mechanisms for grounding a contextualised theorisation of leadership in a wider framework of ethical thought, serving to ensure that in attending to a specific context it does not offend against more general moral principles.

Given the essentially contested nature of values and norms, we do not see it appropriate to propose here any specific values or norms as of general applicability to all theorisations of leadership. However, we do note that implied in our advocacy for the explicit articulation of values and norms to both guide *and* constrain leadership are values and norms of transparency and accountability by theorists, as well a view of leadership as something requiring constraints upon its exercise to safeguard the autonomy of followers.

## Domains of Leadership Activity

*Upon which parts of our lives and in what ways ought leadership be permitted to act?* Until quite recently, as our review of the literature showed, issues in the public, private, earthly and spiritual domains of life were all considered in leadership theorising, and propositions were advanced as to what leaders ought and ought not to do in these various domains. For centuries, theorising leadership thus meant attending to issues of religion and morality, to choices in relation to social, political, economic and military strategy and policy. It meant examining all aspects of the leader's life from cradle to grave and required overt attention to power and how it might legitimately and usefully be deployed. It also often entailed expectations that leaders guide or direct followers in multiple aspects of their lives, such as who to marry, how to raise their children and how to worship god.

Since around the end of WWII, however, the focus of scholarly effort narrowed onto the workplace and to issues of productivity and the psychology of the leader and their followers as it affects their workplace performance. 'New leadership' expanded this focus somewhat to issues of culture, meaning-making, strategy, vision and change; however, against a longer view of the history of leadership thought, the domains of life to which leadership theorising is today directed is remarkably narrow. At the same time, however, 'new leadership' has also treated the self of the follower as a legitimate domain for leadership activity in order to render that self more productive, a development whose political and ethical causes and effects are concerning to us.

In formulating contextualised theorisations of leadership, then, we propose that assessing which domains of life leadership activity ought to attend, and the scope and nature of that involvement, are important but largely ignored aspects of the theory-building process. Doing so requires, for example, consideration of to what extent a leader-manager ought to be able to work on the self of the follower-employee: is that a legitimate domain of life for leadership activity or not? The question of domains is, thus, a question that requires exploring issues of focus and boundaries, as were our earlier questions regarding the challenges shaping leadership, its purpose and the values and norms which inform it.

## The Leader (if Any): Personal Attributes, Behaviours, Rights, Responsibilities and Roles

A given theorisation of leadership need not necessarily provide for formally designated leadership positions. However, assuming that such positions will often be envisaged, the key questions then arise as to *what attributes or behaviours do we need from 'the leader'?* and *what rights, responsibilities and role should they be given?* Importantly, our intention is that these questions be addressed with a given context in mind. Developing answers to these questions demands simultaneous (or prior) attention to other aspects of our framework—the particular set of challenges, value and norms deemed of salience to leadership, the purpose specified for leadership and the particular domains of life to which leadership effort is to be directed. This is because we contend that the kind of leadership approach relevant to the demands of a start-up business, for example, is simply not the same as what is needed in the context of a large-scale, mature organization, and our approach seeks to tailor leadership theory and practice to different contexts.

In formulating an account of 'the leader', assuming for the moment such is deemed useful, some basic assumptions about the nature of 'the self' will need to be considered. The self can be assumed as having a fairly fixed, unitary and conscious nature, an approach which dominates the Western tradition, or, drawing on post-modernist thought as we do here, the self may be seen as fluid, contradictory, produced in interaction and not fully conscious of what drives it. The scope for individual agency relative to structural forces such as social norms, markets and institutional arrangements also warrants consideration in theorising 'the leader'. Assumptions about whether leadership attributes/behaviours/skills are understood as personal traits or as matters to be learned warrant consideration. The theorist might also explore what adopting an admiring, sceptical or hostile stance towards 'the leader' implies for the kinds of boundaries we might place around their rights, responsibilities and role.

Alternatively, 'the leader' could be de-emphasised, as relational and distributed theories of leadership are already doing (e.g., Gronn, 2000; Uhl-Bien & Ospina, 2012), in favour of understanding leadership as a co-produced or shared phenomenon and not something 'possessed' by individuals. However, if a given theorisation is to have 'the leader' as part of its model, then the attributes, behaviours, rights, responsibilities and roles expected of them need specification. Doing this will involve addressing both normative and practical issues about the nature and scope of control and influence that 'the leader' ought reasonably and usefully to have vis-à-vis 'the follower'. Hence, determining this aspect of the theory-building process will also entail consideration of the final two elements of our framework: 'the follower' and the leader-follower relationship.

## The Follower (if Any): Personal Attributes, Behaviours, Rights, Responsibilities and Roles

Given that we have already identified that a contextualised theory of leadership need not necessarily entail the construction of 'the leader', the same applies in relation to 'the follower': if 'leadership' is conceptualised as a co-produced phenomenon, then there is no pressing need to theorise 'the leader' or 'the follower', as such roles are understood as fleeting at best and occurring in processes of interaction. However, where 'the follower' is to form part of a theory, then the same questions we confront in respect of 'the leader' can arise in respect 'the follower': *what attributes or behaviours do we need from 'the follower'?* and *what rights, responsibilities and role should they be given?* These too must be answered in context, informed by a particular set of challenges deemed of salience to leadership, a purpose specified for leadership, a set of values and norms to guide and constrain leadership and a focus on particular domains of life. And, in formulating an account of 'the follower', the same issues to those specified above arise in regards to the assumptions made about the nature of 'the self', individual agency versus structure and traits versus learned behaviours and attributes.

Normatively, we suggest that the desirability of positioning 'the follower' as reliant upon or strongly influenced by 'the leader' be understood as a central concern in formulating an account of 'the follower'. For too long leadership theorising has positioned 'the follower' as an inferior being who needs to be 'improved' by the leader's influence; however, in the context of a knowledge-intensive workplace, for example, such assumptions may simply be counter-productive. Fostering follower autonomy, self-reliance and peer collaboration might instead be the appropriate focus. Treating 'the leader' and 'the follower' as partners in the leadership process could also be provocative in thinking about decision-making rights and processes. If we conceive of followers as those whom leaders exist to serve, this would have the effect of directing leader attention to the issues that concern and interest followers, thereby reversing the normal assumption that leaders are those who know best what matters. What should be apparent from these comments is that the assumptions and expectations made in relation to 'the follower' have a direct effect on what we might then expect or permit from 'the leader'. In the process of theory-building then, moving iteratively between the 'leader' and 'follower' elements of our framework is important.

## The Leader-Follower Relationship: Focus, Purpose, Boundaries

The propositions formulated in determining the place, if any, of 'the leader' and 'the follower' in a given theory of leadership will obviously inform the kind of leader-follower relationship that is then sought. However, we also suggest that specific attention go to theorising *the focus, purpose and boundaries of that relationship*. Here again, our concerns are both normative and practical in orientation: the question of how detailed an understanding 'the leader' and 'the follower' might be expected to have of each other's hopes, fears, dreams, skills, weaknesses, concerns and interests, for example, does not lend itself to a value-neutral, universally correct answer. Assuming 'the leader' is in a position of power over 'the follower', the extent of knowledge that they might legitimately and reasonably have of 'the follower' is a political and ethical issue requiring careful theoretical consideration. The leader-follower relationship in a mass production environment might quite legitimately be less intensive, more distant, than what is needed for leading a team of inexperienced psychologists. As always for us, context matters. Assessing the focus of the relationship, its purpose and the boundaries which are to govern it in light of a given context, and in light of the propositions developed in the other elements of our framework, thus comprises a further dimension of the theory-building process. Where a given theorisation has neither 'the leader' nor 'the follower', then this element will not need to be addressed.

## Using the Framework in the Theory-Building Process

Throughout the course of the book, we will demonstrate two different approaches for using the framework in the theory-building process. In the chapters which examine leading in supervisory management (Chapter 3), HRM (Chapter 4) and leadership scholarship (Chapter 8), our process begins at the top and centre of the framework (Diagram 2.1 above), addressing the question of 'what challenges are relevant to leadership in this context?' The analysis then proceeds clockwise around the outer circle and then moves progressively through the inner circles. This approach demonstrates how the model can be applied in a fairly structured, methodical manner to build up a contextualised theorisation. To provide a contrasting approach to its application, in the chapters which examine leadership in innovation and entrepreneurship (Chapter 5), strategy (Chapter 6) and governance (Chapter 7), the discussion moves more fluidly across the different elements of the framework. This approach demonstrates how the model can be used in a more fluid fashion in the process of building a contextualised theorisation.

We consider both approaches to have legitimacy and merit and offer no prescriptive advice as to which may be preferable, leaving that to users to determine for themselves. We do note, however, that to commence the theorising process by formulating an account of 'the leader' would be to miss the basic point of our approach, namely that it is matters outside of the leader which we argue are key in shaping leadership-practice-in-context. A prior focus on contextual issues (challenges, purpose, values and norms, domains of life), those matters in the outer ring of Diagram 2.1, ought to be used to inform the expectations that then arise of leaders and followers and, hence, their relationship, being those matters in the inner rings of Diagram 2.1.

# Conclusion

Our aim in this chapter has been to explore how the contemporary context affects leadership practice and to lay out our framework for developing *contextualised theorisations* of leadership that can inform *practice-in-context*. We examined six major trends affecting the priorities, possibilities and limitations being placed on leadership practice today. From our analysis of globalisation, the greater influence of financial markets on businesses and the economy, the decline of 'authority' as a source of power, the greater status and influence of women in business and politics, the dispersion of knowledge and information (often enabled by technology) and climate change, we have highlighted how the general landscape for leadership practice today is one that is tenuous, contested, complex and difficult.

Having already argued (in Chapter 1) that generic, universalist approaches to theorising leadership are problematic, we then laid out the seven major elements that we propose are important to consider when formulating context-sensitive and context-specific theorisations of leadership. Our theory-building framework has it that identifying the *challenges* which are of salience to leadership in a given context is a key aspect of the theory-building process, these 'challenges' being either constraints upon the exercise of leadership and/or matters to which leadership efforts ought to be directed. Consideration of the *purpose* of leadership in a given context, examining for what ends is it called into being, aid in further directing the desired focus of effort and generating boundaries for such efforts. Attention to the *values and norms* which ought to guide and constrain leadership, and to the *domains* of leadership activity, meaning in which parts of life and in what ways ought leadership be permitted to act, enable further consideration as to questions of focus and to establishing the ethical basis and boundaries of the intended leadership approach. Whether the theory-building process occurs in a step-by-step manner, or by a more dynamic or iterative process of working through these dimensions of the framework, all these matters help to inform the expectations to be established in respect of *'the leader'* (if any) and *'the follower'* (in any) in regards to their desired personal attributes and behaviours and their rights, responsibilities and role. These matters then inform the focus, purpose and boundaries to be formulated to govern the *leader-follower relationship*.

The analysis presented here, then, indicates in the first instance the general kinds of challenges facing leadership practice in the contemporary context. However, we offer no generic answer to the 'big issues' of the contemporary context. Instead, we propose a framework for building context-specific leadership theories that can inform leadership-practice-in-context. We have sought, in other words, to 'think global' before focussing on how we may theorise 'acting local'. In the remainder of the book, we put this approach to use by formulating theorisations of leadership focussed on specific contexts that commonly arise in organizations today. Our hope is that such efforts to 'act local' can make a difference, both in the immediate context at hand and cumulatively in respect of the wider context in which leadership practice occurs today.

## Note

1 'Kiwi' is a vernacular term for New Zealanders. In political discourse in New Zealand, frequent appeal is made by politicians to 'ordinary Kiwis', seeking to evoke positive connotations of people who are 'hard working', 'down to earth', 'friendly', 'honest', 'family oriented' and 'fair minded'. These popular ideals contrast sharply with the Prime Minister's reputation as a 'smiling assassin' from his time at merchant banking firm Merrill Lynch (Mellor, 2010).

## References

Acker, J. (1990). Hierarchies, jobs, bodies: A theory of gendered organizations. *Gender and Society*, 4(2), 139–158.

Aker, J. C., & Mbiti, I. M. (2010). Mobile phones and economic development in Africa. *Journal of Economic Perspectives*, 24(3), 207–232.

Alvesson, M. (2013). *The triumph of emptiness: Consumption, higher education, and work organization*. Oxford: Oxford University Press.

Alvesson, M., & Sveningsson, S. (2003). Managers doing leadership: The extra-ordinarization of the mundane. *Human Relations*, 56(12), 1435–1459.

Arnold, D., & Hewison, K. (2005). Exploitation in global supply chains: Burmese workers in Mae Sot. *Journal of Contemporary Asia*, 35(3), 319–340.

Banerjee, S. B. (2008). Corporate social responsibility: The good, the bad and the ugly. *Critical Sociology*, 34(1), 51–79.

Banerjee, S. B., & Linstead, S. (2001). Globalization, multiculturalism and other fictions: Colonialism for the new millennium? *Organization*, 8(4), 683–722.

Barbier, E. B. (2012). The green economy post Rio+20. *Science*, 338(6109), 887–888.

Bass, B. M. (1985). *Leadership and performance beyond expectations*. New York: Free Press.

Bauman, Z. (2007). *Consuming life*. Malden, MA: Polity Press.

Bonsón, E., Torres, L., Royo, S., & Flores, F. (2012). Local e-government 2.0: Social media and corporate transparency in municipalities. *Government Information Quarterly*, 29(2), 123–132.

Borel-Saladin, J. M., & Turok, I. N. (2013). The green economy: Incremental change or transformation? *Environmental Policy and Governance*, 23(4), 209–220.

Brown, S. P., & Slegel, L. B. (2005). Mass layoff data indicate outsourcing and off-shoring work. *Monthly Labor Review*, 128(8), 3–10.

Bryson, J. (Ed.). (2010). *Beyond skill: Institutions, organizations and human capability*. Basingstoke: Palgrave Macmillan.

Buckley, P. J., Burton, F., & Mirza, H. (Eds.). (2008). *The strategy and organization of international business*. New York, NY: Macmillan.

Burns, N., & Kedia, S. (2006). The impact of performance-based compensation on misreporting. *Journal of Financial Economics*, 79(1), 35–67.

Cameron, E. (2001). The power of the word: Renaissance and reformation. In E. Cameron (Ed.), *Early modern Europe: An Oxford history* (pp. 63–101). Oxford: Oxford University Press.

Castells, M. (2010). *The rise of the network society* (2nd ed., Vol. 1). Chichester, UK: Wiley-Blackwell.

Cerny, P. G., Menz, G., & Soederberg, S. (2005). Different roads to globalization: Neoliberalism, the competition state, and politics in a more open world. In S. Soederberg, G. Menz, & P. G. Cerny (Eds.), *Internalizing globalization: The rise* of neoliberalism and the decline of national varieties of capitalism (pp. 1–32). Basingstoke, UK: Palgrave Macmillan.

Chadwick, A., & May, C. (2003). Interaction between states and citizens in the age of the internet: "E-Government" in the United States, Britain, and the European Union. *Governance*, 16(2), 271–300.

Chossudovsky, M. (1997). Global financial crisis. *Economic and Political Weekly*, 32(43), 2794–2796.

Christensen, K., & Schneider, B. (2010). Conclusions: Solving the workplace/workforce mismatch. In K. Christensen & B. Schneider (Eds.), *Workplace flexibility: Realigning 20th-century jobs for a 21st-century workforce* (pp. 337–350). Ithaca, NY: Cornell University Press.

Ciulla, J. B. (1995). Leadership ethics: Mapping the terrain. *Business Ethics Quarterly*, 5(1), 5–28.

Collinson, D. (1992). *Managing the shopfloor: Subjectivity, masculinity and workplace culture.* Berlin: Walter de Gruyter.

Collinson, D. (2005). Dialectics of leadership. *Human Relations*, 58(11), 1419–1442.

Collinson, D. (2006). Rethinking followership: A post-structuralist analysis of follower identities. *The Leadership Quarterly*, 17(1), 179–189.

Collinson, D. (2009). Rethinking leadership and followership. In S. R. Clegg & C. Cooper (Eds.), *The Sage Handbook of Organizational Behaviour* (Vol. 2, pp. 251–264). London: Sage.

Conger, J. (1989). *The charismatic leader: Behind the mystique of exceptional leadership.* San Francisco, CA: Jossey-Bass.

Costas, J., & Grey, C. (2014). Bringing secrecy into the open: Towards a theorization of the social processes of organizational secrecy. *Organization Studies*, 35(10), 1423–1447.

Coucke, K., & Sleuwaegen, L. (2008). Offshoring as a survival strategy: Evidence from manufacturing firms in Belgium. *Journal of International Business Studies*, 39(8), 1261–1277.

Crotty, J. (2009). Structural causes of the global financial crisis: A critical assessment of the 'new financial architecture'. *Cambridge Journal of Economics*, 33(4), 563–58.

Doh, J. P. (2005). Offshore outsourcing: Implications for international business and strategic management theory and practice. *Journal of Management Studies*, 42(3), 695–704.

Dörrenbächer, C., & Geppert, M. (2011). *Politics and power in the multinational corporation: The role of institutions, interests and identities.* Cambridge: Cambridge University Press.

Dosi, G., Faillo, M., & Marengo, L. (2008). Organizational capabilities, patterns of knowledge accumulation and governance structures in business firms: An introduction. *Organization Studies*, 29(8–9), 1165–1185.

Douglas, K. M., & Sutton, R. M. (2014). "A giant leap for mankind" but what about women? The role of system-justifying ideologies in predicting attitudes toward sexist language. *Journal of Language and Social Psychology*, 33(6), 667–680.

Dyer, S., Humphries, M., Fitzgibbons, D., & Hurd, F. (2014). *Understanding management critically: A student text.* London: Sage.

Eagly, A. H., & Carli, L. L. (2003). The female leadership advantage: An evaluation of the evidence. *The Leadership Quarterly*, 14(6), 807–834.

Eagly, A. H., Johannesen-Schmidt, M. C., & van Engen, M. L. (2003). Transformational, transactional, and laissez-faire leadership styles: A meta-analysis comparing women and men. *Psychological Bulletin*, 129(4), 569–591.

Efendi, J., Srivastava, A., & Swanson, E. P. (2007). Why do corporate managers misstate financial statements? The role of option compensation and other factors. *Journal of Financial Economics*, 85(3), 667–708.

Fayol, H. (1930). (J. A. Coubrough, Trans.). *Industrial and general administration*. London: Pitman.

Fonterra. (n.d.). Company overview. Retrieved from www.fonterra.com/nz/en/About/Company+Overview.

Foster, J. B. (2007). The financialization of capitalism, editorial. *Monthly Review: An Independent Socialist Magazine*, (April), 1–12.

Foucault, M. (2010). *The Government of Self and Others: Lectures at the College de France, 1982-1983* (G. Burchell, Trans.). Basingstoke, Hampshire: Palgrave Macmillan.

Frenkel, M. (2005). The politics of translation: How state-level political relations affect the cross-national travel of management ideas. *Organization*, 12(2), 275–301.

Gabriel, Y. (1997). Meeting god: When organizational members come face to face with the supreme leader. *Human Relations*, 50(4), 315–342.

Gitlin, T. (1993). *The sixties: Years of hope, days of rage*. New York: Bantam.

Gosling, J., & Mintzberg, H. (2003). The five minds of a manager. *Harvard Business Review*, 81(11), 54–63.

Gowin, E. B. (1915). *The executive and his control of men; a study in personal efficiency*. New York: The Macmillan company.

Gronn, P. (2000). Distributed properties: A new architecture for leadership. *Educational Management Administration and Leadership*, 28, 317–338.

Hafner-Burton, E. M., & Tsutsui, K. (2005). Human rights in a globalizing world: The paradox of empty promises. *American Journal of Sociology*, 110(5), 1373–1411.

Hall, S. (2005). *Peace and freedom: The civil rights and anti-war movements in the 1960s*. Philadelphia: University of Pennsylvania Press.

Harris, J. D. (2008). Financial misrepresentation: Antecedents and performance effects. *Business & Society*, 47(3), 390–401.

Harrison, A., & Scorse, J. (2006). Improving the conditions of workers? Minimum wage legislation and anti-sweatshop activism. *California Management Review*, 48(2), 144–160.

Higgins, W., & Hallström, K. T. (2007). Standardization, globalization and rationalities of government. *Organization*, 14(5), 685–704.

Hodgson, G. M. (2011). The great crash of 2008 and the reform of economics. In J. Michie (Ed.), *The handbook of globalisation* (pp. 518–538). Cheltenham, UK: Edward Elgar.

Hudson, P. (2005). *The industrial revolution*. London, UK: Hodder Arnold.

Inglehart, R. (1977). *The silent revolution: Changing values and political styles among Western publics*. Princeton, NJ: Princeton University Press.

Inglehart, R., & Norris, P. (2003). *Rising tide: Gender equality and cultural change around the world*. Cambridge: Cambridge University Press.

IPCC (2014). Climate change 2014: Synthesis report. *United Nations Intergovernmental Panel on Climate Change*. Retrieved from www.ipcc.ch/report/ar5/syr/.

Johnson, P. J., Lenartowicz, T., & Apud, S. (2006). Cross-cultural competence in international business: Toward a definition and a model. *Journal of International Business Studies*, 37(4), 525–543.

Johnson, S. L., Safad, H., & Faraj, S. (2015). The emergence of online community leadership. *Information Systems Research*, 26(1), 165–187.

Kellerman, B. (2008). *Followership: How followers are creating change and changing leaders*. Boston, MA: Harvard Business Press.

Kellerman, B. (2012). *The end of leadership*. New York: Harper Business.

Kempster, S., Jackson, B., & Conroy, M. (2011). Leadership as purpose: Exploring the role of purpose in leadership practice. *Leadership*, 7(3), 317–334.

Koch, M. (2015). Climate change, capitalism and degrowth trajectories to a global steady-state economy. *International Critical Thought*, 5(4), 439–452.

Kolk, A. (2008). Sustainability, accountability and corporate governance: Exploring multinationals' reporting practices. *Business Strategy and the Environment*, 17(1), 1–15.

Kunda, G. (2006). *Engineering culture: Control and commitment in a high-tech corporation*. Philadelphia, PA: Temple University Press.

Levi, M., & Wall, D. S. (2004). Technologies, security, and privacy in the post-9/11 European information society. *Journal of Law & Society*, 31(2), 194–220.

Lewin, A. Y., & Peeters, C. (2006). Offshoring work: Business hype or the onset of fundamental transformation? *Long Range Planning*, 39(3), 221–239.

Linton, J. D., Klassen, R., & Jayaraman, V. (2007). Sustainable supply chains: An introduction. *Journal of Operations Management*, 25(6), 1075–1082.

Locke, R. M., Qin, F., & Brause, A. (2007). Does monitoring improve labor standards? Lessons from Nike. *Industrial and Labor Relations Review*, 61(1), 3–31.

Luthans, F., & Avolio, B. J. (2003). Authentic leadership: A positive developmental approach. In K. S. Cameron, J. E. Dutton, & R. E. Quinn (Eds.), *Positive organizational scholarship: Foundations for a new discipline* (pp. 241–258). San Francisco: Berrett-Koehler.

Lyon, D. (2014). Surveillance, snowden, and big data: Capacities, consequences, critique. *Big Data & Society*, 1(2), 1–13.

Machiavelli, N. (2005). The prince (W. J. Connell, Trans.). In W. J. Connell (Ed.), *The prince by Niccolo Machiavelli, with related documents*. Boston: Bedford/St Martins.

Magdoff, H., & Sweezy, P. M. (1987). *Stagnation and the financial explosion*. New York, NY: NYU Press.

Marini, M. M. (2000). Values and norms. In E. F. Borgatta & R. J. V. Montgomery (Eds.), *Encyclopedia of sociology* (2nd ed.). New York, NY: MacMillan.

Mayo, M. (2005). *Global citizens: Social movements and the challenge of globalization*. London: Zed Books.

McDonald, P. (2012). Workplace sexual harassment 30 years on: A review of the literature. *International Journal of Management Reviews*, 14(1), 1–17.

Meadowcroft, J. (2007). Who is in charge here? Governance for sustainable development in a complex world*. *Journal of Environmental Policy & Planning*, 9(3–4), 299–314. doi:10.1080/1523908070163154

Meadowcroft, J. (2009). What about the politics? Sustainable development, transition management, and long term energy transitions. *Policy Sciences*, 42(4), 323–340.

Mellor, W. (2010). 'Smiling assassin' targets rich immigrants. *New Zealand Herald*. Retrieved from http://www.nzherald.co.nz/business/news/article.cfm?c_id=3&objectid=10668580

Michie, J. (2011). Globalisation: Introduction and overview. In J. Michie (Ed.), *The handbook of globalisation* (2nd ed., pp. 1–18). Cheltenham, UK: Edward Elgar.

Mintzberg, H. (2009, August 6). The best leadership is good management. Retrieved from businessweek.com.

Moghadam, V. (2015). Gender and globalization: Female labour and women's mobilization. *Journal of World-Systems Research*, 5(2), 366–389.

Morgan, G., & Kristensen, P. H. (2006). The contested space of multinationals: Varieties of institutionalism, varieties of capitalism. *Human Relations*, 59(11), 1467–1490.

Murphy, J. (2007). *The World Bank and global managerialism*. Abingdon, UK: Routledge.

Newlands, D. J., & Hooper, M. J. (Eds.). (2016). *The global business handbook: The eight dimensions of international management*. London: Routledge.

OECD (2010). *Measuring globalization: OECD economic globalisation indicators*. Paris: OECD Publishing. Retrieved from http://dx.doi.org/10.1787/9789264084360-en.

Parker, M. (2002). *Against management: Organization in the age of managerialism*. Oxford: Polity Press.

Paulicelli, E., & Clark, H. (2009). Introduction. In E. Paulicelli & H. Clark (Eds.), *The fabric of cultures: Fashion, identity and globalization* (pp. 1–12). Abingdon, UK: Routledge.

Pearce, W. B., & Pearce, K. A. (2000). Extending the theory of the coordinated management of meaning (CMM) through a community dialogue process. *Communication Theory*, 10(4), 405–423.

Peet, R. (2003). *Unholy trinity: The IMF, World Bank and WTO*. London: Zed Books.

Pfeffer, J. (2009). Shareholders first? Not so fast. *Harvard Business Review*, 87(7/8), 90–91.

Pfeffer, J. (2016). Why the assholes are winning: Money trumps all. *Journal of Management Studies*, 53(4), 663–669.

Plato (1995). (R. Waterfield, Trans.). In J. Annas & R. Waterfield (Eds.), *Statesman*. Cambridge: Cambridge University Press.

Porter, C. E., & Donthu, N. (2006). Using the technology acceptance model to explain how attitudes determine Internet usage: The role of perceived access barriers and demographics. *Journal of Business Research*, 59(9), 999–1007.

Porter, M. (1990). *The competitive advantage of nations*. New York, NY: Free Press.

Prasad, P., Mills, A. J., Elmes, M., & Prasad, A. (Eds.). (1997). *Managing the organizational melting pot: Dilemmas of workplace diversity*. Thousand Oaks, CA: Sage.

Psychogios, A. G. (2007). Towards the transformational leader: Addressing women's leadership style in modern business management. *Journal of Business & Society*, 20(1/2), 169-180.

Radice, H. (2015). *Global capitalism: Selected essays*. Abingdon, UK: Routledge.

Read, E. (2016). John Key's rich list wealth rises to $60m. *Stuff.co.nz*, July 28. Retrieved from www.stuff.co.nz/business/82566495/john-keys-rich-list-wealth-rises-to-60m.

Rich, G. P. (1995). Values and value systems. In F. N. Magill (Ed.), *International encyclopedia of sociology* (Vol. 2, pp. 1473–1477). Chicago, Ill.: Fitzroy Dearborn.

Ross, S. E., Todd, J., Moore, L. A., Beaty, B. L., Wittevrongel, L., & Lin, C. T. (2005). Expectations of patients and physicians regarding patient-accessible medical records. *Journal of Medical Internet Research*, 7(2), 1–8.

Schaefer, S. (2016). The world's largest companies 2016. *Forbes*. Retrieved from www.forbes.com/sites/steveschaefer/2016/05/25/the-worlds-largest-companies-2016/#5d2489f837eb.

Schatz, D., & Bashroush, R. (2016). The impact of repeated data breach events on organisations' market value. *Information and Computer Security*, 24(1), 73–92.

Scholte, J. A. (2005). *Globalization: A critical introduction* (2nd ed.). Basingstoke, UK: Palgrave Macmillan.

Schweigert, F. J. (2007). Learning to lead: Strengthening the practice of community leadership. *Leadership*, 3(3), 325–342.

Senge, P. (2006). *The fifth discipline: The art and practice of the learning organization* (2nd ed.). London: Random House Business.

Sennett, R. (2006). *The culture of the new capitalism*. London: Yale University Press.

Shen, J., Chanda, A., D'netto, B., & Monga, M. (2009). Managing diversity through human resource management: An international perspective and conceptual framework. *The International Journal of Human Resource Management*, 20(2), 235–251.

Sinclair, A. (1998). *Doing leadership differently: Gender, power and sexuality in a changing business culture*. Carlton South, VIC: Melbourne University Press.

Smircich, L., & Morgan, G. (1982). Leadership: The management of meaning. *The Journal of Applied Behavioural Science*, 18(3), 257–273.

Smith, S., & Jamieson, R. (2006). Determining key factors in e-government information system security. *Information Systems Management*, 23(2), 23–32.

Spicer, A., & Fleming, P. (2007). Intervening in the inevitable: Contesting globalization in a public sector organization. *Organization*, 14(4), 517–541.

Springer, S., Birch, K., & McLeavy, J. (2016). An introduction to neoliberalism. In S. Springer, K. Birch, & J. MacLeavy (Eds.), *The handbook of neoliberalism* (pp. 1–14). Abingdon, UK: Routledge.

Standing, G. (2011). *The precariat: The new dangerous class*. London: Bloomsbury Academic.

Stead, V., & Elliott, C. (2009). *Women's leadership*. Basingstoke, UK: Palgrave Macmillan.

Sum, S., Mathews, R. M., Pourghasem, M., & Hughes, I. (2009). Internet use as a predictor of sense of community in older people. *CyberPsychology & Behavior*, 12(2), 235–239.

Terjesen, S., & Singh, V. (2008). Female presence on corporate boards: A multi-country study of environmental context. *Journal of Business Ethics*, 83(1), 55–63.

Tourish, D. (2013). *The dark side of transformational leadership: A critical perspective*. London: Routledge.

Trow, M. (2007). Reflections on the transition from elite to mass to universal access: Forms and phases of higher education in modern societies since WWII. In J. J. F. Forest & P. G. Altbach (Eds.), *International handbook of higher education* (pp. 243–280). Dordrecht: Springer.

Uhl-Bien, M., & Ospina, S. (Eds.). (2012). *Advancing relational leadership research: A dialogue among perspectives*. Charlotte, NC: Information Age Publishing.

UNEP (2013). Green economy and trade trends, challenges and opportunities. *UNEP*. Retrieved from www.unep.org/greeneconomy/GreenEconomyandTrade.

United Nations Women (2016). *Progress of the world's women 2015–2016: Transforming economies, realizing rights*. New York, NY: United Nations. Retrieved from http://progress.unwomen.org/en/2015/.

Vaccaro, A., & Madsen, P. (2009). Corporate dynamic transparency: The new ICT-driven ethics? *Ethics and Information Technology*, 11(2), 113–122.

Webb, M. (2007). *Illusions of security: Global surveillance and democracy in the post-9/11 world*. San Francisco, CA: City Lights.

Wilson, S. (2016). *Thinking differently about leadership: A critical history of leadership studies*. Cheltenham, UK: Edward Elgar.

The World Bank (2016). New Zealand GDP 2015 (current US dollars). Retrieved from http://data.worldbank.org/indicator/NY.GDP.MKTP.CD?locations=NZ.

Wright, K. A. M., & Holland, J. (2014). Leadership and the media: Gendered framings of Julia Gillard's 'sexism and misogyny' speech. *Australian Journal of Political Science*, 49(3), 455–468.

WTO (2003). *Adjusting to trade liberalization: The role of policy, institutions and WTO disciplines*. World Trade Organization. Retrieved from www.wto.org/english/res_e/publications_e/special_studies7_e.htm.

WTO. (2007). World Trade Report 2007: 60 years of the multilteral trading system: What have we learnt? Retrieved from Geneva: https://www.wto.org/english/res_e/booksp_e/anrep_e/world_trade_report07_e.pdf

Yang, J. S., & Krishnan, J. (2005). Audit committees and quarterly earnings management. *International Journal of Auditing*, 9(3), 201–219.

Zhang, X., & Bartol, K. M. (2010). Linking empowering leadership and employee creativity: The influence of psychological empowerment, intrinsic motivation, and creative process engagement. *Academy of Management Journal*, 53(1), 107–128.

# 3 *Leading in* Supervisory Management

## Introduction

In this chapter our attention turns to consider leadership in relation to a context which most contemporary leadership theories have little to say about, that of the supervisory, first-line level of management. Even in the so-called post-bureaucratic era, the structure of most organizations of any size or scale still resembles the traditional hierarchical pyramid, meaning the number of managers reduces the further one moves up the organizational hierarchy until we reach the sole position of CEO. Because of this way of organizing, first-line managers are far and away the most numerous amongst the managerial ranks. They typically have less organizational authority in terms of decision making than their more senior colleagues. At the same time, however, they usually have the greatest amount of day-to-day contact with the non-managerial employees, who themselves normally constitute the bulk of an organization's workforce. Supervisory managers are, therefore, the most numerous and direct source of potential influence upon employees and, hence, leadership. Their importance should be clear, but they have been largely neglected in leadership studies. Grounded in an ethic of care, we imagine here a new approach that seeks to revitalise supervisory leadership.

In the first part of the chapter, we examine existing research so as to gain an understanding of the empirical context in which the work of first-line managers takes place. Of particular interest are the expectations, issues, problems or, in the terms of our conceptual framework, the *challenges* which research has identified as being key features of the context in which supervisory managers work. Understanding these challenges is an essential building block in our effort to formulate a theory of supervisory leadership designed for this particular context. We will posit a specific *purpose* for leadership in this context, this being informed by the challenges which supervisory leadership entails. We then consider the *values* and *norms* which we argue normatively ought to inform such roles, along with the *domains* of life to which we pose supervisory leadership ought to be restricted. These dimensions thus relate to the outer layer of our model for contextualised theory-building (see Diagram 2.1). We then consider the expectations the proceeding analysis implies for leaders, followers and the leader-follower relationships, as per the remaining elements of our theory-building model. As you will see, the central focus we identify for supervisory leadership entails an abiding concern to enhance human well-being through supporting acts and activities that foster individual and collective well-being, experiences that may merely be 'slipped in' to the bounded conditions that organizational life routinely entails. Enabling such experiences due to their intrinsic value, rather than because of their performative potential for serving organizational interests, provides a rationale and scope for supervisory leadership that can make a modest but valuable difference to the daily lives of employees.

## The Work and Work Context of the Supervisor

There is an extensive body of studies which examine the characteristics of managerial work. Some of these, such as Mintzberg's famous study of how CEOs actually spend their time (1973), have greatly influenced contemporary management and organizational theory, challenging earlier prescriptions which sought to portray managerial work as orderly and rational (e.g., Fayol, 1930; Taylor, 1919). Of particular relevance to us here are studies of the work of supervisory, first-line management, which researchers have identified as having some distinctive characteristics that do not simply replicate those identified in studies of middle and senior management work (see Hales, 2005 and Tengblad & Vie, 2012 for recent reviews). This literature has much to tell us, then, about the specific context of supervisory management and, hence, the *challenges* it is expected to deal with.

Hales's (2005) analysis of key studies of supervisory roles conducted between the 1940s and 1970s identified the following common findings:

*Table 3.1* The focus of supervisory work, 1940s–1970s

| Activities | Challenges |
|---|---|
| • work planning, scheduling and allocation<br>• monitoring work volume and compliance with standards<br>• monitoring safety, equipment and housekeeping of the workplace<br>• oversight of the introduction of new technology<br>• responding to unforeseen problems with equipment, production processes or staffing<br>• employee discipline, training and counselling<br>• keeping records<br>• dealing with disputes<br>• assisting employees with operational work | • gap between the supervisor's accountability for performance and their actual authority; the latter is limited to routine rather than broader systemic issues, but performance is affected by systemic issues<br>• a tightly defined role but it simultaneously entails dealing with open ended problems<br>• very limited involvement in wider decision-making within the organization<br>• role conflict due to being caught between the varying expectations of senior management and employees |

Source: Hales, 2005

What emerges here, then, is an organizational context for supervisory work which creates a variety of fast-paced demands on a supervisor's time, requires technical, interpersonal and administrative skills and produces tensions and conflict as a matter of organizational design. The focus and nature of the supervisor's work are clearly important to organizational functioning, given the typical scenario in which employees have not been authorised to determine by and for themselves how the work is to be carried out. The supervisor's role is contrasted with that of the middle manager by virtue of its immediate proximity to the site of work and the workers, the concomitant focus on direct, rather than indirect, control of work and the workforce which such proximity entails and its operational rather than strategic orientation (Hales, 2005). These activities and challenges arise, too, from the key functions of the supervisory role, namely to keep the operational processes of the organization going and to translate business plans into an operational reality (Hales, 2005).

Tengblad and Vie's (2012) more recent review of studies from this same era confirms the traditional focus of supervisory work on production, staffing issues and handling emergencies, resulting in a working day which is multi-faceted and fragmented. Despite these challenges, the supervisor was found to act as a 'shock absorber' of these work pressures, meaning they did not routinely 'transmit' such pressures elsewhere into the organization but, rather, dealt with them directly (Walker & Guest, cited in Tengblad & Vie, 2012). Most of the supervisor's time was found to go to addressing immediate problems and ensuring operational processes remain functioning, despite constant issues arising due to technical or human factors (Wirdenius, cited in Tengblad & Vie, 2012).

However, if all this characterises the supervisory role as identified in studies prior to the 1980s, how has it changed since then? Given the widely reported de-layering that has taken place within organizations, the much greater reliance on information technology, the much talked about shift toward a 'post-bureaucracy' mode of organizing and the intensification of competitive pressures, has the supervisory role changed?

In investigating this very issue it appears that the common assertion that 'everything is changing' (Sturdy & Grey, 2003) does not match the reality when it comes to supervisory roles. Indeed, despite frequent assertions in the popular management literature from the early 1980s onwards that a paradigm shift is needed for business success (e.g., Deal & Kennedy, 1982; Peters & Waterman, 1982), *from* close supervisory control *to* a new approach focussed on shared norms and values and the empowerment of employees, only modest changes to the traditional supervisory role as outlined above were found in Hales's major study (2005). Notably, Hales's study included a high proportion of organizations in the service industry, knowledge-intensive firms and the public sector. These parts of the economy are often held up as being at the forefront of moves toward post-bureaucratic, networked organizations, where strategy, culture and values reduce or eliminate the need for hierarchy, rules and the intensive monitoring of workers (2005). Yet even in these settings, the supervisory role had remained remarkably stable.

Hales's study identifies that a greater responsibility for the overall business performance of a work unit by supervisory managers has occurred in some cases, through the delegation to supervisors of budgetary management and customer interactions previously held by middle managers (2005). Some greater involvement by supervisors in HR processes relating to recruitment, training and staff appraisal is also evident. However, new technologies and practices concerned with meeting quality and/or regulatory requirements have also resulted in an *increase* in the means of, and demand for, supervisory control over work and workers, with the aim of ensuring and improving performance (Hales, 2005). The much-vaunted shift from a control orientation to facilitation, coordination and empowerment, allowing supervisory attention to shift to the overall business management of the work unit, has, therefore, not made its way into the daily reality of most supervisory level management. Instead, a strengthening of the traditional supervisory function has occurred through greater performance monitoring and reporting, often supported by technology, while at the same time, the role has been broadened somewhat, through increased responsibility for the management of personnel, budgetary and customer issues (Hales, 2005). Hales posits that a reluctance by senior management to trust non-managerial employees to themselves maintain quality and output lies at the heart of this continued emphasis on supervision.

Tengblad and Vie's (2012) more recent review of the literature on managerial work behaviour reinforces Hales's general point—that the kind of work and work practices of managers has remained remarkably stable, in organizations that themselves remain largely bureaucratic or, at most, somewhat post-bureaucratic in form and nature. However, they also identify the greater focus in more recent times on the emotional, political and symbolic aspects that come with managerial work. Managing relationships, negotiating and seeking to influence peers, employees and other stakeholders and making ongoing efforts to render one's actions appear as legitimate and credible feature in many studies as key challenges involved in managerial work at all levels (e.g., Kunda, 2006; Tengblad & Vie, 2012; Watson, 1994). Conceptualising organizations as having or being 'cultures' which can or need to be 'managed', along with the idea that the 'management of meaning' is a key function performed by managers, have also become prominent symbolic concerns for managerial work in recent decades (Smircich & Morgan, 1982; Morgan, 2006).

Teaching textbooks and popular books focussed on supervisory management, meanwhile, provide a further indication as to the scope of issues that are considered relevant today, as books of this nature seek to position themselves as being strongly attuned to contemporary trends in practice (e.g., Belker, McCormick & Topchik, 2012; O'Brien Carelli, 2010;

Robbins, DeCenzo & Wolter, 2015). In such texts, common topics comprise the traditional focus on managerial planning and goal setting, determining roles and organizational structures, securing staffing resources, monitoring performance and decision making. These are complemented by a focus on canonical organizational behaviour topics, such as motivation, communication, conflict and stress, teamwork, leadership (typically conceptualised as 'influencing others' by offering direction, encouragement, support and consideration) and employee and group development (e.g., Greer & Plunkett, 2007; Mosley, Mosley & Pietri, 2008; Newstrom, 2013; Robbins et al., 2015). Basic human resources practices such as performance appraisals, dealing with disciplinary issues and an understanding of labour laws and health and safety requirements also commonly feature.

The scope of topics addressed in teaching textbooks and popular books aimed at supervisory management is, then, largely consistent with what the earlier discussion would indicate. The absence in such texts of a focus on budgetary and customer management, topics indicated as of growing relevance by Hales (2005), likely reflect disciplinary boundaries in how tertiary institutions organize the teaching of supervisory knowledge, rather than a view that such matters are not relevant to supervisors. The impact of new technology, the emergence of a more diverse workforce, managing change and post-bureaucratic modes of organizing are commonly identified in such texts as contemporary issues which pose new challenges and opportunities for supervisors. However, at the same time, and confirming Hales (2005) and Tengblad and Vie (2012), there is a tendency to argue that 'the fundamentals' of the role are relatively stable. The orientation in such teaching and popular texts is, of course, typically managerialist and functionalist, hence, the tensions and ambiguities noted earlier as central features of supervisory work are routinely minimised, glossed over or treated as a 'problem' that can be solved via individual skill and effort: harmony is presumed achievable.

From a variety of empirical and teaching/practice-oriented literature on managerial work, then, we may understand that the context in which supervisory managers work is fast-paced, multi-faceted, fragmented, oriented to immediate issues of production and service delivery and requires a mix of technical, administrative and interpersonal skills. The challenges of having wide-ranging responsibilities but limited formal authority, of limited involvement in wider decision-making and of being caught between the expectations of employees and senior management are the lot of the supervisor in most instances.

To this picture, we may add what the vast literature on employee experiences of work demonstrates, namely that many employees routinely find their work and work context problematic in varying ways. Common concerns for employees include work that is boring (Molstad, 1986; Rose, 1975; Ulrich, 1998), stressful (Johan Hauge, Skogstad & Einarsen, 2007; Johnson, Cooper, Cartwright, Taylor & Millet, 2005), insecure and poorly paid (Kalleberg, 2011; Standing, 2011), excessively controlled, surveilled and having performance standards that are onerous to meet (Green, 2006; Sewell, Barker & Nyberg, 2012; Weckert, 2005). At the same time, employees routinely seek intellectual and interpersonal stimulation and development, along with a sense of purpose and meaning, from their work (Rose, 1975; Silverman, 1970; Sennett, 1999). Moreover, whether manager or employee, our professional identity constitutes an important source of our sense of self and social status (Knights & Willmott, 1999; Sennett, 1999; Standing, 2011). The supervisory manager encounters all these employee expectations directly, at the same time as they are tasked with maintaining or improving work output and quality. Navigating these demands entails considerable political, emotional and relational effort, yet for these managers, whose positioning is at the lowest level in the managerial hierarchy, there typically exists limited leverage they can exert upon those above them. All these matters, then, constitute the key *challenges* with which leadership in this context must contend. Given all this, how might we conceive of the *purpose* of leadership in this context?

## The Question of Purpose in Revitalising Supervisory Leadership

The question of the purpose of leadership directs us to think about the kinds of ends or results for which leadership is called into being and, we think, to contemplate the kinds of means to be deemed acceptable in striving to secure the desired ends. You may recall that in Chapter 2, we developed a general statement of purpose for leadership as *"enabling the achievement of shared goals, via means that are consistent with shared values"*, and we think this is of relevance to supervisory leadership. However, a more tailored, context-specific approach is also possible, and that is what we lay out below.

In thinking about a *purpose* for supervisory leadership, we are cognisant of the limited authority and organizational power which supervisory managers typically have and of their challenging work context. Consequently, we adopt the pragmatist stance that the structural and systemic challenges considered above (Hales, 2005; Tengblad & Vie, 2012) are not matters which a theory of supervisory leadership need try to overcome or eliminate as, barring dramatic changes in the typical structure of organizations and work, such efforts would be unlikely to succeed in most instances. We suggest instead, then, that these challenges be understood as constraints within which supervisory leadership arises, constraints which it seeks to ameliorate or lessen where possible, but not matters which it seeks, as its purpose, to overcome. We acknowledge the limited scope of ambition this demonstrates on our part, but believe it would be irresponsible to propose a purpose for supervisory leadership that is systemically and structurally beyond the scope of supervisors to address in most instances. While it is admirable to have bold aspirations, it is also sensible to have achievable aims, and we err here towards that which is achievable.

However, more boldly, we do wish to resist the common tendency found in most contemporary leadership theorising to focus on instrumental ends, framing, justifying and measuring leadership by way of its contribution to concerns with productivity and performativity which serve commercial, organizational interests (Alvesson & Deetz, 2000; Collinson, 2011; Wilson, 2016). We think supervisory leadership, to be of distinctive and intrinsic value, can desirably have a purpose that does not render it simply a servant to the interests of employers and businesses. It need not be constituted in such a way as to make it just another mechanism for achieving organizational goals. *Management* knowledge, tools, processes and practices are already designed to address issues of efficiency and performativity, and for all managers, these concerns are central to their role. Instead, a valuable *leadership* contribution for supervisory managers, we propose, is one directed toward addressing non-instrumental human needs. Such a purpose will sit in a relation of tension with the demands of management, never to be fully and finally reconciled, always to be juggled, grabbed at tactically as and when opportunities arise. However, its very distinctiveness from managerial interests is what makes it worth pursuing and is why it constitutes leadership, rather than management by another name. Our proposal, then, is that a desirable purpose for supervisory leadership is *to support individual and collective well-being in the work group for which the supervisor holds authority*. This purpose centres the moral grounding of supervisory leadership in an ethic of care (Clement, 1996; Gilligan, 1982; Larrabee, 1993).

This statement of purpose requires careful unpacking to clarify its focus and its boundaries. By 'well-being', we refer to the diverse set of physical, intellectual, aesthetic, emotional, creative, cultural, spiritual, individual and interpersonal stimuli that bring value, meaning and purpose to our lives. It means those experiences that make us feel happy, fulfilled and enriched, enabling our development as people and allowing us to express, share and connect our unique selves with others. The value of such experiences is not to be measured in terms of improved productivity, employee morale or some other instrumental benefit for the employing organization: what matters is the intrinsic worth of such experiences and how supervisory leadership can help support such experiences arising in the workplace context. Our interest in these matters is informed by the growing focus on humanistic values and social responsibility in business (Pirson & Lawrence, 2010; Waddock, Bodwell & Graves, 2002).

We understand that this purpose may sometimes align and at other times conflict with the supervisor's managerial responsibilities, potentially invoking ethical or political dilemmas. Organizations are sites of competing demands, of conflict and contestation, as well as being sites of co-operative endeavour (Fineman, Gabriel & Sims, 2010; Knights & Willmott, 1999). We see no merit in pretending this is not so or trying, through fallacious reasoning, to purport that a purpose for supervisory leadership can somehow be crafted in a manner that would avoid or somehow dissolve such dynamics. We expect, then, that the experience of supervisory leadership will demand of such leaders ongoing judgement calls about the how, when, to what extent and in what ways this statement of purpose can be enacted. Our later discussion of the values and norms which we propose ought to inform supervisory leadership, and the expectations we see as relevant to leaders and followers in this context, may aid in the making of such judgement calls.

This framing, however, implies that leadership may merely be something that is 'slipped in' to existing interactions and work practices, in ways that are subtle in nature and possibly modest in effect, but which still have a positive value and meaning to those involved. As we have suggested earlier, a more constrained view of what we expect from leadership is something we are broadly advocating, given the concerns we identified in Chapter 1 with the more grandiose notions of charismatic, visionary, transformational leadership which have prevailed in recent decades. Enacting, or at least attempting to act in accordance with this statement of purpose may, then, arise via ostensibly mundane means, such as demonstrating a genuine interest in, and concern for, the employees for whom the supervisor has formal authority. Diverse practices such as encouraging conversations in the tea room that enable people to experience a sense of community with workmates, reading stories together, sharing food from our different cultures, listening to music or engaging in dance, yoga, tai chi or some other bodily practice, are all simple but potentially meaningful and valuable activities that could be supported by supervisory leaders in pursuit of this purpose. Shared engagement in sociomaterial organizing practices of this type influence how people feel about themselves, their work and others and can generate a sense of "belonging, recognition and respect between diverse people" (Keevers & Sykes, 2016, p. 1644; also Sennett, 2003; Sinclair, 2007). As managerial prescriptions for workplace action are rarely, if ever, complete and absolute (Fineman, Yiannis & Sims, 2010; Parker, 2002), multiple opportunities to render our work place experiences more humanely enriching do exist and we believe that it is into these gaps that supervisory leadership efforts can be slipped to positive effect. Diagram 3.1 offers a metaphorical representation of the contextual 'space' in which supervisory leadership emerges, one where the requirements determined by management may occupy much of the field of action whilst nonetheless remaining incomplete.

The specific emphasis in this purpose statement on the *support* of individual and collective well-being means, importantly, that supervisors need not themselves be front and centre of such activities, but could instead focus their leadership efforts on encouraging others to bring such experiences into our workplaces. This framing is, then, consciously designed to guard against a leader-centric monopolising of acts of leadership, seeing instead that these may come from any quarter. Relatedly, then, an important boundary in this statement of purpose is that it does not rely on the presumption that the supervisory leader knows best what others need for their well-being or what

The workplace space

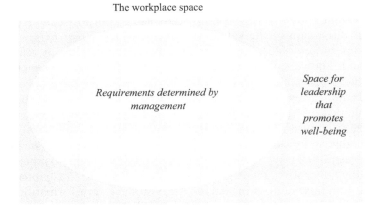

*Requirements determined by*
*management*

*Space for*
*leadership*
*that*
*promotes*
*well-being*

*Diagram 3.1* The workplace space, managerial requirements and the space for leadership

result someone should be striving for when engaged in something intended to foster their well-being. Unlike most 'new leadership' theories, where it is presumed or asserted that leaders do indeed know how and in what particular direction to guide their follower's personal development (e.g., Bass, 1985; Bennis & Nanus, 1985), no such presumption is made here. The focus here is on *supporting* individual and collective well-being, which is quite different from guiding or directing efforts to achieve that which the leader has determined followers need, from a presumed position of superior insight and knowledge (Sinclair, 2007; Wilson, 2016).

No doubt for some the approach proposed here seems rather humdrum and ordinary. Or, perhaps, it may seem too much like a 'motherhood and apple pie' version of leadership, an interpretation which, we think, thereby reminds us of the strongly gendered nature of how leadership in typically conceived and represented (Bell & Sinclair, 2016; Stead & Elliott, 2009). Indeed, insofar as an ethic of care, which provides the moral foundation for this approach, itself emerged from feminist theorising (e.g., Clement, 1996; Larrabee, 1993), it is not unsurprising that what we propose may seem feminised in its orientation. Certainly, it stands in stark contrast to the dominant, masculinist view, which would demand of supervisors that they articulate a vision, generate intellectual, emotional and moral excitement and find ways to transform how their followers understand reality and themselves (e.g., Bass, 1985; Bennis & Nanus, 1985; Conger, 1989). For us, however, the context of supervisory work which we examined earlier indicates these conventional approaches are not realistic or relevant. This is not because supervisors are somehow presumed inadequate but, rather, because the conventional account of leadership fails to address their context and the genuine constraints it poses. Accounting for leadership in ways that pay heed to such contextual, structural and cultural constraints is, indeed, central to what motivates this book.

We are not interested, then, in advancing propositions about leadership which are likely to render what supervisors can realistically hope to achieve in their workplaces as always lacking when compared with some idealistic but unrealistic account of what constitutes leadership. Research has already shown that managers experience stress and even existential identity crises when trying to reconcile their daily reality with the expectations generated by 'new leadership' theorists (Ford, Harding & Learmonth, 2008), so we do not wish to compound this problem. Moreover, to be tempted to decry the intrinsic practical and moral value of supporting individual and collective well-being in the small ways that we suggest could be helpful seems rather to miss the fundamental point that our lives are lived moment to moment, not as grand designs. Being agentic and nurturing in those moments to the best extent that one is able, given other demands, constitutes a profoundly pro-social mode of being and practice.

To work in an environment where such care is offered without an instrumental motive strikes us as a workplace worth aiming for. Supervisory leadership, then, which has as its purpose *supporting individual and collective well-being* may seem modest, mundane, homely and entirely prosaic, but its effects could nonetheless be of genuine value to the people involved. Moreover, insofar as the acts and activities which foster well-being need only be *supported*, rather than exclusively enacted, by the supervisor, participation by all is encouraged. This enables a distribution of the leadership contribution, from which people may experience personal development, and it serves to strengthen the collective capability of the group, which is a form of community building (Gronn, 2000; Sinclair, 2007).

In encouraging participation by all in acts and activities designed to foster human well-being, an approach that is cast here as constituting leadership, democratic values and practices are fostered, providing a counter-point to the typically top-down, non-democratic nature of organizational decision making (Parker, 2002). In an operational work context where there is so often an unceasing, hectic demand to produce and serve the needs of the organization and its customers, finding ways to 'slip in' acts and activities that make people feel known by and cared for by their colleagues and which provide, even momentarily, a sense of well-being, will not absolve supervisors or employees of the demands and constraints of their work context. However, it may alleviate some suffering and serve to support that which makes our lives feel they are worth living. Supervisory leadership which serves such a purpose is therefore worth promoting.

## Values and Norms for Supervisory Leadership

Turning now to the next key question in our framework for theory building, we ask *what values and norms ought to guide and constrain leadership in this setting?* By this stage in the theory-building process, certain matters, namely the challenges of salience to leadership in this context and the purpose we have proposed for it, are now to be taken as 'givens' as we advance the theorisation. As a consequence, the value and norms of care and respect for others, and of supporting acts and activities that foster human well-being, are clearly central normative features of supervisory leadership as conceptualised here. These expectations, however, are deliberately framed in non-paternalistic, non-directive terms, such that self-determination has a place in establishing what constitutes the kind of care or respect that is sought, or what kinds of acts and activities support human well-being, rather than these being matters about which the leader knows best. In this sense, then, an underpinning value of the model proposed for supervisory leadership is that of the irreducible equality as persons that exists between the supervisory leader and those in their work group, meaning that actions *taken in the name of leadership* that serve to constrain the autonomy of others are normatively prohibited, unless such constraints prevent harm to others. However, reflecting the pragmatist framing within which supervisory leadership as theorised here emerges, we note that this same prohibition is not expected to apply to actions conducted as part of the supervisor's *managerial* responsibilities, where norms and values applicable to the exercise of management authority will apply.

We have also acknowledged that our approach to supervisory leadership will, at times, sit in some tension with supervisors' managerial responsibilities, arguing that leadership which supports individual and collective well-being as its purpose is something we see being 'slipped in' to the work context of supervisors and the employees they supervise. Hence, further normative dimensions of the approach include a tolerance for paradox, conflict and ambiguity, these being connected with a pluralist rather than unitarist view of the nature of workplace dynamics, along with a pragmatist stance as regard the potential and scope of impact of leadership in a supervisory context. However, an eye for the incremental or opportunistic enactment of non-instrumental values and norms in the otherwise intentionally instrumental context of a workplace is also inferred as a value guiding supervisory leadership. This means the pragmatist stance should not be taken to simply imply a passive acceptance of the status quo. Instead, supervisory leadership may emerge momentarily, seeking to construct even brief experiences of human well-being whenever and wherever possible, due to their intrinsic worth. This concern to foster human well-being within a workplace context to the greatest extent possible, then, constitutes the key underpinning value guiding and constraining supervisory leadership.

## Domains of Leadership Activity

The next aspect of our model to be addressed requires us to consider *upon which parts of our lives and in what ways ought supervisory leadership be permitted to act*? These questions are intended to demand further consideration of the boundaries intended to be placed on leadership action to further ensure its ethical grounding.

Given the purpose proposed for supervisory leadership along with the values and norms intended to govern its enactment, the risk of treating other persons as means not ends has been minimised in the theorisation as sketched thus far. We have, in other words, sought to construct supervisory leadership on ethical, non-instrumental, non-paternalistic, non-directive and pro-social grounds. The focus on fostering human well-being which we propose for supervisory leadership, however, does clearly imply a crossing of the boundary lines between what the work and work context typically *requires* that we share of ourselves to fulfil our duties and those other, more personal, aspects of our selves which are *not* part of what our work and work context requires of us. Sharing of one's personal interests, pleasures and concerns beyond those relevant to work requirements is, of course, entirely commonplace—and is often an important aspect of people's social connectivity and support system (Eisenberg & Witten, 1987; Sias & Cahill, 1998). Nonetheless, to actively encourage this sharing of personal information in the name of supervisory leadership does create the risk that the knowledge gained could later be deployed to serve managerial interests.

To address this risk, we propose that while supervisory leadership, as formulated here, may legitimately enter into the personal domain, the knowledge gained through that ought not to be later deployed for managerial purposes. To do so would constitute an ethical breach of supervisory leadership as we have formulated it. Moreover, the non-directive orientation of supervisory leadership, captured by its purpose of *supporting* individual and collective well-being, means that when engaging in the personal domain, the intent is not to try to change other people, as is clearly envisaged by transformational leadership theory, but, more modestly, simply to support acts and activities which enrich, nourish and bring pleasure and meaning to others. Overall, then, supervisory leadership may participate in the personal domain but in a non-directive, non-instrumental manner, and its aim is not to colonise the follower's psyche. The knowledge obtained from this engagement with the personal domain may not then be utilised for managerial purposes without thereby breaching the values, norms and purpose intended of supervisory leadership. These prescriptions provide further normative boundaries around the nature and scope of supervisory leadership.

## Leader Personal Attributes, Behaviours, Rights, Responsibilities and Role

Thus far, our efforts to formulate a theory of supervisory leadership have examined the 'outer layer' of our theory-building model (see Diagram 2.2). We have examined the challenges of salience to leadership in this context, identified a purpose in light of that, proposed a set of values and norms and scoped the domains of life in which it engages and on what basis. This means we are now ready to turn our attention to ask, given these matters, *what are the personal attributes, behaviours, rights, responsibilities and role of the supervisory leader* we envisage? In considering these leader-related issues, we seek to draw out what is implied by the preceding analysis as to the expectations held here of supervisory leaders.

The approach proposed indicates that the supervisory leader is expected to be one who has the intellectual, emotional and ethical capacity to cope with a paradoxical expectation: that their leadership contribution demands both high principle and pragmatism, placed as it is within the constraints posed by their managerial responsibilities. At the core of this approach sits an ethic of care as the principle moral foundation and motivating force for supervisory leadership. Supporting acts or activities that foster human well-being is the raison d'etre for this form of leadership; hence, a concern and empathy for others is a core expectation for the supervisory leader. Whilst there is no blanket prohibition here on being 'self-regarding', the supervisory leader does need to be 'other-regarding' (Taylor & Wolfram, 1968) to adhere to the purpose, values and norms of leadership proposed here.

This ethic of care, however, arises within the constraints of operational and managerial demands, even at the same time as it seeks to ameliorate any negative effects arising from those demands via incremental, opportunistic tactics of 'slipping in' acts and activities intended to foster human well-being. The supervisory leader thus operates in a space of tension, ambiguity and paradox—meaning, in turn, that the various skills, temperament and beliefs that equip people to cope with such demands will be required.

Issues of principle derived from the ethic of care, and from the value and norms outlined earlier, create the expectation that supervisory leaders respect, in a serious, mindful and considered manner, the autonomy of others to be self-determining in regards to what fosters their well-being. This means, too, adherence to the principle of the irreducible equality of all persons, such that their manner of engagement with others when enacting a leadership contribution is normally expected to be non-directive, non-paternalistic, inclusive and tolerant of difference. They are also expected to demonstrate the principled capacity to hold information gained from their leadership engagement separate from the exercise of their managerial authority, this also being part of the paradoxical expectations placed here on supervisory leadership.

However, this level of attentiveness to respecting others' autonomy should not be taken to imply that a passive, 'hands off' approach on the part of the supervisory leader is envisaged. Committing to an ethic of care constitutes an *active* responsibility: the leader is expected to take action of some kind to foster human well-being. Moreover, being respectful, tolerant, inclusive and non-directive does not mean, following Marcuse, simply accepting all views as equally valid and meritorious. Supervisory leaders ought not to "protect false words and wrong deeds which demonstrate that they contradict and counteract the possibilities of liberation" (Marcuse, 2007, p. 37). Their concern should be to promote human well-being and to counteract that which is founded in oppression, exploitation, prejudice, denigration or other sources of harm. This implies a bias for action, not a laissez faire approach. It implies, too, the willingness to take a stand on ethical and moral issues and to challenge others when their words or actions breach the values and moral principles highlighted here as of central concern. Not only diplomacy but also courage is indicated.

In terms of pragmatism, the expectation is for an agentic, opportunistic orientation, actively seeking out opportunities to 'slip in' acts and activities designed to foster human well-being. Yet at the same time, the nature and scope of such contributions is to be pragmatically accepted as a limited approach to leadership, one that is constrained by their operating context. Leadership arises, here, in the 'gaps' left by organizational demands. However, despite this limitation its intrinsic value, derived from its purpose and values, ought to be grasped as powerful motivation for the supervisory leader to sustain their effort.

In operationalising supervisory leadership, seeking to deal with the differences of opinion that will inevitably arise without recourse to positional authority will demand skill in negotiation, conflict management and, in many situations, cross-cultural communication. Active listening and appreciative inquiry are implied as key practices. Fostering the trust that will be needed to build a workplace community that is a safe and supportive space for its members implies a willingness on the part of the supervisory leader to share their own hopes and fears, along with a careful concern to honour confidences and keep commitments.

Overall, what should be evident is that while supervisory leadership may be modest in scope, style and possibly impact, the kinds of personal capabilities its exercise relies on are neither simple nor straight-forward. Its effective enactment demands considerable interpersonal sensitivity, organizational savvy and clarity as to one's moral commitments. That its exercise cannot be reduced to a precise set of skills points to its grounding being not in mere matters of technique. Notions of 'character', 'temperament', 'mindset' or an 'orientation' toward care for others are perhaps more helpful frames for understanding these expectations. Moreover, fostering these capacities involves an ongoing process of 'becoming' rather than of 'being', where grappling with the variable needs and concerns of others, alongside one's own anxieties and limitations, demands moment to moment attention as to what is present and what might be possible (Ladkin, 2010; Sinclair, 2007).

The rights and responsibilities of supervisory leaders are, meanwhile, intended to be governed by the parameters set by the purpose, values and norms and domains of leadership examined earlier. This means, for example, that while supervisory leaders are granted, here, both the right and the responsibility to support acts and activities that foster human well-being, in exercising those powers they must be simultaneously cognisant of the values, norms and domains that provide boundaries over the scope and nature of those powers. Hence supervisory leaders, according to this formulation, ought to be empowered to challenge ideas and actions that are harmful of human well-being; however, they are expected to exercise this challenge in ways that remains respectful of individual autonomy and which does not conflate their managerial authority and leadership role. And, while they are empowered to support actions consistent with the purpose of leadership, this does not extend to being the sole determinant of what those actions might comprise or to determining what is in someone else's best interests: the supervisory leader is not empowered here to 'know best' what others need for their well-being. Moreover, the capacity to initiate acts and activities that foster human well-being is not an exclusive right or responsibility which only the supervisory leader holds. Rather, this capacity is left open on an equal basis to all members of the group. In determining leader rights and responsibilities, then, both the positive obligations and the boundaries of action are to be found by reference to what has been set by the purpose, values, norms and domains of life in which supervisory leadership is to function.

In determining the role of supervisory leaders, these matters also provide the governing orientation, hence the role can be understood as supporting acts and activities that foster human well-being in a manner consistent with the prescribed values, norms and domains of action. In exercising this role, the various practices we identified earlier which are intended to solicit the active contribution from all members have particular importance, because the leadership role is not presumed exclusive to the supervisor alone. Granted, we do assume that the supervisory leader is the only one who will need to grapple with the tensions that arise between their managerial responsibilities and their leadership contribution. However, given the purpose we propose here is to *support* acts and activities that foster human well-being, any and all group members can therefore make such a leadership contribution. Barring the expectations which are tied solely to the interface with managerial responsibilities, then, the potentially distributed nature of the leadership role implies that the personal capabilities we have outlined here will be of relevance to other members of the group when seeking to make leadership contributions. If they exercise this role infrequently, the level of accomplishment may be less, however, the basic orientation and approach are expected to be similar.

Overall, the supervisory leader as sketched here is no hero insofar as their contributions may be modest, their style of engagement with others may be low-key and their powers and scope of action are constrained. They are not expected to offer a bold vision or to transform others. They are not placed on the pedestal as the role model for others to seek to mimic. They are, however, expected to be a person of moral substance, who engages mindfully and skilfully with others in promoting positive developments within their sphere of influence. They do this in spite of the constraints that daily operations and organizational demands place upon them and other employees and in spite of the tension their leadership role may create relative to their managerial responsibilities. They combine, or move between, principle and pragmatism, serving to foster morally meritorious aims but often by small deeds of momentary effect. It may be tempting to regard this kind of leader as offering but a stepping stone to something 'bigger' and 'better', however to do so underestimates, we think, the capability expected here and the value this kind of leader can bring to a group.

## Follower Personal Attributes, Behaviours, Rights, Responsibilities and Role

The follower is not expected to be a passenger in this formulation. While they may be a recipient or beneficiary of initiatives developed as a result of the supervisor's leadership contribution, followers may equally step into playing a leadership role by initiating acts and activities that foster human well-being. Indeed, the more often this happens, the better the group will likely become as a source of support and development for its members. The supervisory leader, as we have seen, is expected to seek to elicit this kind of initiative from followers by seeking out their contribution and supporting it. The position of someone as a follower in this formulation then, is not fixed but is fluid: acts of leadership are open to all. When followers engage in leadership, the expectations of leaders explained above, barring those tied directly to the supervisor's managerial authority, will apply. *Qua* follower, however, what expectations are implied by our formulation?

The personal attributes expected of followers here could be thought of in very restricted terms. A degree of receptivity to others' efforts in offering acts or activities intended to promote well-being is implied as a minimum. An expectation of avoiding harm to others, and acceptance that one ought to treat others in ways that respects their autonomy and irreducible inequality, are indicated. A willingness to accept membership of the group as a community with shared interests, rather than as a merely functional configuration of employees to meet organizational needs, also seems a minimum requirement. However, these expectations constitute a fairly passive view of the follower.

If we instead regard followership as agentic in nature, then actively engaging with what others have proposed as acts or activities to foster well-being is implied in order to explore the potentialities these experiences offer. This willingness to explore what others propose relies on an openness to different ideas and experiences and a respect for what others can offer. It suggests, moreover, that being a follower requires a contribution, a willingness to participate, to positively accept a member role and to seek to contribute to the values, norms and life of the group. From these understandings, then, the same core expectation as applied to supervisory leaders, namely that they be oriented toward providing care and respect to others in non-directive, non-paternalistic ways, is expected of followers. Followers, then, are expected here to be engaged community members, not mere observers. To simply sit back and let others do all the work entailed in sustaining a sense of community and fostering well-being within that community is to fail in one's role as a follower.

A similar approach applies as regards the rights and responsibilities of followers, namely that the purpose, values, norms and domains of action provide the governing framework for what is permitted and promoted in the name of leadership. Insofar as followers may take on a leadership role at any time, by initiating actions consistent with the purpose of leadership, the rights and responsibilities which then arise are the same as defined above for supervisory leaders (other than those expectations which relate specifically to the connection between their managerial authority and their leadership contributions). *Qua* followers, meanwhile, a key right is to be protected from leadership (or peer) efforts that wrongfully seek to dominate or dictate matters that are properly a question of individual autonomy, while a key responsibility is a willingness to share ideas and experiences that will contribute to the group's well-being. In this regard, then, it again becomes clear that a consistently passive, non-engaged stance would constitute a failure to meet the expectations of followers in this model. Importantly, however, this does not limit the follower's right to refuse to engage on any particular activity, should the individual deem that matter unconducive to their well-being. This protection is important if collective efforts are not to unduly impose themselves on individuals. Following, like leading, may thus be something one does intermittently, rather that it being a fixed role or personal attribute.

Overall, then, while followers *qua* followers have some specific rights and responsibilities and play a different role from that of the leader, their status as such is not fixed in this formulation. Followership and leadership here are, thus, not fundamentally matters of the self but, rather, of the role one plays within the group. At any point the follower may make a leadership contribution and, in so doing, take on the expectations held of the leader, barring those matters tied to the supervisor's managerial authority. Moreover, to contribute fully as a follower relies on adherence to the same caring orientation, and the same constraints as to what is permitted, as are given here to leaders via the purpose, values, norms and domains which govern this form of leadership.

This approach, however, ought not to be understood as conflating leadership and followership, as the expectations are not identical. There are differences, primarily in the extent to which the supervisory leader is expected to take ongoing responsibility to support that which fosters human well-being, whereas this responsibility may be taken up only intermittently by the follower or perhaps not at all. The supervisory leadership responsibility demands sustained effort and, in all likelihood, will see greater confidence and competence emerge over time in exercising leadership. Followers' right to protection from leadership efforts that they experience as impeding their right to self-determination is also a distinctive point of difference, reflecting that relations of power have not been removed from this formulation, despite the efforts made to constrain leadership action to that which is beneficial and acceptable to followers. While these differences are important, as the boundary between leading and following is always open the potential exists for all to engage in both forms of social contribution and, thus, to experience leadership from both sides. This, in turn, may foster both better leadership and better followership.

## The Leader-Follower Relationship

The preceding analysis of the attributes, behaviours, rights, responsibilities and roles of both leaders and followers serves to inform our understanding of the desired nature of that relationship. Unavoidably, given the supervisor's managerial authority, there are power dynamics here. However, the approach as framed provides much that serves to protect the follower from the abusive exercise of power and to instead direct the supervisory leader toward actions that are empowering for followers. Given the orientation is toward the creation and sustenance of a community in which both care for others and the protection of personal autonomy are central concerns, the intended relationship is one of mutual support, respect and sharing.

Hierarchical divisions of labour, responsibility and authority continue to provide the backdrop for this relationship, nested as it is within a wider organizational setting where different priorities, values and forces than those guiding supervisory leadership (as proposed here) are at play. Consequently, we think the prospects of dependency dynamics developing, whereby followers *need* leaders to initiate, guide and provide sense-making, because they are unaccustomed to undertaking such activities themselves, remains a risk. However, this risk is at least mitigated by two factors. The first is the clear distinction made between the purpose and practices of *leadership* we propose, which is oriented around an ethic of care, and the supervisor's *managerial* responsibility and role, which is oriented to issues of production, service delivery and efficiency. Secondly, the approach here is that the supervisory leader is not one who 'knows best' what others need: they are not expected to be priest, seer, counsellor, wise wo/man, visionary, therapist or any other role which implies they have superior knowledge and insight into the future or the needs of others. They are expected, much more simply and modestly, to support acts and activities that others will find positive for their well-being. Moreover, it is also the case that followers may engage in acts of leadership themselves at any point, which also guards against the risk of dependency relationship developing. If there is a therapeutic dimension to this relationship it derives from the purpose of leadership as proposed here and resides in the group experience: all are expected to feel nourished by the acts and activities within the group which foster human well-being.

Overall, the relationship between leader and follower as proposed here is grounded in respect, mutual support, care, trust and sharing. Its power dynamics seek to guard against dependency or domination and offer scope for the empowerment of both leader and follower. There is an expectation that learning can flow in both directions. The focus of effort is intended to go to that which nourishes and sustains human well-being, hence the relationship is founded in pro-social values, norms and purposes and offers scope for both individual and collective development.

Table 3.2 summarises our model of supervisory leadership.

*Table 3.2* Supervisory leadership: a summary

| Component | Key issues and ideas |
| --- | --- |
| Challenges | Supervisory work is fast-paced, multi-faceted and fragmented. |
| | Supervisors primary focus is on controlling and sustaining production or service delivery. |
| | Supervisors have wide-ranging responsibilities but limited formal authority or involvement in wider decision making. |
| | Many employees experience their work/work context as difficult or stressful. |
| | Employees routinely seek intellectual and interpersonal stimulation and development opportunities from their work |
| | Our professional identity constitutes an important source of our sense of self and social status |
| | Supervisors are caught between the expectations of employees and senior management |
| Purpose of leadership | To support individual and collective well-being in the work group for which the supervisor holds authority |
| Values and norms | Ethics of care as the core value and orientation |
| | Respect for others |
| | Non-directive, non-paternalistic basis of engaging with others, to assure self-determination as to what supports their sense of 'well-being' |
| Domains | Work and personal via trust-based disclosure |
| | Personal information obtained through leadership efforts cannot be used for managerial purposes without breaching the ethical expectations of supervisory leadership |
| Leader | Motivated by an ethic of care |
| | Has the intellectual, emotional and ethical capacity to cope with the tensions, ambiguity and paradox involved in supervisory leadership |
| | Sustained active effort in seeking out opportunities to foster human well-being |
| | Respectful, inclusive and tolerant—but will take a stand on ethical and moral issues |
| | Skilled in negotiation, conflict management, listening, appreciative inquiry |

| Component | Key issues and ideas |
|---|---|
| Follower | May step into making a leadership contribution at any time |
| | Actively engages with others' ideas and participates in the life of the community in a respectful, caring, non-directive manner |
| | Right to not be dominated by others and to choose not to participate in particular activities |
| | Responsibility to share ideas and experiences that contribute to the group's purpose |
| Leader-follower relationship | Mutual support, respect, care, trust and sharing |
| | Learning from each other |
| | Focus on that which nourishes and sustains human well-being |

## Conclusion

The direct engagement which supervisory managers have with non-managerial employees means they have a critical leadership contribution to make in terms of how people get treated at work. While pragmatically accepting that managerial requirements demand a focus on issues of quality, service and output, in this chapter we have identified an alternative, complementary space, or focus, through which supervisors can make a leadership contribution. This places the focus on supporting acts and activities that foster human well-being, an approach derived from an ethic of care and thereby separated out from instrumental concerns with productivity. We envisage these leadership initiatives being 'slipped in' to existing workplace interactions in ways that may be subtle or modest in effect but which nonetheless have intrinsic value.

This approach to leadership is grounded in care and respect for others, framed in non-paternalistic, non-directive terms, thereby valuing self-determination. It provides a qualitatively different basis for engagement than the instrumentality routinely at play in manager-worker interaction, shifting the focus on to how persons in a work group can support each other's well-being. Leadership here is also intended to be a role or contribution that is not exclusive to the supervisor, but can instead be distributed amongst members of the work group. Recognising the tensions that may arise between a supervisor's managerial responsibilities and their leadership contribution means a tolerance for paradox, conflict and ambiguity, along with a pluralist view of workplace dynamics, are also important normative features of this approach.

Quite possibly supervisory leadership, as crafted here, may seem too modest in its ambition when compared with more common ideals of leadership as comprising bold visions and transformational change. However, by taking seriously the context of supervisory management we argue there is considerable ambition in this model. Its successful enactment would not come easily in an environment of constant operational pressures, where employees are so often disillusioned by the nature of their work or workplace. Indeed, in this very context, bold visions and transformational change so often result in job losses, the intensification of work or 'flexible' employment practices which benefit organizations in the short term, but often not those who work in them. Yet even if these pressures are present, the potential always remains, moment to moment, to demonstrate care for others. Supervisory leadership which supports a work group to forge itself into a community built on an ethic of care and respect will provide a counterweight to organizational demands, creating a space in which our shared humanity can shine through to sustain and strengthen us for the challenges we encounter.

## References

Alvesson, M., & Deetz, S. A. (2000). *Doing critical management research*. London: Sage.

Bass, B. M. (1985). *Leadership and performance beyond expectations*. New York: Free Press.

Bell, E., & Sinclair, A. (2016). Bodies, sexualities and women leaders in popular culture: From spectacle to meta-picture. *Gender in Management: An International Journal*, 31(5/6), 322–338.

Belker, L. B., McCormick, J., & Topchik, G. S. (2012). *The first-time manager* (6th ed.). New York, NY: American Management Association.

Bennis, W. G., & Nanus, B. (1985). *Leaders: The strategies for taking charge*. New York: Harper & Row.

Clement, G. (1996). *Care, autonomy, and justice: Feminism and the ethic of care*. Boulder, CO: Westview.

Collinson, D. (2011). Critical leadership studies. In A. Bryman, D. Collinson, K. Grint, B. Jackson, & M. Uhl-Bien (Eds.), *The Sage handbook of leadership* (pp. 181–194). London: Sage.

Conger, J. (1989). The charismatic leader: Behind the mystique of exceptional leadership. San Francisco, CA: Jossey-Bass.

Deal, T. E., & Kennedy, A. A. (1982). *Corporate cultures: The rites and rituals of corporate life*. Reading, MA: Addison-Wesley.

Eisenberg, E. M., & Witten, M. G. (1987). Reconsidering openness in organizational communication. *The Academy of Management Review*, 12(3), 418–426.

Fayol, H. (1930). (J. A. Coubrough, Trans.). *Industrial and general administration*. London: Pitman.

Fineman, S., Yiannis, G., & Sims, D. (2010). *Organizing and organizations* (4th ed.). London: Sage.

Ford, J., Harding, N., & Learmonth, M. (2008). *Leadership as identity: Constructions and deconstructions*. Basingstoke: Palgrave Macmillan.

Gilligan, C. (1982). *In a different voice: Psychological theory and women's development*. Cambridge, MA: Harvard University Press.

Green, F. (2006). *Demanding work: The paradox of job quality in the affluent economy*. Princeton, NJ: Princeton University Press.

Greer, C. R., & Plunkett, W. R. (2007). *Supervisory management* (11th ed.). Upper Saddle River, NJ: Pearson Prentice Hall.

Gronn, P. (2000). Distributed properties: A new architecture for leadership. Educational Management Administration and Leadership, 28, 317–338.

Hales, C. (2005). Rooted in supervision, branching into management: Continuity and change in the role of first-line manager. *Journal of Management Studies*, 42(3), 471–506.

Johan Hauge, L., Skogstad, A., & Einarsen, S. (2007). Relationships between stressful work environments and bullying: Results of a large representative study. *Work & Stress*, 21(3), 220–242.

Johnson, S., Cooper, C., Cartwright, S. I. D., Taylor, P., & Millet, C. (2005). The experience of work related stress across occupations. *Journal of Managerial Psychology*, 20(2), 178–187.

Kalleberg, A. L. (2011). *Good jobs, bad jobs: The rise of polarized and precarious employment systems in the United States, 1970s to 2000s*. New York: Russell Sage Foundation.

Keevers, L., & Sykes, C. (2016). Food and music matters: Affective relations and practices in social justice organizations. *Human Relations*, 69(8), 1643–1668.

Knights, D., & Willmott, H. (1999). *Management lives: Power and identity in work organizations*. London: Sage.

Kunda, G. (2006). *Engineering culture: Control and commitment in a high-tech corporation*. Philadelphia, PA: Temple University Press.

Ladkin, D. (2010). *Rethinking leadership: A new look at old leadership questions*. Cheltenham, UK: Edward Elgar.

Larrabee, M. J. (Ed.). (1993). *An ethic of care: Feminist and interdisciplinary perspectives*. New York: Routledge.

Marcuse, H. (2007). In A. Feenberg & W. Liess (Eds.), *The essential Marcuse: Selected writings of philosopher and social critic Herbert Marcuse*. Boston, MA: Beacon Press.

Mintzberg, H. (1973). *The nature of managerial work*. New York: Harper & Row.

Molstad, C. (1986). Choosing and coping with boring work. *Journal of Contemporary Ethnography*, 15(2), 215–236.

Morgan, G. (2006). *Images of organization* (2th ed.). Thousand Oaks, CA: Sage.

Mosley, Jr., D. C., Mosley, Sr., D. C., & Pietri, P. H. (2008). *Supervisory management: The art of inspiring, empowering, and developing people*. Mason, OH: South-Western Cengage Learning.

Newstrom, J. W. (2013). *Supervision: Managing for results* (10th ed.). New York, NY: McGraw Hill.

O'Brien Carelli, A. (2010). *The truth about supervision: Coaching, teamwork, interviewing, appraisals, 360° assessments, delegation, and recognition* (2nd ed.). Springfield, IL: Charles C. Thomas.

Parker, M. (2002). *Against management: Organization in the age of managerialism*. Oxford: Polity Press.

Peters, T., & Waterman, R. H. (1982). *In search of excellence: Lessons from America's best-run companies*. Sydney: Harper & Row.

Pirson, M. A., & Lawrence, P. R. (2010). Humanism in business towards a paradigm shift? *Journal of Business Ethics*, 93(4), 553–565.

Robbins, S. R., DeCenzo, D. A., & Wolter, R. M. (2015). *Supervision today!* (8th ed.). Boston, MA: Pearson.

Rose, M. (1975). *Industrial behaviour: Theoretical development since Taylor*. New York, NY: Penguin Books.

Sennett, R. (1999). *The corrosion of character: The personal consequences of work in the new capitalism*. New York, NY: Norton.

Sennett, R. (2003). *Respect in a world of inequality*. New York: Norton and company.

Sewell, G., Barker, J. R., & Nyberg, D. (2012). Working under intensive surveil-lance: When does 'measuring everything that moves' become intolerable? *Human Relations*, 65(2), 189–215.

Sias, P. M., & Cahill, D. J. (1998). From coworkers to friends: The development of peer friendships in the workplace. *Western Journal of Communication*, 62(3), 273–299.

Silverman, D. (1970). *The theory of organisations*. London: Heinemann Educational.

Sinclair, A. (2007). *Leadership for the disillusioned: Moving beyond myths and heroes to leading that liberates*. Crows Nest, New South Wales: Allen & Unwin.

Smircich, L., & Morgan, G. (1982). Leadership: The management of meaning. *The Journal of Applied Behavioural Science*, 18(3), 257–273.

Standing, G. (2011). *The precariat: The new dangerous class*. London: Bloomsbury Academic.

Stead, V., & Elliott, C. (2009). *Women's leadership*. Basingstoke, UK: Palgrave Macmillan.

Sturdy, A., & Grey, C. (2003). Beneath and beyond organizational change manage-ment: Exploring alternatives. *Organization*, 10(4), 651–662.

Taylor, F. S. (1919). *The principles of scientific management*. New York: Harper & Brothers.

Taylor, G., & Wolfram, S. (1968). The self-regarding and other-regarding virtues. *The Philosophical Quarterly*, 18(72), 238–248.

Tengblad, S., & Vie, O. E. (2012). Management in practice: Overview of classic stud-ies on managerial work. In S. Tengblad (Ed.), *The work of managers: Towards a practice theory of management* (pp. 18–46). Oxford: Oxford University Press.

Ulrich, D. (1998). Intellectual capital = Competence x commitment. *Sloan Manage-ment Review*, 39(2), 15–26.

Waddock, S. A., Bodwell, C., & Graves, S. B. (2002). Responsibility: The new busi-ness imperative. *The Academy of Management Executive*, 16(2), 132–148.

Watson, T. J. (1994). *In search of management: Culture, chaos and control in mana-gerial work*. London: Routledge.

Weckert, J. (Ed.). (2005). *Electronic monitoring in the workplace: Controversies and solutions*. London: Idea Group.

Wilson, S. (2016). *Thinking differently about leadership: A critical history of leader-ship studies*. Cheltenham, UK: Edward Elgar.

# 4    *Leading in* Human Resource Management

## Introduction

'Human resource leadership' is not necessarily a widely understood phenomenon. While formal roles and practices for managing human resources are by now ubiquitous across small, medium and large organizations, human resource management (HRM) has for many years struggled to assert itself (Wright, Dunford & Snell, 2001; Nkomo & Ensley, 1999). From a worker's perspective, human resource managers are often more likely to be seen as untrustworthy agents for the shareholders than employee advocates and leaders. From an organizational perspective, HRM is regularly excluded from executive levels, and where granted organizational influence through strategic HRM approaches or otherwise, it has been accused of failing to deliver (Hammond, 2005; Bolton & Houlihan, 2007). Furthermore, while HRM has been framed as a means to develop leadership in others, it is far less likely to be seen as performing leadership itself.

Increasingly, however, the status of HRM as a leadership function has emerged. In practice, there has for some time been a loud lament about the paucity of individuals who are adequately prepared to take up the 'demanding' and 'visionary' role of leading HRM in (especially) large organizations. It is likely, too, that many HR managers view themselves as performing leadership. Academic research, however, has been slow to follow suit. While extensive calls have been made by scholars for the recognition of HR as a strategic partner in organizations, there has been only minimal consideration of the nature of leadership in such strategic roles (although see Caldwell, Truong, Linh & Tuan, 2011). Indeed, the extensive scholarly fields of HRM and leadership studies have developed largely independently (Den Hartog & Boon, 2013), and at the time we were preparing this chapter, a call for papers was circulating for a special issue of *Human Resource Management Review* on 'Bridging Leadership and HRM' (Leroy, Den Hartog & Segers, 2015). The editors of this special issue pointed to the problem of translation between leadership theory and the practice of HR managers and identified the urgent need to "theoretically link leadership research with HRM research".

In this context, anyone attempting to 'revitalise' HR leadership needs to take a step back to ask "how far has HR leadership come in its theorisation and practice?" and "to what extent might traditional and emergent HRM and leadership approaches complement, contradict or progress each other?" If we are willing to concede that the understanding of HR leadership itself is still nascent, the question then becomes "can HR leadership be developed in a way that will avoid some of the pitfalls of the distinct models of HRM and organizational leadership developed in the past?"

In this chapter, we will briefly outline the early formation of the HRM function as described in the literature and draw connections to the concept of leadership. We will identify some of the problems for a new and vital HR leadership that this formation poses. We will then consider the challenges that currently face HRM in association with the opportunities and threats that have been identified in academic analysis of HRM, leadership and organizational practice. Specifically, we will draw on three domains in which we see HR leadership currently (though often implicitly) conceptualised, consisting of: the recruitment of senior HRM professionals, the development of HRM leaders through popular and professionalised HR competency frameworks, and mainstream and critical scholarly accounts of the HRM function. This groundwork is necessary before we begin to move through the framework for theorising leadership outlined in Chapter 2. By taking this approach, we offer one orientation to HR leadership that aims to be sustainable, ethical and contribute to the enhancement of human and organizational capability.

## The Evolution of Human Resource Management as Leadership

The history of human resource management in organizations is 'relatively long and humble' (Cohen, 2015). From the first time that one individual recruited, managed and compensated another for their work, the HR function was born. Early formalised forms of HRM were emergent through the late 19th and early 20th centuries in Europe, the United States of America, Japan, Britain and later in some of the former British colonies. The early role of industrial 'welfare worker' was built on deep Christian and charitable commitments to the well-being of workers held by many large employers in Britain, but was further prompted by the introduction of legislation in the early 1900s designed to ensure adequate safety and working conditions of factory workers (Berridge, 1992). Later payroll administrators, employment record-keepers and then dedicated work units with the responsibility of 'personnel' management and administration emerged in the first half of the 20th century (Kaufman, 2007). While, some have argued that the early versions of HRM had embedded in them a strategic and integrating role for organizations through an employee advocacy function (e.g., Jacques, 1999; Kaufman, 2007; Lengnick-Hall, Lengnick-Hall, Andrade & Drake, 2009), traces of this were largely absent from the majority of accounts of 'personnel management' and 'Industrial Relations' roles in American and European organizations into the 1960s. While there were exceptions (e.g., large, non-unionised US companies, large Japanese companies in the primary sector), the image and status of the human resource function became diminished between 1950s and the 1980s as it became framed as an administration and service role, a tool, to implement a range of personnel activities (Kaufman, 2007).

As an operational and administrative arm of organizations, personnel management took on the (often low-status) role of organizing a collection of discrete practices or disciplines relating to the recruitment, retention, development and payment of staff. By this time, the welfare and employee advocacy role evident in early models of the HR function were all but gone. While in the 1980s, the dominance of the descriptor 'personnel management' began to give way to 'human resource management' along with the re-introduction of a more integrated function, the vestiges of this low status has endured. Combined with the problems of dynamic economic conditions and rapid fluctuations of hiring and shedding employees in recent decades, HRM has had to continually fight to justify its position in organizations (Cohen, 2015; Dunford, Snell & Wright, 2001).

But in the last 30 years, the status and ability for human resource management to influence and participate in leading organizations has arguably increased. Two main areas of development in theorising HRM seem to have contributed to this shift through the 1980s—2000s: (1) the growing promotion and acceptance of viewing organizations as complex systems and the theorisation of integrated models of strategic human resource management as part of this (e.g. Walker, 1978; Devanna, Fombrun & Tichy, 1984), and (2) the theorisation of high-performance and high-commitment work systems and related debates about 'hard' and 'soft' HRM approaches (e.g., Appelbaum, Bailey, Berg & Kalleberg, 2000; Alvesson, 2009).

Building on shifting trends in organizational theory through the 1970s and 80s, and as a response to the perceived functional fragmentation, low status and limited influence of HRM, theorists began to conceptualise a cohesive, linked network of human resource practices as part of the larger open organizational system. Beer, Spector, Lawrence, Quinn & Walton (1984), for example, offered one of the first systems models of HRM which acknowledged the influence of external and internal factors. While this and other systemic models such as Fromburn and colleague's Matching model (Devanna, Fombrun & Tichy, 1984) identified links between organizational strategy and HRM policies and practices, these early phases of what would become strategic human resource management (SHRM) struggled to develop a convincing theoretical base (Wright & McMahan, 2011). Analysis during the 1980s and 1990s was often split between two key approaches with little overlap. On the one hand, emphasis shifted attention from discrete HR functions (e.g. recruitment, training, reward and compensation etc.) to finding complementarity and optimal configuration between these (horizontal integration) (e.g., MacDuffie, 1995; Ichniowski, Shaw & Prennush, 1997; Appelbaum et al., 2000). On the other hand, theorists such as Schuler and Jackson (1987), Wright and Snell (1991), and Guest (1987) used a foundation of strategic management theory (e.g., Porter, 1980; Miles & Snow, 1978) to emphasise vertical integration between the external context, business strategy and HR (Dunford et al., 2001). While the full potential of systems thinking for HRM was somewhat constrained through these partial approaches, they did provide the basis for the more integrative SHRM approaches we see today that incorporate both vertical and horizontal integration. Martín-Alcázar, Romero-Fernández and Sánchez-Gardey (2005), for example, combine contingent, configurational and contextual approaches to offer a systems model where SHRM is defined as: "the integrated set of practices, policies and strategies through which organizations manage their human capital, that influences and is influenced by the business strategies, the organizational context and the socio-economic context" (p. 651).

High-performance work systems and related high-commitment management models built on integrated systems models of HRM but shifted the focus to reforming the quality of work systems to achieve superior organizational performance and productivity (Boxall & Macky, 2009; Beer, 2009; Guest, Michie, Conway & Sheehan, 2003). High-performance work systems have been argued to bring productivity benefits to organizations and commitment, satisfaction and participation benefits to workers. An enduring debate in this field has been between the 'hard' utilitarian and instrumental approaches to HRM and the 'softer' more developmental and humanist approaches that identify that workers are not merely raw resources to be utilised for organizational gains but are motivated, inspired, and excited by enriched working environments in which they can contribute and innovate (Storey, 1995). The extent to which high-performance/high-commitment HRM facilitates voice, participation and engagement has become of particular interest. Alongside reducing union density and legislatively restricted trade union influence through the 1990s in places like New Zealand, high-performance work systems potentially offered alternative 'in-house' mechanisms to hear from, engage and involve their staff in processes of 'continuous improvement'.

Together, these developing approaches brought with them three crucial ways of linking human resource management with enhanced organizational influence and leadership. First, the argument that human resource management functions had to be planned and designed in an optimal configuration highlighted the need for high level HR managers who had the expertise and oversight required for effective coordination. Second, the strategic alignment of human resource systems with environmentally contingent organizational objectives reinvigorated the need for high level collaboration between senior HR managers and other senior executives and external organizational stakeholders. This opened up the potential for 'HR leaders' to be seen as equivalent to their counterparts, the CFOs and COOs. The third set of debates relating to high-performance/high-commitment models of HRM has highlighted issues of worker participation, voice, development and commitment. This emphasis has shifted the understanding of HRM as driven by technical management and control, to one that must inspire, incite and motivate employee commitment and engagement—"to win the hearts and minds" of employees.

## Uncertain Foundations for Building HR Leadership?

Given the familiar narrative of the evolution of HRM sketched out above, it is perhaps not surprising that many HR practitioners, academics and commentators now argue that HR needs to be at the 'c-suite table' (Urlich, cited in Moore, 2011). Indeed, SHRM has been viewed as a direct attempt "to better position human resources within the managerial hierarchy" (Nkomo & Ensley, 1999, p. 342), which some argue has led to "exciting opportunities for unprecedented leadership" (Erikson, 2009, p. 378). However, despite three decades of debate regarding HRM's strategic and high-performance/high-commitment approaches, its relationship with leadership has gained only narrow direct attention in academic analysis. Even in highly integrated and developed theories of SHRM which argue for the pivotal role of HRM at the top table, the concept of leadership is typically only considered in regard to how HRM may build the capability of other organizational members to lead (e.g., Wright et al., 2001; Compton, 2009). Through selection, succession planning, stretch assignments, leadership development workshops and the like, leadership is something HRM facilitates; far less often is it seen as something it enacts itself. This presents a rather paradoxical foundation upon which we might revise HR leadership. Given that the relationship between HRM and leadership is typically conceived through HRM's mandate to develop leadership in others through a set of personnel practices, there may also be a risk of arriving at what Mabey and Mayrhofer (2015) have identified as a "reduction of leadership to a set of morally neutral techniques coupled with the danger and deficiency of dominant functionalist, means-end understanding" (described by Harney, 2016, p. 1)? This risk is quite real given that the theoretical shifts which have arguably elevated HRM to possess leadership status within the organization hierarchy have also brought with them increasing emphasis on instrumental, unitarist and short-termist approaches to HRM (Bolton & Houlihan, 2007). The value of people within an organization has become increasingly narrowly defined as holding the potential to further organizations' performance and productivity if managed appropriately through increasingly advanced, and as we discuss below, technological strategies. Even so called 'soft' approaches that emphasise engagement, commitment and participation are undertaken in the name of improving the bottom-line or, if we want to be more generous, the organizational 'reason for being' (Rucci, 2009). There has been an excising of humanity from the human resource function in that worker outcomes are continually deferred in the pursuit of organizational outcomes (Bolton & Houlihan, 2007; Guest, 2011; Lindley, 1984; Warren, 2000). As Nkomo and Ensley (1999) have previously argued,

> The shift to human resource management was positioned as a means of demonstrating the significance of humans as resources in organizations. Yet, the shift appears to be more about arguing for the importance and legitimacy of human resource professionals. Ironically, the 'humans' of human resource management seem to have ended right up where we started from, as commodities.
>
> (p. 343)

Certainly, a foundation of unitarist, instrumental models of HRM alongside functionalist notions of leadership development provide a very distant starting point from our aspirations for a revitalised leadership articulated earlier in this book, which seeks to "enable shared goals of a given community via means that are consistent with shared values". This raises a key dilemma for our revitalisation of HR leadership—is it possible to grasp current opportunities to influence and shape organization through HR leadership in a way that does not fall back on some of the flaws of dominant HRM and leadership theory that have already been highlighted by critical scholars? In the following section, we consider this question as we move through our framework for theorising leadership as set out in Chapter 2.

## Revitalising HR Leadership

Any new theorisation of HR leadership must necessarily attend to how organizations understand and utilise HRM. Recruitment advertisements for HRM leaders offer a unique insight into how organizations currently perceive the challenging context in which HR leaders must operate, the purposes of HR leadership and associated values, skills, knowledge and attributes of actors in the HR leadership process. On a single day in early 2016, we drew a complete set of 38 recruitment advertisements advertising senior HRM roles on the leading job vacancy website in New Zealand.[1] We have also traced through increasingly popular 'HR competency frameworks' (e.g., Ulrich, 2013; HRINZ, 2016) and mainstream scholarly accounts of HRM. We draw on these three sources of data as well as more critical debates to firstly identify some of the key challenges to which HR leadership must respond now and in the future and then go on to consider the appropriate purposes, values and norms, and domains in which HR leadership should be enacted. In alignment with our arguments elsewhere in the book we paint a picture of a revitalised HR leadership which is founded in an ethical and moral orientation towards supporting the well-being and human capability of all organizational community members and in turn necessarily refigure the leader and the follower within the leadership process.

## What Are the Challenges That HR Leadership Must Address?

For many decades, HRM has oriented itself around a pivotal challenge: how to obtain increased and measurable gains in organizational outcomes of investments made in human resources. The focus has primarily been on enhancing worker productivity for improved organizational performance and HRM has developed increasingly specialised tools and strategies for this purpose. However, as it has been noted by many commentators and scholars, the context of HRM is rapidly changing, and the demands on HR leadership to meet this purpose have extended and deepened (e.g., Colakoglu, Lepak & Hong, 2006; Erikson, 2009; Farnham, 2010). Indeed, our highly diverse sample of New Zealand organizations seeking their next HR leader describe their organizational context almost uniformly as 'demanding and complex', 'dynamic and fast paced', 'exciting', 'challenging' and 'changing'. As we have previously argued in Chapter 2, dynamism of the organizational context brings with it particular challenges for leadership generally, but these take on specific relevance in the context of an emerging HR leadership function.

An expanding global and competitive context for organizations bring the challenge of acutely apparent differentials in employment legislation and conditions across nation states (minimum wage, protections etc.). The global mobility of workforces means that HR leaders must plan recruitment, selection, development and compensation practices both competitively and fairly. A more diverse and global workforce including varying experience, needs, expectations and patterns of life-cycle have also thrown into sharp relief the inadequacy of traditional career pathways, compensation plans, rigid working arrangements and static training opportunities to meet worker's needs. In this context, it is likely that increasingly bespoke working arrangements and development opportunities relevant to individual requirements (voiced by workers and understood by the organization) will be necessary.

Globalisation of work and workforces also suggests that if it was ever possible to manipulate organizational culture for better performance (which, we might argue, it wasn't), the effectiveness of cultural management will become ever more evasive in a context in which: organizational boundaries are fluid within sectors and between national and international regions; where workers' careers span diverse organizations and professions; and where there is greater need for interorganizational collaboration and partnership as part of international markets. HRM will need to rely more deeply on the approaches, professionalism and knowledge of the workers that flow in and out of the organization rather than attempt to drive culture change from the top down.

Through the continued dominance of SHRM models, the connection between the management of people resources and bottom-line performance has gained a great deal of attention. However, as organizations have become increasingly influenced by financial markets and susceptible to radical market fluctuations, such strategic alignment has required constant re-articulation. For example, developing 'business cases' for diversity management, culture programmes or training programmes have been a central strategy undertaken by HRM professionals in leading change at an organizational level. However, due to equivocal evidence of longitudinal effects on performance and rapid cycles of organizational expansion and retraction, the value of such programmes to the bottom-line must be constantly rehearsed. There will be a need for flexibility in HR practices that align with fluctuating numbers of employees and shifting skill and knowledge portfolios of organizations.

As we have previously described, there has been a 'decline of authority' in organizational and political contexts. This has occurred at the same time as the HRM function has sought higher levels of organizational status and influence through models of SHRM. HRM has arrived at the party late and is now faced with the challenge of building an HR leadership function when traditional sources of power and influence are being reformed and the ties between organizational hierarchy and leadership weakened. As Nkomo and Ensley (1999) described over 15 years ago, in its striving for influence "HRM appears to be in a permanent stage of 'becoming' significant" (p. 339). Ongoing questions of the legitimacy of HRM as a leadership function hold the potential risk of HRM slipping into practices of 'petty tyranny' (Ashforth, 1994) in which HR leaders, grasping, attempt to hold their tenuous power over others. This shifting context poses the challenge of HRM articulating a purpose and gaining influence through means not solely embedded in legitimised ranks of hierarchy. If HR leadership can be exercised by other means, HRM may be better protected from market fluctuations and shifting prioritisation in organizations.

It is certainly the case that while we have witnessed a decline in authority broadly, the 'harder' edge of HRM, including the ability to exert direct managerial surveillance and control across our organizations, has expanded in recent years through technical innovation. Just a few examples include: intensive online screening in recruitment and selection (e.g., drawing on personal online profiles of applicants) (Anderson, 2003; Jeske & Shultz, 2015), tracking and building of individual personnel files for enhanced 'talent management', measuring working pace and productivity at team and individual levels for compensation and performance management and monitoring working time and the technology use of workers for personal and organizational purposes (Moussa, 2015; Mishra & Crampton, 1998). Thus, as a strategic 'business partner' for organizations, HRM has become expert in developing technologies and strategies for increasingly close control and surveillance of workers and has developed and implemented these tools for the use of line managers through to chief operating officers. However, these affordances of technology also carry ethical and moral questions for HRM relating to privacy, freedom and fairness (Barratt, 2003; Moussa, 2015; Searle, 2006). For example, digital job advertising, recruitment and selection processes have the potential to reduce or enhance traditional patterns of inequality. Increased availability and access to job information, online application functionality and automated screening of applicants may on the one hand open up opportunities to a different range of applicants. But on the other hand, digital recruitment processes can also restrict access of information opportunity to individuals who possess the appropriate technological resources and, at the same time, increase the likelihood of discrimination by recruiters who make quick initial decisions about candidates' suitability on the basis of information about the personal and leisure activities of applicants and observable characteristics relating to their gender, race, age, class and general appearance (Jeske & Shultz, 2015; Searle, 2006).

We have outlined here just a selection of the challenges that the complex and demanding context of modern organizations throw up for HRM. In the face of global competition for mobile and diverse workforces, HR leadership must establish employment conditions that are competitive and fair. HR leaders need to understand individual characteristics and needs of workers and to develop models of working that are bespoke, varied, and adaptable to meet workers' needs. HR leadership will also need to build an ability to influence from domains other than legitimised hierarchies and to consider carefully the ethical implications of using emergent technologies for advanced surveillance and control. Together, such matters suggest to us the need for a redefinition of the challenge around which HR leadership must orient. We set the challenge of HR leadership to be a question of how to obtain increased and measurable outcomes of investments made (capital, labour and physical resource) for *all* members of the organizational community in ways that are consistent with shared values and ethics of that community. This re-framed question provides the basis for a different type of purpose than is commonly described in dominant HRM literature.

## Clarity of Purpose and Dual Agendas

Given the complex context outlined above, what purpose should we then hold for HR leadership? In explaining the strategic role of HRM, Rucci (2009) states that the "core purpose for the HR profession should look something like this: To build organizational capabilities that help achieve sustained value creation, by focusing the commitment of people's energy, effort and ideas on a common vision" (p. 138). While Rucci explains that his definition incorporates an orientation to 'value creation' that far exceeds economic value, and to 'common vision' as shared purpose, the requirement for worker's commitment and ideas for the sole purpose of progressing organizational goals overrides any attention to the needs of the individual.

Without any reflection on the desirability or not of organizations acting *on* individual workers, Rucci asserts that the goal of SHRM must be to inspire and harness worker commitment to the extent that they might arrive at work having thought through and solved an organizational problem in their time off (p. 139). In this vision of strategic and high-performance/high-commitment HRM, workers are never wholly freed from pursuing organizational purpose.

We have provided Rucci's definition here not to single out his particular analysis as problematic but, rather, as an exemplar of the ways in which the majority of HRM scholarship (even when a prioritisation of *shared* values is made explicit) slips into utilitarian forms of manipulation and control of workers for organizational ends. This is an approach which perhaps unsurprisingly appears deeply embedded in the ways that many organizations perceive and frame their own strategic HR leadership function. Without exception, the employment advertisements of New Zealand and multi-national organizations that we looked at identified the key purpose of HR leadership in terms of delivering on business strategy through the effective management of people—but without very much to say about the people themselves. For example, organizations described the overall purpose of HR leadership roles to "design talent policies, processes and programmes that support the development, execution and consistent delivery of business strategy" to "play a pivotal role in the development of high quality human resource strategies and the ongoing development and delivery of services that contribute to the successful achievement of the Department's overall objectives", and to "[d]evelop an annual 'People Plan' that aligns with wider business plan". To deliver on these objectives, HR leaders are required to lead "the development and implementation of relevant organizational strategies", to provide "strategic and intellectual leadership" and to "lead a business transformation and drive cultural change to directly contribute to the strategic direction of the business". Leadership in relation to more specific HR functional domains was also described in relation to remuneration, talent management, performance management, culture management, stakeholder engagement, health and safety and training and development.

Moreover, even in areas in which we might expect the purpose to shift towards a stronger focus on supporting and contributing to the well-being of employees in the organizational community (such as the latter three listed above), the focus is consistently on engaging in these tasks for the purpose of furthering business strategy. Developing, engaging or protecting others from harm was consistently associated with meeting the objectives of the organization rather than meeting the needs of individual staff themselves. We see this orientation in competency frameworks also, in which meeting employee needs is a means to an end, a pathway to achieve the core purpose of organizational objectives. Taken to the extreme, one competency framework from a national association for HR professionals suggests HR leaders must "develop, lead and implement strategies that use health, safety and well-being to enhance business effectiveness and achieve strategic objectives" (HRINZ, 2016). The expectations of HR leadership are thus entirely instrumental and unitarist in orientation. Somehow, even the health and safety of workers are not for their own benefit.

So schooled are we in strategic approaches to HRM, the obvious response from organizations and commentators to our highlighting of this focus might be 'but of course'. As prominent HRM scholar and commentator David Ulrich argues:

> HR departments are not designed to provide corporate therapy or as social or health and happiness retreats. HR professionals must create the practices that make employees more competitive, not more comfortable. . . . The HR function does not own compliance—managers do. HR practices do not exist to make employees happy but to help them become committed. HR professionals must help managers commit employees and administer policies.
>
> (Ulrich, 2013, p. 18)

While Urlich's (2013) low prioritisation of employee needs and outcomes in this passage is clear, employees, he argues, remain important. Indeed, one of the four core functions that Ulrich consigns to HR leaders in his text from which the quotation above was drawn is to be an 'Employee Champion'. If we return to Rucci, we find there, too, that the very best HR professionals 'are employee advocates'. Rucci goes on to explain a similar inconsistency in his own writing about the role of SHRM:

> Despite all of the prior rhetoric in this chapter, this is the final (seemingly inconsistent?) requirement for effective HR professionals. Beyond helping organizations create value, beyond being strategic, beyond being business relevant, have real courage of conviction about your 'ultimate' role as an advocate for employees.
>
> (Rucci, 2009, p. 147)

Rucci suggests the employee advocacy role involves protecting the dignity of people and that rather than being inconsistent with the core purpose of HRM, it is in fact the "very foundation of this purpose". The advocacy role of the HR leader here is so important, so 'foundational', that it is first introduced in the bottom third of the last page of a ten-page chapter. In this type of influential account of SHRM, the employee is at once made visible and invisible: in this swift sleight of hand, if you blink, you will miss it. The likely outcome of HRM professionals trying to manage such a 'seemingly inconsistent' and contradictory dual agenda is that the weight of emphasis is given to the instrumental, commercial considerations, while any human concerns are pushed down and buried, as reflected in our analysis of job advertisements above.

Even high-commitment/high-performance models (significant in heightening attention to relationships, communication and culture alongside technical management strategies) provide an impoverished orientation when they are singly focussed on practices for the enhancement of organizational capability to the exclusion of the humans within the organization. In response, and amidst the rise of SHRM in the late 1990s, a number of critical scholars have begun to search for the missing or invisible human in HRM (e.g., see special issue on the 'Human and Inhuman' of HRM edited by Steyaert & Janssens, 1999). Nkomo and Ensley (1999) for example, wondered what HRM would look like if it rejected the temptation to engage in continual reassertion of a 'strategic' and central organizational role and rather, consciously and carefully worked from the 'perilous' and 'marginal' space between "the demands of top management for organizational effectiveness and the interests and well-being of humans in organizations" (p. 345). These authors advocate for HRM to create "a space in which to champion humans". That is, not to act as an employee voice, but rather as "a voice for articulating the meaning of human beyond the 'capital' emphasis it has been given", holding open the potential to speak against inequality, exploitation and subordination of workers (Nkomo & Ensley, 1999, p. 345).

Since that time, the call for HRM to re-figure its purpose in ways that build up and contribute to the health and well-being of humans in organizations has strengthened although remains marginal. Bolton and Houlihan (2007) describe one such approach of building 'thick' employment relationships that recognise the "multiple (and sometimes contradictory) motivations" of HRM and responds with a model of 'reciprocal obligation' between workers and organizations based on trust, autonomy and respect (p. 10). Other critical HR scholars have attended to humanist principles that they believe should underpin HRM. Over 30 years ago, Clyde Lindley (1984) advocated for a Rogerian approach to HRM based on two core principles that aim at 1) "Helping the person to realize his/her potentials and 2) [acknowledging] that each person has inner resources to grow and become a fully functioning person" (p. 504). More recently, others have built on Amartya Sen's human capability approach (Sen, 1993; 1999) to argue that the purpose of HRM should be turned to building 'human capability' and the consideration of "how people can achieve lives of value to them" (Bryson, 2010, p. 3). As Bryson notes: "Human capability, described by Sen (1999) as the ability to lead lives we value and have reason to value, provides a much needed counterpoint to the largely organizationally instrumental and human capital assumptions that have dominated debates on work" (p. 3).

The human capability approach to organizations and work as described by Bryson and others is based on the notion that all members of an organizational community possess certain rights. Bryson (2013) describes these as the right to:

be alive, to live in physical security and to be healthy . . . be knowledgeable, to understand and reason, and to have the skills to participate in
society . . . enjoy a comfortable standard of living, with independence
and security . . . engage in productive and valued activities . . . enjoy individual, family and social life . . . participate in decision-making, have a
voice and influence . . . being and expressing yourself, having self-respect
and knowing you will be protected and treated fairly by the law.

(p. 564)

This approach draws attention to why individuals engage in organizations
in the first place and underscores "the freedom to live a life that [is] person-
ally perceived as valuable and that the capability to perform work for an
organization [is] merely a means towards that end" (Bryson, 2010, p. 199).

Drawing from a cross-sector empirical study, Bryson and O'Neil (2010)
note that there are a number of institutional and organizational drivers and
constraints which shape the extent to which organizations may facilitate
the building of human capability including the economic setting; the role
of the state/public policy; educational arrangements; cultural/ideological
legacies; philosophy of economic and working life; and key organizational structures and practices. Bryson and O'Neil also found a number of
employee factors that influenced the extent to which human capability was
built, including proactive behaviour to seek out opportunities and shape
the work environment to suit their needs. Those with the strongest sense of
self-efficacy, confidence and awareness of their rights and responsibilities
were the best prepared for being involved in the building of human capability of themselves and others. To support the development of such characteristics in individuals, HR leaders have a role in facilitating the collective
formation and articulation of reciprocal rights and responsibilities of all
members and to provide opportunities for workers to have a voice, exercise
control and make a meaningful contribution to decision making in organizations. Bryson and O'Neil (2010) found in their empirical research that
such support was consistently associated with the development of human
capability. The same carries for HR leadership in regard to the leadership
of HRM teams.

In re-centring the 'human' in human resource management, we are advocating for a formation of HR leadership in which there is a clear ethical
and moral commitment to all members of the organization. Our proposed
focus for HR leadership then is: *to build capability and facilitate all members of the organizational community to achieve their potential so that they
may lead lives that they value.* In the language of SHRM this purpose must
become a core 'strategic aim' of the organization (and HRM) alongside
"building organizational capabilities" (Rucci, 2009). Such a purpose shifts
a top-down HR focus from the management and control of employees for
the enhancement of organizational outcomes, to recognizing the rights, but
also joint responsibilities, of all members to collectively work together for

shared goals. This orientation assumes a revision of the values and norms that must underpin HR leadership, as discussed below.

## Values and Norms

A human capability approach for HR leadership provides an ethical anchor around which central values relate to recognition, reciprocity, integrity, dignity, autonomy and trust between all members of the organization. This approach asserts a mutual obligation of employees, managers, HR professionals and the organization more broadly to participate and collaborate openly and fairly to ensure capability is built. HR leaders ought, therefore, to design jobs that offer quality work, in which employees are paid fairly, have opportunities to progress and are extended the resources and freedom to do their job.

In order for organizations to know and understand workers' needs and capabilities, to develop truly shared visions, there must be full opportunity for voice, collaboration and shared decision making. This involves a commitment to redress inequality internally and within the broad economic network in which the organization is situated. As Bryson and O'Neil (2010) argue, "those in precarious employment or low-quality jobs are more likely to be women, young, an ethnic minority, and less-skilled and less-educated (Tucker, 2002; Spoonley, 2010), thus, relative to other social groups, have less capability to live the life they value" (p. 205).

Clearly, the above implies significant change in many organizational practices should be sought in the name of HR leadership. Hence, we are advocating here a self-consciously long-term view in policy-making, practices and decision making as part of this. In arguing for a long-term orientation, and one that attends to reducing inequality and building capability, we are not naive to the conflicting pressures that limit the potential for HR leaders to enact such change in organizations. For example, dynamic, fast-moving contexts tend to encourage short-term responses even if these are not sustainable; flexible employment of workers can be responsive and save costs but at the same time may limit individual skill and knowledge development due to the insecurity of the employment relationship for both organisation and worker. A human capability approach to HR leadership, however, offers a stable ethical value, rather than a priority which may shift with changing pressures. It establishes the basis for rich and mutually beneficial interactions on a daily basis through high participation, sharing of ideas, individual growth, while also building human and organizational capability for the long term.

## Domains of HR Leadership

With a core purpose to facilitate and contribute to the health and well-being of organizational members, and underpinning values of human capability, reciprocity and mutual obligation, the question of which domains and in what ways should we attempt to enact HR leadership is confronting. HRM has traditionally sought to *act on* employees, to enhance their individual motivation, commitment and creativity through policies, practices, culture management, training and performance-based contracts for service. It is envisioned that appropriate management practices and HR policies will 'put to work' personal as well as professional networks of workers, will draw on the creative and innovative potential of workers' diversity and will induce workers to offer up unpaid as well as paid labour to further progress organizational goals (Fleming & Sturdy, 2011; Martínez Lucio, 2008; Weiskopf & Munro, 2012).

Even where top-down tight control has been replaced by a more passive approach to 'harness' or 'capture' individuals' natural propensity to innovate, solve problems or bond with others, the domain of influence of HR has been extended far beyond traditional boundaries of work and organization. As Fleming (2014) remarks, during the mid-1990s, there was a shift in which human resource managers and organizations more broadly moved from attempting to align all organizational members to a single manufactured culture for productivity to, rather, encourage workers to express their idiosyncrasies, interests, diversity, sexual orientation, politics and other characteristics traditionally prohibited from the workplace. At the same time, workers are encouraged to see their job as extending beyond traditional workplace boundaries "so that ideas, skills and potential value-adding efforts that occur in a cafe, at home or even on holiday might be captured by the firm" (Fleming, 2014, p. 878).

By contrast, we argue that the domains in which HR leadership should act needs to be restricted. That is not to imply that HR leaders should be indifferent to the quality of life that workers are able to achieve, but rather to act within the much more constrained domain of the workplace and to accept the right to freedom of workers. The surveillance of both work and home life through tracking personal profiles on social media, blanket drug testing even where roles pose no risk to human safety, contracted obligations relating to diet and smoking habits and monitoring computer use in the workplace are not part of our vision for HR leadership. These are examples in which attention to individual and personal activities and characteristics are used as a means to control and punish, rather than build on the trustful and shared approach to leadership we envision in which formally prescribed 'leaders' and 'followers' participate.

## Leaders and Followers in HR Leadership

As we have discussed previously, much leadership theory positions the 'leader' within the leadership process as an elevated individual with almost superhuman capabilities to inspire and motivate passive followers. From the systemic SHRM approach, the individualised, deliberate leader can also be unearthed, a formally designated, unitary agent with specified authority and responsibility, who acts upon their subordinates to direct, vision, inspire and coordinate for the benefit of the organization and wealth creation. As one recruitment advertisement said, the HR leader they appoint will "Be a leader that leads from the front". However, aspirations towards becoming a 'transformational leader' for example, one with vision, charisma and the ability to inspire others to action, may create mechanisms for dependence rather than empowerment. By contrast, a focus on human capability in HR leadership disrupts the traditional static roles of leader and follower; it acknowledges the individual values, interests, capabilities, energy, resources and limitations of all actors contribute to the leadership process.

A core contribution of our orientation to HR leadership, then, is the recasting of 'followers' as actors with their own potentials, capabilities, needs and valued outcomes. Drawing from Bolton and Houlihan (2007), we propose that to include 'humanity' in the HR leadership process means to understand leaders, managers, employees, all, as "[s]ocial actors who are capable of moral commitment, who are involved with society and whose activities take place within multiple and layered frameworks of action" (p. 7). Further, our approach assumes that all actors in the organizational community have inner resources to enact leadership themselves, so that they may shape their working lives in ways which they value. As we argue below, this ethical orientation is essential to the viability of the HR leadership we envision, in that it provides a centerpoint around which shifting and or conflicting priorities may move and places the responsibility of leadership within a broader relationship of mutual obligation and involvement so that it does not fall solely on a single 'leader'.

Above, we have argued that the dual agenda of value creation and employee advocacy typically described for HRM has the potential to stretch HR leaders almost to breaking point. The skills, knowledge and attributes expected of HR leaders by mainstream theorists, professional bodies and organizations are similarly intimidating. Senior human resource managers are leaders with direct reports as well as strategic responsibilities; they must lead upwards and downwards. Given the diverse responsibilities and accountabilities of their position, HR leaders are expected to be high-performing hybrids that can draw from deep experience and knowledge in technical management, strategic design and people and relationship development. As one advertisement for an HR leader in a large educational institute describes, the desirable candidate as "experienced, business partner who is able to think strategically and offer pragmatic operational advice with a particular strength in coaching and developing". HR leaders are at once "in charge of the daily operations" of the HR unit and required to play the role of 'strategic partner' with 'strong business acumen'. Furthermore, organizations are seeking leaders possessing a vast range of personal characteristics, including: 'energy', 'passion', 'self-motivation', and 'confidence', 'proactivity', 'innovation' and 'creative flair', and 'pragmatism', 'attention to details and deadlines', 'sound analytical thinking', 'ability to prioritise' and 'strong time management and organization skills'. As one large multi-national organization describes, HR leaders are required to '[b]ring it all together' with "key accountabilities [that] will cover Strategic Initiatives, Operational Effectiveness, Financial Management and Internal & External Customer Management".

SHRM scholars and professional bodies have developed competency frameworks to guide the development of such hybrid individuals (e.g., HRINZ, 2016; Ulrich, 2013). For example, New Zealand's HR professional association, the Human Resource Institute of New Zealand suggests HR leadership must be enacted in HR delivery, strategic contribution, business knowledge, business technology and have personal credibility (HRINZ, 2016). Similarly, Ulrich (2013) identifies four primary roles of human resource professionals: strategic player, administrative expert, employee champion and change agent and that these roles need to be undertaken simultaneously by HR practitioners. Rucci also describes "the very best HR professionals" will: have personal credibility and excellent professional skills, be business people and change agents, and be employee advocates (p. 146–147). He goes on to note, "We should expect HR professionals and executives to be no less a business person and leader than we expect from a CFO, a general manager or a CEO" (Rucci, 2009, p. 146). Competency frameworks, organizational recruitment practices and dominant HRM theory propose HR leaders need to possess a mind-boggling range of capabilities, and any given context may demand a different set of capabilities of any particular individual leader. This leaves the HR leader as potentially over-stretched and vulnerable to shifting demands.

In a similar fashion to the role of the follower in dominant leadership discourse described in earlier parts of this book, the workers' voice in the human resource equation has largely been neglected in dominant conceptualisations of HRM (Guest, 2011; Donnelly & Proctor-Thomson, 2010). Certainly, the figure of the follower in the recruitment advertisements and competency frameworks we reviewed was barely perceptible. Where they were mentioned, typically in regard to the HR team, staff are positioned as requiring motivation, training and inspiration. The human capability approach, in contrast, insists that workers and managers alike are motivated by specific values and needs and have the capacity to enact leadership in some contexts and in response to some circumstances. In particular, the involvement and leadership of workers in regard to operational improvement, the shaping of quality jobs, the evaluation of the ethical nature of a decision and the protection of health and safety of selves and others are important examples of this.

Finally, rather than 'leading from the front' HR leaders and followers alike can more modestly act as 'ethical stewards' (Caldwell et al., 2011), with the specific strategic aim of enhancing organizational and human capability simultaneously. That is, to consistently raise and think through questions within organizational decision-making processes and change programmes from an ethical and values-based standpoint that is collectively defined by the members in that organization. This might entail asking how a particular proposal looks from a long-term sustainability view or considering how a new practice might impact on equality for diverse members of the organizational community. From this perspective, the leader/follower relationship is fluid but always embedded in notions of reciprocity, trust and collaboration. We consider all staff, whether within formal roles of leadership or not, to be responsible and accountable to the organizational community broadly, for engaging in the identification of goals, establishing moral and ethical foundations, making improvements, identifying opportunities for growth and development and keeping self and others safe. At times, those in subordinate positions will lead in areas in which they have knowledge, commitment, expertise and energy, while at other times, it will be the role of the formally designated leader to ensure organizational members can fulfil their capability. In particular, HR leaders have a unique leadership role in establishing the size of and duties of jobs, the contracts used to employ workers, the ways in which data is collected and used by managers regarding performance and decisions about recruitment, training, development and compensation. These are areas that will have a direct impact on the opportunity for building human capability.

## Conclusion

In this chapter, we have sought to articulate a revised model for HR leadership that takes an explicitly ethical role in the facilitation of human and organizational capability. We have described a model founded in reciprocal relationships of mutual obligation between all members of the organizational community. Table 4.1 summarises our revitalisation of HR leadership based on the articulation of the challenges and tensions HR leadership faces, a revised purpose, the values and norms which we argue must underpin this approach, the domains to which HR leaders should constrain their intended influence and the figuration of the actors and their relationships within the HR leadership process.

While there has been growing academic and organizational interest in ethical orientations to HRM, our approach explicitly places 'humanity' and the building of human capability at its heart as a core strategic aim of HRM. Our approach might seem idealistic or lofty, but there are numerous real world examples which demonstrate the relevance and necessity of our approach. One significant example writ large in the current New Zealand context is how organizations are attempting to respond to new legislation guiding policy and practice for ensuring health and safety at work. In Box 4.1, we have provided a brief consideration of the alignment of our model for a revitalised HR leadership with promoting organizational health and safety in New Zealand.

As a final point, it is important to note here that the relationship between supervisors, line managers and HR leaders is a close one. If we compare the summary framework for HR leadership provided here in Table 4.1 with that

*Table 4.1* HRM leadership: a summary

| Component | Key issues and ideas | |
|---|---|---|
| Challenges | HRM's leadership status and influence within organizations is precarious and vulnerable to market fluctuations. | |
| | The environment in which HRM must operate is fast-paced and multi-faceted. | |
| | International and highly mobile workforces and multi-national organization raises issues for companies in the provision of fair and equitable work conditions. | |
| | Emerging technologies have afforded opportunities for extended monitoring and control of workers but also bring with them intensified ethical concerns. | |
| | HRM work requires an extensive mix of technical, administrative and interpersonal skills at operational and strategic levels | |
| | HRM professionals face inconsistencies and tensions between responsibilities to advance the organization's strategic aims and valuing employees to the extent to which they can fulfil those goals. | |
| Purpose of leadership | To build capability and facilitate all members of the organizational community to achieve their potential so that they may lead lives that they value. | |
| Values and norms | Oriented towards building human capability<br>Reciprocity<br>Mutual obligation<br>Long-term view<br>Autonomy | Trust<br>Assumption of value and potential of all<br>Freedom to undertake work in ways that health and well-being is retained |
| Domains | Restricted to work domain but with care for quality of life and extent to which members can live lives that they value. | |
| Leader | Formal authority for overseeing the planning, policy and practice of people management | |
| | Orients own decision making and action around shared ethical commitments and calls others to do the same. | |
| | Obligation to provide opportunities for all members to contribute, take up leadership roles and to exercise voice and control | |
| Follower | Possesses interests, concerns and ideas that can be shared within the workplace for the purposes of meeting shared goals. | |
| | Obligation to participate and contribute to shaping work and organization in ways that lead to building of human capability. | |
| | Take leadership roles in areas that will contribute to human capability draw from shared values and norms of community, and extend shared goals. | |
| Leader-follower relationship | Collaborative and participatory | |
| | Shared leadership for identifying goals, establishing moral and ethical foundation, making improvements, identifying opportunities for growth and development, keeping self and others safe. | |

of supervisory leadership described earlier in Chapter 3, we see significant overlap. Of course, HR leadership involves the day-to-day operation of the HR function and in this respect, our vision of supervisory leadership is relevant. But in addition, a unique and primary contribution of HR leadership can come in the form of planning, policy and high-level implementation of people management practices across organizations. For example, HRM professionals are often the architects of the sophisticated tracking and management technologies that are used by line managers and senior executives alike. But, if our vision of HR leadership is to be fulfilled, there must be a heavy reliance by HR leaders on colleagues in supervisory roles to facilitate opportunities for employees to: participate, give voice, articulate their needs and ideas and determine optimal ways of fulfilling their work. Similarly, the role of HR leadership is set within a broader context of governance, strategy setting and organizing for innovation. It is these areas of leadership to which we now turn.

---

### Box 4.1 HR leadership and human capability for health and safety at work

The Health and Safety at Work Act 2015 (HSWA) came into effect in New Zealand on 4 April, 2016. The law was introduced with the aim of reducing the unacceptably high number of deaths and injuries occurring at work every year. In recent years, there have been some devastating, high-profile and fatal breaches of health and safety in New Zealand organizations, and the national record for health and safety year on year is poor in relation to international comparisons, such as Australia and the UK (Independent Taskforce on Workplace Health and Safety, 2013). The new legislation provides an expanded definition of hazard and explicitly outlines the rights and responsibilities of all organizational members in the protection of health and safety (including the business itself, health and safety officers, employees and any others within the workplace). The act establishes increased personal responsibility and liability for directors and senior management, formal requirements for employee participation in managing health and safety and increased penalties for breaches.

The legislation changes have been met with concern, worry and even resistance amidst overblown concern that organizations will need to abolish apparently wholesome and reasonable practice or risk breaching the new health and safety regulations. Two examples include widespread media coverage of schools who feel they need to restrict activities for children (e.g., tree climbing, school camps) and building companies worried they will need harnesses for simple ladder use (Watkins, 2015).

The ambivalence in which health and safety regulations are traditionally met as demonstrated here have in part led to an explicit model of mutual obligation written into the new act. The act seeks to ensure the health and safety of all members of the organizational community through a model of shared rights and responsibilities. It is explicitly written into the act that senior leaders, HR leaders and employees must be involved in the collective monitoring and response to safety risks. Workers must have the freedom to work in ways that are healthy and safe, they must take leadership when a health and safety issue needs to be addressed and they must be able to trust that their managers and the organization are similarly working towards providing a safe working environment and will be responsive to health and safety concerns when they are raised. In contrast to the previously dominant 'thin' notion of employee participation to meet health and safety minimum standards, HR leadership which is underpinned by a human capability approach offers much to organizations seeking to protect health and safety at work. It promotes the building of a 'thicker' (Bolton & Houlihan, 2007) employment relationship founded in a reciprocal commitment-based model in which participation and voice are central to maintaining high-quality, healthy and sustainable work.

## Note

1 A keyword search for 'human resource' and 'leadership' on www.seek.co.nz returned 172 jobs listed on 18 January, 2016. From this list, we included all advertisements that advertised for senior HR managers. Advertised roles included: 'HR Manager', 'People Manager', 'HR leader', 'Senior HR advisor', and 'People and capability business partner'. More specialised roles relating to senior levels of the HR function were also included: ER consultant, OD consultant, Training and OD manager. All roles in which less than five years of experience was required or where the job titles indicated a lower organizational level were excluded, e.g., payroll analyst, HR analyst, HR coordinator, HR advisor. This is not to discount the possibility of HRM leadership being required and enacted at lower organizational levels. Generalised senior management roles with explicitly stated HR responsibilities but not considered an HR role were also excluded, e.g., senior architect, general manager, branch manager, nurse manager, site manager, clinical manager. The final 38 advertisements reflected a vast array of organizations from large public sector policy and operational agencies, large national and multi-national organizations, educational and training institutions and medium-sized and smaller regional organizations. Legal, accountancy, finance, retail, design, services and consultancy sectors were represented.

## References

Alvesson, M. (2009). Critical perspectives on strategic HRM. In J. Storey, P. Wright, & D. Ulrich (Eds.), *The Routledge companion to strategic HRM*, (p. 52–68). Abingdon, UK: Routledge.

Anderson, N. (2003). Applicant and recruiter reactions to new technology in selection: A critical review and agenda for future research. *International Journal of Selection and Assessment*, 11(2/3), 121–36.

Appelbaum, E., Bailey, T., Berg, P., & Kalleberg, A. (2000). *Manufacturing advantage: Why high-performance work systems pay off*. Ithaca: ILR Press.

Ashforth, B. (1994). Petty tyranny in organizations. *Human Relations*, 47, 755–778.

Barratt, E. (2003). Foucault, HRM and the ethos of the critical management scholar. *Journal of Management Studies*, 40, 1069–1087.

Beer, M. (2009). *High commitment high performance: How to build a resilient organization for sustained advantage*. San Francisco: Jossey-Bass.

Beer, M., Spector, B., Lawrence, P. R., Quinn Mills, D., & Walton, R. E. (1984). *Human resource management*. New York: Free Press.

Berridge, J. (1992). Human resource management in Britain. *Employee Relations*, 14(5), 62–92.

Bolton, S., & Houlihan, M. (2007). Beginning the search for the H in HRM. In S. Bolton & M. Houlihan (Eds.), *Searching for the human in human resource management*, Chapter 1. Basingstoke: Palgrave Macmillan.

Boxall, P., & Macky, K. (2009). Research and theory on high-performance work systems: Progressing the high involvement stream. *Human Resource Management Journal*, 19(1), 3–23.

Bryson, J. (Ed.). (2010). *Beyond skill: Institutions, organizations and human capability*. Basingstoke: Palgrave Macmillan.

Bryson, J. (2013). Putting skill in its place. *Journal of Education and Work*, 28(5), 551–570.

Bryson, J., & O'Neil, P. (2010). A frameowrk for developing human capaibility at work. In J Bryson (Ed), *Beyond skill: Institutions, organizations and human capability*, Chapter 10. Basingstoke: Palgrave Macmillan.

Caldwell, C., Truong, D. X., Linh, P. T., & Tuan, A. (2011). Strategic human resource management as ethical stewardship. *Journal of Business Ethics*, 98(1), 171–182.

Cohen, D. J. (2015). HR past, present and future: A call for consistent practices and a focus on competencies. *Human Resource Management Review*, 25, 205–215.

Colakoglu, S., Lepak, D. P., & Hong, Y. (2006). Measuring HRM effectiveness: Considering multiple stakeholders in a global context. *Human Resource Management Review, Special Issue: The New World of Work and Organizations*, 16(2), 209–218.

Compton, R. (2009). Towards an integrated model of strategic human resource management: An Australian case study. *Research and Practice in Human Resource Management*, 17(2), 81–93.

Den Hartog, D., & Boon, C. (2013). HRM and leadership. In S. Bach & M. R. Edwards (Eds.), *Managing human resources: Human resource management in transition* (5th ed.). Chapter 10, p. 198–218. Chichester, Sussex: John Wiley & Sons.

Devanna, M. A., Fombrun, C. J., & Tichy, N. M. (1984). *Strategic human resource management*. New York: Wiley.

Donnelly, N., & Proctor-Thomson, S. B. (2010). Workplace sustainability and employee voice. In M. Clarke (Ed.), *Readings in HRM and sustainability*, Chapter 9, p. 117–132. Sydney: Tilde University Press.

Dunford, B. B., Snell, S. A., & Wright, P. M. (2001). Human resources and the resource based view of the firm. *CAHRS Working Paper #01–03*. Ithaca, NY: Cornell University, School of Industrial and Labor Relations, Center for Advanced Human Resource Studies.

Erikson, T. J. (2009). The changing context for HR. In J. Storey, P. Wright, & D. Ulrich (Eds.), *The Routledge companion to strategic HRM*, p. 377–389. Abindon, UK: Routledge.

Farnham, D. (2010). *Human resource management in context* (3rd ed.). London: Chartered Institute of Personnel and Development (CIPD).

Fleming, P. (2014). Review article: When 'life itself' goes to work: Reviewing shifts in organizational life through the lens of biopower. *Human Relations*, 67, 875–901.

Fleming P., & Sturdy, A. (2011). Being yourself in the electronic sweatshop: New forms of normative control. *Human Relations*, 64(2), 177–200.

Fombrun, C. J., Tichy, N. M., & Devanna, M. A. (1984). *Strategic human resource management*. New York: Wiley.

Guest, D. E. (1987). Human resource management and industrial relations. *Journal of Management Studies*, 24(5), 503–521.

Guest, D. E. (2011). Human resource management and performance: Still searching for some answers. *Human Resource Management Journal*, 21(1), 3–13.

Guest, D. E., Michie, J., Conway, N., & Sheehan, M. (2003). Human resource management and performance. *British Journal of Industrial Relations*, 41(2), 291–314.

Hammond, K. H. (2005). Why we hate HR. *Fast Company*, 97, 40.

Harney, B. (2016). Book review: Developing leadership: Questions business schools don't ask. *Management Learning*, 47(5), 626-627.

HRINZ (2016). HRINZ HR competency model. *HRINZ website*. Retrieved from www.hrinz.org.nz/Site/My_HR_Career/Competencies/default.aspx.

Ichniowski, C., Shaw, K., & Prennush, G. (1997). The effects of human resource management practices on productivity: A study of steel finishing lines. *American Economic Review*, 87(3), 291–313.

Independent Taskforce on Workplace Health and Safety (2013). The report of the independent taskforce on workplace health and safety; He korowa i whakaru-ruhau. Wellington: Independent Taskforce on Workplace Health and Safety (ITWHS), Retrieved 5 January, 2017 from http://hstaskforce.govt.nz/index.asp

Jacques, R. (1999). Developing a tactical approach to engaging with 'strategic' HRM, *Organization*, 6(2), 199–222.

Jeske, D., & Shultz, K. S. (2015). Using social media content for screening in recruitment and selection: Pros and cons. *Work, Employment and Society*, 30(3), 535–546.

Kaufman, B. E. (2007). The development of HRM in historical and international perspective. In P. Boxall, J. Purcell, & P. M. Wright (Eds.), *The Oxford handbook of human resource management* (pp. 19–47). Oxford: Oxford University Press.

Lengnick-Hall, M. L., Lengnick-Hall, C. A., Andrade, L. S., & Drake, B. (2009). Strategic human resource management: The evolution of the field. *Human Resource Management Review*, 19(2), 64–85.

Leroy, H., Den Hartog, D., & Segers, J. (2015). Call for papers, special issue: Bridging leadership & HRM—theory and research. *Human Resource Management Review*, June 23, 2016. Retrieved from https://esg.uqam.ca/upload/files/Appels_%C3%A0_communications/HRMR_-Bridging_Leadership__HRM_-_theory__research.pdf.

Lindley, C. J. (1984). Putting "Human" into human resource management. *Public Personnel Management*, 13, 501–510.

Mabey, C., & Mayrhofer, W. (Eds.). (2015). *Developing leadership: Questions business schools don't ask*. Thousand Oaks, CA: Sage.

MacDuffie, J. P. (1995). Human resource bundles and manufacturing performance: Organizational logic and flexible production systems in the world auto industry. *Industrial and Labor Relations Review*, 48(2), 197–221.

Martín-Alcázar, F., Romero-Fernández, P. M., & Sánchez-Gardey, G. (2005). Strategic human resource management: Integrating the universalistic, contingent, configurational and contextual perspectives. *The International Journal of Human Resource Management*, 16(5), 633–659.

Martínez Lucio, M. (2008). The organization of human resource strategies: Narratives and power in understanding labour management. In S. Clegg & C. L. Cooper (Eds.), *The Sage handbook of organizational behavior* (pp. 323–39). London: Sage.

Miles, R., & Snow, C. (1978). Organizational strategy, structure, and process. McGraw-Hill: New York.

Mishra, J. M., & Crampton, S. M. (1998). Employee monitoring: Privacy in the workplace? *S.A.M. Advanced Management Journal*, 63(3), 4.

Moore, K. (2011). Dave Ulrich on why HR should be at the C-suite table. *Forbes*, May 30. Retrieved from www.forbes.com/sites/karlmoore/2011/05/30/dave-ulrich-on-why-hr-should-be-at-the-c-suite-table/#7a5953536465.

Moussa, M. (2015). Monitoring employee behaviour through the use of technology and issues of employee privacy in America. *Sage Open*, (April–June), 1–13.

Nkomo, S. M., & Ensley, M. D. (1999). Deja Vu: Human resource management's courtship of strategic management. *Organization*, 6, 339–348.

Porter, M. E. (1980). *Competitive strategy*. Free Press: New York.

Rucci, A. J. (2009). The pursuit of HR's core purpose. In J. Storey, P. Wright, & D. Ulrich (Eds.), *The Routledge companion to strategic HRM*, Chapter 9. Abingdon, UK: Routledge.

Schuler, R., & Jackson, S. (1987). Linking competitive strategies with human resource management practices. *The Academy of Management Executive*, 1(3), 207–219.

Searle, R. H. (2006). New technology: The potential impact of surveillance techniques in recruitment practices, *Personnel Review*, 35(3), 336–351.

Sen, A. (1993). Capability and wellbeing. In M. Nussbaum & A. Sen (Eds.), *The quality of life* (pp. 30–53). Oxford: Oxford University Press.

Sen, A. (1999). *Development as freedom*. Oxford: Oxford University Press.

Spoonley, P. (2010). New ways of working: Changing labour markets in 21st century New Zealand. In J. Bryson (Ed.), *Beyond skill: Institutions, organizations and human capability*, Chapter 10, p. 79–102. Basingstoke: Palgrave Macmillan.

Steyaert, C., & Janssens, M. (1999). Human and inhuman resource management: Saving the subject of HRM. *Organization*, 6, 181–198.

Storey, J. (Ed.). (1995). *Human resource management: A critical text*. London: Routledge.

Tucker, D. (2002). 'Precarious' non-standard employment. Labour Market Policy Group. Wellington: Department of Labour.

Ulrich, D. (2013). *Human resource champions: The next agenda for adding value and delivering results*. Boston: Harvard Business Press.

Walker, J. (1978). Linking human resource planning and strategic planning. *Human Resource Planning*, 1, 1–18.

Warren, R. C. (2000). Putting the person back into human resource management. *Business and Professional Ethics Journal*, 19(3&4), 181–198.

Watkins, T. (2015). National's health and safety legislation its lightbulb moment. *Stuff Website*, August 26. Retrieved from www.stuff.co.nz/national/politics/opinion/71467660/Nationals-health-and-safety-legislation-its-lightbulb-moment.

Weiskopf, R., & Munro, I. (2012). Management of human capital: Discipline, security and controlled circulation in HRM. *Organization*, 19, 685–702.

Wright, P. M., Dunford, B. B., & Snell, S. A. (2001). Human resources and the resource based view of the firm. *Journal of Management*, 27(6), 701–721.

Wright, P. M., & McMahan, G. C. (2011). Exploring human capital: Putting 'human' back into strategic human resource management. *Human Resource Management Journal*, 21, 93–104.

Wright, P. M., & Snell, S. A. (1991). Toward an integrative view of strategic human resource management. *Human Resource Management Review*, 1(3), 203–225.

# 5 *Leading in* Innovation and Entrepreneurship

## Introduction

Everybody these days wants more innovation and more entrepreneurship. Businesses, governments, schools, sports teams, and not-for-profit organizations all want to be seen to be more innovative and entrepreneurial, to be leading in a way that encourages the elements that inspire innovation and entrepreneurship. And they are investing increasing amounts of resource toward encouraging this. Cities, regions and countries compete with one another to attract 'talent' to their innovation ecosystems. Innovation workshops are designed and run for schoolchildren; corporate training programmes seek to make employees think and act more like innovators and engage in entrepreneurial activities; government and university grants to lure the best entrepreneurial researchers have been established; journalistic quests seek to find the start-ups that could become the next big thing; regional funding is generated to create business hubs and 'bootcamps' for budding entrepreneurs; and so on. Interest in such activities has become almost frenzied. In fact, of all the topics covered in this book, innovation and entrepreneurship are probably the only to have come close to generating the kind of interest and 'buzz' that leadership itself has created in the past two decades and may even be surpassing that level now.

This interest raises two important challenges for our study of leading in innovation and entrepreneurship, matters that haven't been adequately considered or researched to this point, largely because leadership, innovation and entrepreneurship have been treated as separate research domains by researchers who specialise in one or the other field. Consequently, there has been a vast amount of work done on all three of these matters separately, but far less on how the three phenomena interrelate.

So, if we want to explore how leadership can inspire more effective innovation and entrepreneurship and also, by association, how a greater understanding of innovation and entrepreneurship can revitalise thinking about leadership, we need to think further about two questions: where does innovation and entrepreneurship come from? And, subsequently, how can these sources of innovation and entrepreneurship be led effectively?

The first question is easy to answer: innovation and entrepreneurship come from individuals and groups being given some degree of free rein and some encouragement to try and to fail (and learn from this failure). There is a wide range of research on this topic (see Bilton & Cummings, 2010 or Tidd & Bessant, 2009 for a review of this literature; or Amabile, 1998 and Amabile & Khaire, 2008, for accessible summaries of what this research means for organizations), but the idea can be illustrated with a couple of Antipodean stories and one from China and a quotation from an American leader of innovation.

The first story is about an Australian government department that was criticised for being one of the least innovative of ministries at the time (around 2012). In investigating why, the major reason was determined to be that the department saw its primary stakeholder and the person for whom the organization's strategy was developed as the Minister. The Minister (or so the department's leadership believed) was interested in things running smoothly and in there being 'no cock-ups' (to use the Australian phrase). No wonder the department wasn't innovative or staff weren't keen to express entrepreneurial ideas. If they really wanted to become more innovative, the department's staff, customers and alliance partners needed to be engaged in strategy development, to be seen as the key stakeholders in the department and to be given some licence to bring new ideas to the table (Cummings & Angwin, 2015, p. 44ff.).

The second story relates a comprehensive study of strategies in New Zealand's public sector. Over 100 strategic planning documents were reviewed and scored in terms of a number of categories, including their articulation of a clear vision and goals, the identification of opportunities and threat, the articulation of human capabilities within the organization and its partnerships. The area where these reports scored lowest, and by some degree, was the latter: human capabilities. In showing the results to senior ministers, the reasoning as to why this was the case was clear: leaders in these organization were happy to articulate external reasons for potential success and failure, but less keen to put the existence of internal strengths and weaknesses 'above the parapet'. An abundance of capability might lead to things being taken away, while a lack might lead higher ups to point the finger at an organization's leaders as to why they hadn't been developed. But the result of this conservatism was plainly understood: a discouragement of human capability development and thus risk taking, innovation and entrepreneurship within these organizations and government in general, and the need to address this was clear (McGuiness Institute, 2016).

The story from China may be geographically removed from the previous two, but it is intellectually related. Recently, the Chinese government announced a major initiative: 'Made in China 2025'. The idea behind this is to greatly increase the percentage of products that are designed and made in China, rather than manufactured in China but designed elsewhere. Interestingly, China is the only country in the world where SWOT

(Strengths, Weaknesses, Opportunities and Threats) analysis (an approach which has internal capabilities or strengths at the forefront) is not the most popular strategy development tool (Cummings & Angwin, 2015). In China, the most popular tool is one that helps determine external opportunities and threats: PEST analysis (PEST stands for Political, Economic, Social, Technological). And this indicates what needs to be done. The Chinese recognise that for Made in China to work, for it to become a more innovative and entrepreneurial country, more emphasis and value need to be placed on giving the sources of these things—individuals and groups—more creative freedom and input. Innovations cannot be forced from the top down.

And, finally, the quotation. When Jeff Immelt took over as CEO of General Electric from Jack Welch, he admitted that the hardest thing to balance was knowing when to steer and encourage and when to get out of the way and let people alone. In a company that rose and fell on the strength of innovations and entrepreneurial behaviours, in keeping with the personality of its founder (Thomas Edison), these issues were of central concern to how he approached leadership. As he told the *Herald Tribune* in an interview, "When you run General Electric, there are seven to twelve times a year when you have to say, 'You're doing it my way'. If you do it eighteen times, the good people will leave. If you do it three times, the company falls apart" (Nocera, 2007).

Just as the general context in which leaders must act is increasingly characterised by ambiguity, complexity and paradox, as we outlined in Chapter 2, so too are innovation and entrepreneurship. As we have argued elsewhere (Bilton & Cummings, 2010), innovation is powered by the bisociation of the discipline that leads to discovery, with the free thinking that allows for creativity. And, effective entrepreneurial activity generally stems from loose dilettante wandering combined with a focussed diligence on achieving clear goals. In short, leading innovation and entrepreneurship is a delicate balance: not too little encouragement and direction setting, but not too much, either. Grappling with these tensions are, we argue, the core challenge involved in leading in innovation and entrepreneurship. It means that conventional modes of leadership may be more likely to kill value-adding innovation and entrepreneurship, rather than enable it.

Which brings us back to the second question. Now that we are clear about where innovation and entrepreneurship come from, this question can be more clearly stated as: from where and how can we lead innovation and entrepreneurship, when these things require some intervention but in a way that paradoxically lets things alone? This question is more difficult to answer. But attempting to answer it is the focus of the remainder of this chapter. As mentioned in Chapter 2, in this and the next two chapters, the approach taken moves fluidly across the different elements of our theory-building framework (Diagram 2.1) to demonstrate how the model can be used in an iterative fashion in the process of building a contextualised theorization.

## From Where Should Innovation and Entrepreneurship Be Led?

> You say that you have no keenness of wit. Be it so; but there are many other things of which you cannot say that nature has not endowed you. Show those qualities then which are perfectly in your power: sincerity, gravity, patience, contentment with your lot, frankness, dislike of superfluity, freedom from pettiness. Do you not see how many [leadership] qualities you are immediately able to exhibit, as to which you have no excuse of natural incapacity and unfitness?
>
> Marcus Aurelius, *Meditations* (text in brackets added), (1945).

Around the time that the Made in China initiative was being formulated (c. 2010), one of the best-selling books in China was Marcus Aurelius's *Meditations* (1945), originally written in the 2nd century AD. This seems unlikely, but if you read what is one the earliest complete treatises on the nature of leadership, you can see how Aurelius's writings, which are ascetic, rational and almost Confucian in tone, might appeal to thinkers in both the East and West.

But while *Meditations* is currently well known in China, it is now largely overlooked in the English-speaking world. This is a great shame, given that it contains a passage that we believe best sums up the qualities required for leading innovation and entrepreneurship, in two centring ways.

Firstly, while innovation can provide organizational life-blood and entrepreneurial drive can give the organization legs, it takes a quite different set of attributes and behaviours to establish and lead an enterprise beyond the beachheads established through these activities. The challenge of holding together a chaotically diverse and often necessarily egotistical band of innovators and entrepreneurial spirits, be they those driving the expansion of an empire or the development of an organization, requires a quiet, strong and relatively ego-free *centre*. Hence, the leadership that coordinates and inspires innovation, entrepreneurship and organization comes from 'the middle', providing a solid centre for the creativity of teams and individuals to hitch on to. If entrepreneurship is about providing force or impetus to the innovation that lies at the heart of a creative enterprise, the leadership role in this context is about providing a gravitational hub, to ensure that things don't spin out in conflicting orbits.

Secondly, leading the strategic dimensions of a creative enterprise requires someone, or a group, that is *centred*. We'll unpack this idea in the paragraphs below.

A question often asked is "are leaders born or made?" (Jackson & Parry, 2011). Aurelius provides us with a nice answer with regard to forming the leadership lynchpin between innovation, entrepreneurship and an organizational setting: they are neither.

Often, people will claim that they are not leaders. They were not born with, or they failed to acquire, the attributes we in the modern world conventionally associate with leadership: charisma, searing intellect, a strong jaw. However, to assume that leadership traits are heroic and either God-gifted or added in at a later stage is to miss Aurelius's important point. We may lack an innate 'keenness of wit', for example. But the qualities Aurelius describes—sincerity, patience, contentment with your lot, frankness, dislike of superfluity, freedom from pettiness—are not traits we are born with (as any parent well knows!); nor are they skills which can be acquired from training, consultants or business schools.

These qualities are more like habits than traits or skills. They develop slowly. And they come with experience and mindful attention to our actions and how they affect others. Aurelius would probably class them as 'virtues', because we must continue to restrain our baser instincts to enact them. They come to us as we become more 'centred' and mature with time and experience. Consistent with the ideas we discussed in our examination of supervisory and HRM leadership, what we find here again, then, is an approach grounded in daily habits of thought and action which are not heroic or grand, but which require a sustained effort to make a constructive contribution.

Hence, it is not so much, as is commonly purported now, that everybody is a leader. Or, alternatively, that nobody can lead apart from a sainted few. Aurelius indicates that everybody has the *potential* to mature into a leader. The qualities he describes are possible for any human; the challenge is to enact them consistently to the point where they become habitual and we become centred in this way.

In *Leading Quietly*, Joseph Badaracco paints a picture of how this type of leader may appear:

> They're often not at the top of organizations. They often don't have the spotlight or publicity on them. They think of themselves modestly; they often don't think of themselves as leaders. But they are acting *quietly*, effectively, with political astuteness, to basically make things better, sometimes much better than they would be otherwise.
>
> (2002, p. 3)

It is a picture, like that painted by Marcus Aurelius, that requires us to think differently about what it means to be a leader of innovation and entrepreneurship.

Innovation and entrepreneurship require leadership that quietly joins the diverse elements and energies that contribute to their development. And this, we argue, requires leadership not from the top or front, but from the middle, where the purpose is *centring the organization's focus and direction and, simultaneously, ensuring sufficient latitude and support exists for the creativity that drives innovation and entrepreneurship to flourish*. In the remainder of this chapter, recent arguments and ideas that are all pointing us towards the importance of 'leading from the middle' are explored in laying out our theorisation for leadership in this context. Finally, some examples of such practice in action are discussed.

## All Roads Lead to the Middle

A 2007 article in *Scientific American Mind* called "The New Psychology of Leadership" (Reicher et. al., 2007) outlined the case for leading not from the top or the front, but leading instead from the middle. In a world where leadership is about working to enable and shape what people want to do, rather than telling them or showing them what to do, leaders rely upon constituent support and co-operation. In this context, leadership can thus no longer be a 'top-down' process, relying on the leader's intelligence, charisma or other extraordinary traits to captivate and dominate the minds of followers. Rather, to gain the credibility necessary to attract followers, leaders must position themselves among the group not above it. It follows, then, that leader attributes and behaviours should personify the shared values of a group, rather than being in some way superior or extra-ordinary.

This new concept of leadership was backed up by a growing number of research studies showing that most people would prefer a leader who is considerate and dedicated over one who is highly intelligent and that they value the sort of mature leadership qualities that Marcus Aurelius alluded to, like being down-to-earth, trustworthy or dependable.

The box below contains more details about the research behind the article, but it is also clear that this notion of leading from the middle, rather than just from the top, is part of a groundswell of changes in business thinking about leadership and the complex, ambiguous and paradoxical contexts in which organizations are situated, matters which we examined in our introductory chapters.

---

### Box 5.1 The new psychology of leadership

1. A new psychology of leadership suggests that effective leaders must understand the values and opinions of their followers—rather than assuming absolute authority—to enable a productive dialogue with team members about what the group stands for and thus how it should act.
2. According to this new approach, no fixed set of personality traits can assure good leadership because the most desirable traits depend on the nature of the group being led.
3. Leaders who adopt this strategy must try not only to fit in with their group but also to shape the group's identity in a way that makes their own agenda and policies appear to be an expression of that identity.

From "The New Psychology of Leadership" by Stephen Reicher, Alexander Haslam and Michael Platow, *Scientific American Mind*, August/September 2007.

In the following pages, we examine some key ideas and challenges that are of particular salience to leadership in the context of innovation and entrepreneurship. Analysis of these helps identify relevant values and norms, domains of action as well as the kinds of attributes, behaviours and roles involved in leadership of innovation and entrepreneurship. Examining these issues takes us further towards understanding the importance of leading innovation and entrepreneurship from the middle. They are:

- the rise of the 'knowledge age';
- working with the 'wisdom of crowds';
- the importance of the 'gut instinct' and intuition;
- appreciating 'tipping points' rather than charging into the fray;
- the power of networks and relationships; and
- moving from IQ to many Q's.

## The Rise of the 'Knowledge Age'

In the 1990s, Arie De Geus (1997) declared that we were entering a new 'knowledge society' in a book called *The Living Company*. He describes this historical development as follows:

- Economic theory suggests that there are three sources of wealth: land and natural resources, capital, and labour. Until the late Middle Ages, the critical factor was *land*. Those who possessed and controlled land controlled the accumulation of wealth.
- But as nation states formed and became concerned with expansion, the *capital* to finance expansionary endeavours became more valuable. During the 'Age of Capitalism' that ensued, the modern company developed. Capital was made available for the wealth-creating processes of the venturer, and the old trade and craft guilds broke apart. There evolved competing companies and enterprises and a market which gave the speculative owners of capital great control over human resources. Capital now held greater utility than land or labour.
- The past 50 years, however, have seen a shift from one dominated by capital to one based on labour and, in particular, the *knowledge* possessed by labour. Changes in the banking system since 1945, globalisation and technological advances have made capital easier to access, move around, share and invest. At the same time, restrictions on land and natural resource use mean that possession of land has become less of a driver. Increasing cross-border competition and the subsequent complexity of work have fed the need for inventiveness or creativity, resulting in people, rather than land or capital, to become the dominant economic resource for companies. Those people who had knowledge and knew how to apply it (and the firms

which recruited them) would henceforth be the wealthiest. This shift has become visible in the rise, since the 1950s, of material asset-poor but knowledge-rich companies, such as international auditing firms, management consultancies, advertising and media businesses and IT providers.

Globalisation, 'footloose' labour and the growth in information technology mean that organizational knowledge is now not only the most valuable commodity, it is also more mobile than ever. David Ogilvy famously remarked that the assets of his advertising agency went up and down in the lifts. More recently an advertising executive described his business to us as engaging in a 'war for talent', with each agency competing to recruit the brightest people before their rivals, then leasing them out to clients. And this war for talent presents some unique challenges for leadership, both in respect of innovation and entrepreneurship but also, as discussed earlier, in HRM.

Successful firms are often now 'middle-men' or brokers between the owners of capital and the owners of knowledge. Indeed, a recent study of the academic business literature confirms a massive spike in interest in 'knowledge' in the 1990s and early 2000s and predicts that leadership will need to become more dexterous and 'political' to be effective in an environment where knowledge is king (Bilton & Cummings, 2010). With an increase in the value and power of the 'knowledge worker', the leader's role is less 'command and control' oriented and more focussed on facilitation, enabling, mentoring and coaching. This applies especially to the creative industries, where people are valuable but volatile assets and keeping 'the talent' happy has long been a key task for leaders. But as we enter De Geus's 'knowledge society', knowledge, and in particular knowing how to retain and use knowledgeable people, will become everybody's business.

## Working With the 'Wisdom of Crowds'

*New Yorker* columnist James Surowiecki (2005) began his book, *The Wisdom of Crowds* (with the cumbersome but descriptive sub-title: "Why the Many are Smarter than the Few and How Collective Wisdom Shapes Business, Economies, Societies, and Nations"), with a 100-hundred-year-old story of a sprightly 85-year-old scientist and a fat ox. British scientist Francis Galton's studies of human behaviour, and his fascination with the new science of eugenics, had left him with little faith in the intelligence of the 'average' person. As he walked around a country fair near his home in Plymouth, he observed a weight-judging competition where around 800 bystanders wrote what they guessed as the weight of an ox on display on a ticket. Some were expert breeders, but most were interested laypeople. This struck Galton as an interesting set of data, and once the contest was complete, he asked the organizers if he could have the tickets. He carried out a number of statistical experiments and found, to his surprise, that the mean of all 800 estimates was extremely accurate. The mean was 1,197 pounds. The actual weight: 1,198 pounds. The scientist conceded that "The result seems more creditable to the trustworthiness of a democratic judgment than might have been expected" (Galton, 1907, p. 451). Surowiecki connected this story to a range of subsequent anecdotes and more recent experiments and research that explained how collective wisdom is generally better than individual guess-work.

More recently some have questioned Suroweicki's faith in crowds, citing failing financial markets as examples of crowd-think gone awry. But this is to miss Surowiecki's emphasis on the pluralism and diversity of crowds and Galton's stress on 'democratic' judgement. Crowds are wise only if they are diverse and paying attention. The problem with financial markets in the global financial crisis was that too many people weren't paying proper attention, and there was not a critical mass of divergent dissenters among those who were. Moreover, since *The Wisdom of Crowds* was published, further studies have pointed to the power of plurality in helping guide decision making. Indeed, one study published in 2008 in *Psychological Science* showed that the average of two guesses made by the same person at different times are also significantly better than one.

What might all this mean for leading in the context of innovation and entrepreneurship today? Notwithstanding the need for leaders to make judgement calls at particular points (recall the comments of Jeffrey Immelt in the introduction to this chapter), gung-ho leadership from the top or front may not be such a good thing. Inclusive consulting across a range of people is more useful. Valuing diversity of perspective and adopting the norm that debate is to be encouraged are important. And, leaders should pause and consult widely before making those judgement calls.

## The Importance of the 'Gut Instinct' and Intuition

A further stream of recent research orient leadership to the middle in a physiological sense. This is the rediscovery of the positive influence of the 'gut'—or instinct and intuition—in management. The primary populariser of this view is another *New Yorker* columnist, Malcolm Gladwell. His book *Blink: The Power of Thinking without Thinking* (2005) instantly gained a huge readership, partly because of the fervour that his previous work, *The Tipping Point*, had generated (and which we discuss next).

Gladwell organized a fantastic array of examples to demonstrate that decisions seemingly made in an instant can be as good, if not better, than those made more consciously or deliberately, because of a phenomenon that Gladwell terms 'thin-slicing'. This is where our 'gut instinct' very quickly senses a pattern that enables us to sift out irrelevant information, develop a 'hunch' and then act on this very quickly. Because our unconscious mind, or gut, is so good at this, it often delivers a better response than more protracted forms of rational analysis.

It is important to point out that some have been misled by *Blink* and the simplistic interpretations it has spawned. The title, and subsequent associations with making 'snap judgements', not looking before leaping and acting impulsively can lead people to forget that intuition is not just based on impulse. Quite the opposite. In actual fact, relying more on our gut instinct is about accessing *deeper* feelings and memories, getting beyond experiences that may be at the top of our conscious minds and connecting into a series of other physiological senses tuned by millennia of evolutionary development.

Those works and scientists that Gladwell drew upon, such as *Gut Feelings: The Intelligence of the Unconscious* by Gerd Gigerenzer (2007) and *The Second Brain: The Scientific Basis of Gut Instinct* by Michael Gershon (1998), go into greater detail about the mechanics of how the hundreds of millions of nerve cells in and around our guts can act independently from, and in association with, our brains as we make decisions. Gershon in particular is credited with rediscovering the existence of the gut as a 'second brain' in the 1960s. It was widely discussed decades before this, but the subsequent knowledge that was developed was side-lined, eclipsed and forgotten by medicine. Now he is at the forefront of the field exploring this phenomenon: neurogastroenterology. There is now a wide range of evidence suggesting that the stomach (particularly in combination with a mind that knows how to use it) can be a source of very good judgement. It is not so much that less thinking is better but, rather, that thinking should incorporate and value a diversity of senses. Leading in the context of innovation and entrepreneurship, then, where sensing which ideas have potential and which don't, includes the domain of the gut and bodily senses more broadly.

Intuition is also being rediscovered in leadership studies, too. Noel Tichy and Warren Bennis's (2007) book *How Winning Leaders Make Great Calls* looks extensively at the importance of good judgement with regard to decision making and the role that intuition plays in this. Good leaders in this respect, they argue, need to gain experience and gather 'domain knowledge', but self-knowledge and self-confidence must be a corollary. As the CEO of General Electric, Jeffrey Immelt told Tichy and Bennis: "I make every decision, but get lots of advice. . . . It's 'What do you think?' What do you think? What do you think? Then boom. I decide".

There is a parallel between the heroic leader at 'the top' and the 'genius' artist. However, Robert Weisberg (2006) has noted that when artists appear to be making impulsive creative decisions, they are very often drawing upon domain-specific expertise and accumulated wisdom and memory. These less glamorous precedents often remain unacknowledged. The other authors cited here remind us that individual, intuitive 'judgement calls' that may appear 'heroic' very often draw upon exposure to a wider range of collective experiences and perspectives than the conscious mind might allow or admit. Leading from the middle better enables us to access such resources.

## Tipping Rather Than Charging

Gladwell's previous book had an even more pervasive effect on modern culture than *Blink*. *The Tipping Point's* big idea is that big ideas aren't really that different from other ideas: it's just that they reach a tipping point, a critical mass or threshold at which their momentum becomes unstoppable, like a virus that becomes an epidemic (2000). Gladwell describes the 'three rules of epidemics', or the three agents of change that lead to the tipping points of epidemics, as 'the law of the few', 'the stickiness factor' and 'the power of context'.

Understanding these rules, claims Gladwell, can help people manage toward desired tipping points. Firstly, it pays to know that, as with systems thinking's '80/20' principle (where it is generally 20 per cent of the system's components that account for 80 per cent of its value) or marketing's focus on 'early adopters' (who will influence others to follow them into using a new product or service), it is much more effective to target those people who have the power to influence others than rely on a formal hierarchy, random selection or treating all things equally. Secondly, it pays to know that no idea will spread unless it is communicated in a way that resonates and 'sticks' with people, particularly with that key 20 per cent (more on this in the next chapter). Finally, it pays to know that no idea will spread quickly unless it fits with and can latch into the environment or context in which it is seeking to embed itself.

It is easy to see how the tipping point logic would contribute to our approach of leading from the middle. Instead of issuing blanket proclamations from on high, leaders should position themselves near the relational centre of an organization, understand that organization's key players, identity and context and then seek to attract the influencers and connectors (see the next topic) toward a vision in order to virally spread messages that tip an organization toward greater innovation and entrepreneurship.

## The Power of Networks and Relationships

One of Gladwell's most memorable illustrative stories in *The Tipping Point* compares the two men who rode out simultaneously on the night of 18 April, 1775, to raise the alarm that America's Revolutionary War had begun. William Dawes rode south. Paul Revere rode north. But despite both men coming from similar backgrounds and the towns they rode through being demographically alike, only one man raised an army. Gladwell, like many others before him, asked what might account for the difference.

The answer, according to Gladwell, and to the authors of an article entitled "How to Build your Network" (Uzzi & Dunlap, 2005), was that Revere was at once a gatherer of information and a connector of people and a great salesman or communicator. He knew what to say, how best to say it and the best people to say it to. Whereas Dawes spread the word in a linear fashion with an additive effect, Revere created an exponential multiplier that had the effect of a virus. Revere was like a super conductor: a connecter who connected to other connectors. Like that famous shampoo commercial from the 1970s: "*She told 2 friends, who told 2 friends, who told 2 friends. . .*", networks of connectors allow information and influence to multiply geometrically ($4 \times 4 \times 4 = 64$) rather than progress arithmetically ($4 + 4 + 4 = 12$).

A 2009 article applies this network thinking to Post-GFC recessionary times (Byham, 2009) and recommends that prospective leaders should engage in 'courageous networking'. To gain information, the author recommends you get to know those people who know things that can help you to connect and grow your network. Those people may not be 'bosses'. As he explains, it's better to think about who are the critical people in a supply chain or an information system. Knowing somebody in the legal department may open up a network of contacts able to provide insights into major challenges an organization is facing. Knowing the person who implements office moves can help you to connect with people who are being promoted within the organization. Knowing someone who knows how to 'read' social networking sites may help you to gather multiple insights into what is about to be hot and what is about to be not.

There is now much evidence, both high and low brow, about the value of networking for a leader. From the world of neural science, we now understand that adults can reason, recall and combine ideas more effectively than children, despite having brains that are more 'set in their ways' and which are the same physical size (the human brain stops getting larger at six years), because they have grown more than one neural network, and these networks can both operate independently and collaboratively. In the world of pop management, guru-extraordinaire Tom Peters (1990) updated Bill Clinton's famous slogan 'It's the economy, stupid' into a mantra for what should matter to leading in the context of innovation and entrepreneurship: 'It's relationships, stupid'. The value of networks in the creative industries is often described in terms of a shift from 'know-how' to 'know-who'. Leading innovation and entrepreneurship effectively, from the middle, means being able, through one's abilities *and* through one's networks, to move quickly from the top to the bottom of an organization or from the organization to the wider environment to capture the mood and spread the word.

## From IQ to Many Q's

In simpler times, there was one widely recognised quotient of how effective or bright a person might be: IQ. Reflective of the changes outlined above, there are now many 'Q's' to compete with cerebral intelligence. Most of these can be related to what were once seen as more humble or 'lower-order' faculties.

- Intelligence Quotient (IQ): A measure of *intellectual* proficiency.
- Technical Quotient (TQ): A measure of *technical* proficiency in achieving certain tasks.
- Experience Quotient (XQ): A measure of types of *experience* related to the task or role.
- Motivational Quotient (MQ): A measure of one's *motivation* to achieve and to grow.
- People Quotient (PQ or EQ): A measure of *emotional* awareness and, subsequently, of a person's ability to work co-operatively with others.
- Learning Quotient (LQ): A measure of one's ability to *learn* and adapt to new skills, behaviours and beliefs.
- Cultural Quotient (CQ): A measure of a person's ability to understand and operate across different *cultures* and situations.
- Social Quotient (SQ): A measure of one's ability to *socialise*, mix and get on with others (Bilton & Cummings, 2010).

The list will no doubt continue to grow. Indeed, we could develop a case for an additional PolQ (political quotient), IntQ (intuition quotient), TipQ (tipping quotient) and NQ (networking quotient) based on the discussion above.

While it may be helpful for a leader of innovation and entrepreneurship to have all of these characteristics, we suggest that for future leaders who are good at harnessing creativity, a relatively low score in the first three categories (intelligence, technical proficiency and relevant experience) will be less important than any deficiencies in the last five Q's (motivation, emotional intelligence, learning ability, cultural awareness, social skills).

The major management consultancies have changed their recruitment profiles and advertising accordingly. When it comes to leadership, recruiters are less interested in measuring extraordinary abilities and achievements and more interested in the leader's ability to facilitate the achievements of others, like a good Sherpa or caddy (which have become some of the images used in recent print advertising for 'The Big Four' consulting companies).

## Summary: Leading From the Middle for Innovation and Entrepreneurship

Figure 5.1 offers a summary of the challenges, ideas and trends discussed above which inform our view of the growing importance of leading from the middle in the context of innovation and entrepreneurship.

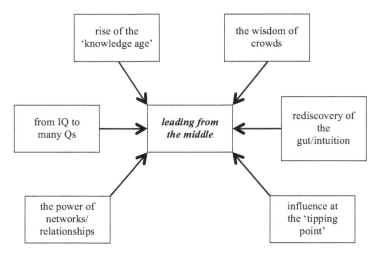

*Figure 5.1* Factors informing 'leading from the middle'

## Beyond Heroic Leaders

At the beginning of the last century, Max Weber (1947) conceptualised three types of leaders: traditional leaders, those who gained their authority from their traditional associations with power (monarchs, Popes and so on); rational-legal leaders, those who ruled by secular decrees and appeals to rational frameworks (Prime Ministers, scientists etc.); and those whose charisma furnished them with followers, for better or for worse (Jesus, Nelson Mandela, Bono, Hitler etc.). Weber believed that only charismatic leaders might deliver us from the rather gloomy and cold bureaucratic world that his social history foretold.

In the chaos that surrounded WWI and beyond, the notion of charismatic leaders as saviours gained further support. The dictatorships which led the world into a second war did undermine enthusiasm for the charismatic hero leader. But work that emerged in the 1970s and beyond (particularly that of James McGregor Burns (1978) on transformational leaders and their special attributes) reignited the Western world's belief in great leaders, standing on a podium or leading from the front, promising salvation.

The first decades of the 21st century have seen another shift, however. There is now a solid body of work shaping a fourth archetype: the less-elevated, 'anti-heroic' or 'post-heroic', leader. Jim Collins, author of *Built to Last* (Collins & Porras, 2005) and *From Good to Great* (2001), was recently asked for some leadership tips based on his research for these books. Collins suggests that two of the best things that good leaders do in new creativity-seeking organizations is to create a 'not-to-do list' and increase their 'questions-to-statements ratio' (Bilton & Cummings, 2010). Old-style, charismatic hero-leaders tended to take on huge workloads and proclaim their own decisions and points of view. In today's complex business environments, the post-heroic leader can no longer monopolise all the key decisions—other lower-level managers want to be heard and are looking to create or make their own marks. So for every new ongoing task put on their 'to-do' Collins argues that one must be put, like an accounting balance, on the 'not-to-do-list' and delegated. In a similar vein, the good leaders in Collins's studies were Socratic—they lead by asking questions and debating the answers.

The same is true in arts organizations as well. In theatre rehearsals, researchers have observed the great directors asking lots of questions (Bilton & Cummings, 2010). This model of leadership is concerned primarily with the way that problems are framed, rather than attempting to solve them. This distinction between 'problem-solving' and 'problem-engagement' is echoed in creativity theory; a genuinely creative approach to a problem does not merely provide an answer: it fundamentally changes the way we think (Bilton & Cummings, 2010).

The arrival of the post-heroic era can be seen in the most observed CEO transition of an innovation driven organization over the past 20 years. When Jeffrey Immelt replaced Jack Welch at GE, the contrast could not have been starker. The jumper-wearing Immelt appeared altogether softer, more empathetic, calm, humble, unflappable than the hard-nosed, 'heroic' Walsh. Immelt was recently named by the *International Herald Tribune* (Nocera, 2007) as the 'prototype CEO' for a world in which people follow "not because they have to, but because they want to": a good listener, consensus builder and ambassador.

Indeed, what is remarkable about GE, and one of the main reasons it has continued to prosper (relatively speaking) while the conglomerate has been pronounced an archaic organizational form, may be that it has a great talent for bringing forth the right leader for the context of the times. In its 130 years, it has only had nine chief executives, and only one might be considered less than successful. This is not to say that post-heroic leaders don't have to make tough calls, rather that they know when to and when not to. Recall Immelt's quotation from the head of this chapter: "When you run General Electric, there are seven to twelve times a year when you have to say, 'You're doing it my way'. If you do it eighteen times, the good people will leave. If you do it three times, the company falls apart" (Nocera, 2007). The secret of post-heroic leadership may be having a sense of where this middle ground is.

This is well and good in theory, but what about this mode of leadership in practice? The following section lays out our guidance, drawn from the issues discussed above, which can be applied to the practical tasks of leading when innovation and entrepreneurship are imperatives.

## The Practice of Leading From the Middle

Throughout this chapter, we have suggested that the leadership which enables innovation and entrepreneurship requires the embrace of dichotomous elements. In what follows, we examine in detail the kinds of attributes, behaviours, roles, responsibilities, norms and values that are needed from both leaders and followers to foster innovation and entrepreneurship. We argue that leadership in this context means switching between two paradoxical processes. Leadership which enables innovation and entrepreneurial activity, whether by an individual leader or a leadership team, depends upon *interacting* with people and ideas inside and outside the organization and at the same time *envisioning* a clear way forward by abstracting away from these detailed interactions and seeing the bigger picture. To understand how this dichotomy plays out in practice, the framework discussed below identifies four key dimensions of this form of leadership. These are linked by a central 'shift key' in the middle, designed to encourages leaders to recognise the importance of tilting back and forth between them.

We may better grasp this idea of leadership which enables innovation and entrepreneurship as a combination of envisioning and interacting through a sporting analogy. In sport, it is standard practice for the playing captain to be positioned in the midfield in football or as quarterback in American Football, or down the spine of a team (hooker, number 8, halfback, centre) in rugby. By leading from the middle they can see the game develop and are better positioned to interact with team-mates. But there are many other leadership positions in a professional sports organization, from the managers and CEOs to the coaches, stars and scouts. Typically, the coaches and managers will take a broader, more conceptual perspective, *envisioning*

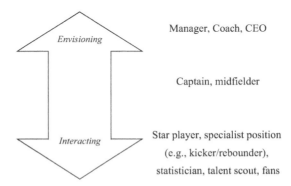

*Figure 5.2* Leading from the middle: a sporting analogy

Adapted from a diagram in Bilton and Cummings (2010). Used with permission from the authors.

strategies and future targets, whilst those closer to the action will take a more specialised and detailed view, *interacting* with others and with the immediate tasks of running the team. For the team to perform, all these positions must function in harmony.

While the diagram above explains the spread from envisioning to interacting, the positions outlined on the right also point to a second dichotomy, between an *internal* and an *external* orientation to the organization or team. At the envisioning level, a coach should be focussed on the internal world of the team, but the CEO or leadership team must be mindful of the wider commercial and competitive environment. At the level of interaction, particular players will be immersed in particular games, whereas the scout and the statistician must be looking outside and ahead.

We think that when innovation is important for the effective leadership of business, government and third-sector organizations then this sporting analogy is of direct relevance. Organizational leaders should also shift from an internal orientation focussing on what is happening inside the organization to an external orientation connecting to the wider world, to customers (who like fans can be inspiring or distracting), financial stakeholders and 'the wisdom of crowds'. And as a successful sports team will require more than one leader if it is to create effective results, so a successful business will need to tap more than one leadership 'key' to keep innovation and entrepreneurship ticking over and on track.

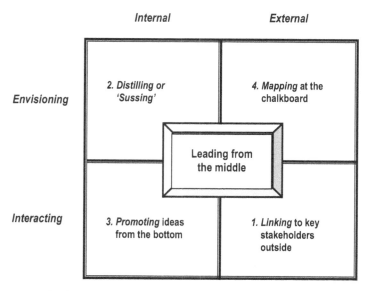

*Figure 5.3* Leadership 'from the middle' matrix

Based on the 'Leadership Keypad' developed in Bilton and Cummings (2010). Adapted with permission from the authors.

Layering this internal/external dialectic across our envisioning/interacting dichotomy creates a picture of four elements that can, and should, be accessed by leaders seeking to promote and enable innovation and entrepreneurship. Leading from the middle thus occupies a position midway along either axis, the best place from which to switch in an agile fashion between internal and external perspectives, and between envisioning and interactive 'leading by doing'. The different leadership dimensions are illustrated in the figure below, with 'leading from the middle' depicted as a shift key, allowing us to conceptualise toggling up and down and across the other dimensions.

We consider each of these dimensions of leadership which enables innovation and entrepreneurship in more detail in the paragraphs that follow, supported by illustrative examples.

### 1. Be A Conduit Linking the Outside With the Inside of the Organization

In an interesting example of leading innovation in an innovative way, Procter & Gamble CEO A. G. Lafely recently set a goal of having 50 per cent of its innovations being sourced from outside of the company. The decision fits with Lafely's view of the leadership priorities of the CEO. In an article called "What Only the CEO Can Do" published in the *Harvard Business Review* in (2009), Lafely pays tribute to his leadership mentor, the great Peter Drucker. Drucker (1994) had outlined that a CEO should be the link between the Inside that is 'the organization', and the Outside of society, economy, technology and customers.

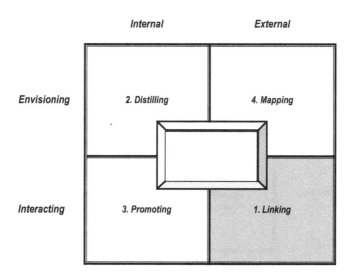

*Figure 5.4* Leading by linking

Adapted from Bilton and Cummings (2010). Used with permission from the authors.

Building on this perspective, Lafely summarises his view of the CEOs primary function as follows:

- Conventional wisdom suggests that the CEO is primarily a coach and a utility infielder in baseball, dropping in to solve problems where they crop up.
- In fact, however, the CEO has a very specific job that only he or she can do: link the external world with the internal organization.
- It's a job that *only* the CEO can do because everybody else in the organization focuses much more narrowly and almost always internally.
- It's a job that the CEO *must* do because without the outside there is no inside.

Hence, the primary task of the CEO is to "define the meaningful outside" for their organization, determining who the external stakeholders are, prioritising the ones that matter the most and consequently determining how those key interactions might be evaluated. We define this leadership approach as *linking*. Research carried out in the late 1990s emphasises the importance of this prioritisation. It found that firms who used stakeholder analysis indiscriminately generally performed worse than those who ignored their stakeholders. The implication is that attempting to satisfy too many and too varied a group of stakeholder demands, instead of prioritising between them, can paralyse an organization (Cummings, 2002).

In order to assess which stakeholders should be prioritised, it is useful first to map them. One way of doing this is to use a power/interest grid which identifies the level of power a stakeholder has to influence the firm and the level of interest they have in supporting or opposing a particular strategy. Those with high interest in influencing and high power to influence are key, and they should be given top priority with regard to relationship building and lobbying efforts.

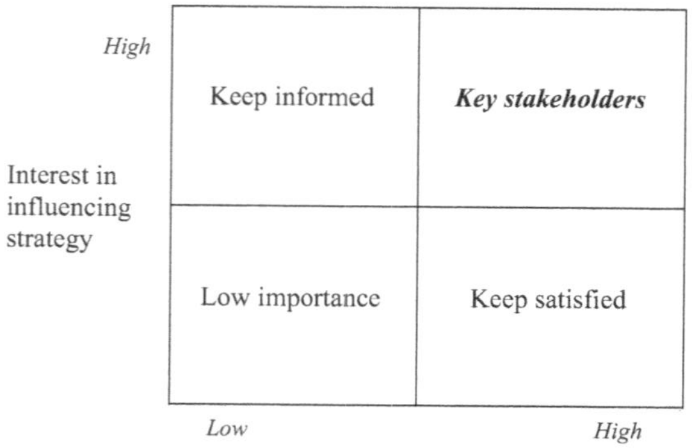

*Figure 5.5* Mendelow's (1991) stakeholder power/interest matrix

Adaptation of Mendelow's stakeholder model from Cummings and Angwin (2015). Used with permission from the authors.

For example, when Steve Jobs said: "We do no market research, we just want to make great products", it was an indication that Apple's key stakeholders are the design team and its links with the wider world of design and design influences, rather than customers or competitors in the technology market.

For Proctor & Gamble, focussing on defining the meaningful outside helped Lafely to understand that the key external interaction was with customers. "Without consumers, there is no P&G", he explained. "Therefore, our [most] meaningful results come from two critical moments of truth: first, when a consumer chooses to buy a P&G product over all others in the store, and second, when she or a family member uses the product at home. Although other external stakeholders have important demands, when there's a conflict, we resolve it in favour of the one who matters most: the consumer".

Subsequently, this is why and how Lafely came to see the importance of half of P&Gs innovations coming from outside the organization: they should be driven by consumers, or, more accurately, from the interaction between P&G employees and consumers. Hence, almost every P&G office and innovation centre now has consumers working inside with employees.

Having identified the primary task of the CEO as defining the meaningful outside, Lafely then outlines the other imperatives for the CEO:

- Deciding what business you are in. "Where should you play to win? Where should you not play at all?" This resonates with the view that effective leadership of strategic matters (which we focus on more directly in the next chapter) is as much about knowing what the organization doesn't do as it is about what the organization does;
- Balancing present and future—being satisfied with short-term goals which are 'good enough' and prioritising long-term aims, so that you are not tempted to sacrifice your future at the altar of the quick win; and
- Shaping values and standards.

Linking efforts, as articulated here, are an important aspect of leadership which enables innovation and entrepreneurship because they help provide some boundaries to help focus the innovative and entrepreneurial efforts that, absent such boundaries, may detract from the organization's mission, purpose or strategy. The last of Lafely's priorities—shaping values and standards—moves us onto the second key on our leadership pad: distilling or 'sussing' a broad sense of direction. This too is particularly relevant to leadership which enables innovation and entrepreneurship, because it also addresses boundary issues.

## 2. Get to the Heart (or Gut) of Things to Distil Simple Guiding Messages

Work done on the external/interactive key of *linking* (identifying and prioritising stakeholders) will help when the leadership toggles up and across to the internal/envisioning key: a perspective that we term distilling or

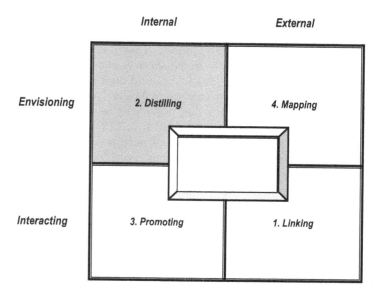

Internal External

Envisioning

Interacting

*Figure 5.6* Leading as distilling

Adapted from Bilton and Cummings (2010). Used with permission from the authors.

*'sussing'*. The alternative term 'suss' is useful because it is also an acronym for a desired outcome of this element of leading innovation and entrepreneurship just enough, but not too much. SUSS stands for: Simple Unifying Strategic Statements. Such a statement can function like a good vision—see the box below for Drucker's classic, and still relevant, view of a good vision's characteristics (which most company visions fail to meet). However, a SUSS statement is generally more colloquial and shorter than a vision statement: it 'sizes up' a strategy and distils its essence into an internal rallying call that is memorable and unifying and, we think, is a key aspect of leadership that enables innovation and entrepreneurship.

---

## Box 5.2 Drucker's five principles of a good vision

1. *brief* (not a long-winded "hero sandwich of good intentions");
2. *true* to the particular company's focus and character;
3. *understandable* to all employees;
4. *inspirational*; and
5. *verifiable*, so that progress and success can be determined.

Adaptation of Peter Drucker's ideas from Cummings & Angwin (2015). Used with permission from the authors.

The first characteristic of sussing is simplicity, boiling down complex ideas into a distilled essence. When Mark Wood became CEO of The Prudential in the UK a few years ago, he inherited an organization with a formal statement of purpose much like any large financial services company: *Prudential plc provides retail financial products and services and fund management to many millions of customers worldwide . . .* and on it went for another 150 words. But it was also a company that seemed to lack a clear view of how it was different and what it, in particular, was trying to achieve.

While Wood (Angwin & Cummings, 2011, p. 219) recognised the necessity of the professional-looking statement of purpose quoted above, he also appreciated the need to distil something that could focus the minds of people internally on what the company actually stood for and which could actually enable clear decision making. In a speech to employees not long after he became CEO, he began to grasp the nettle:

> Above all else we have worked, first and foremost, to ensure that our customers, in their old age, can afford to eat, to heat their homes, to take the style of holiday they are used to, replace worn out clothes, and continue to tend the garden they love and live in the home in which they are comfortable.

This was what made the Prudential different. It wasn't playing the quick high-risk, high-return game that most of its competitors were. It should be focussed on the solid, good-growth, for the long-term, nest-egg investments. Wood went on to distil the following SUSS-line for the Pru: Helping Old People Eat. It doesn't sound much like a corporate vision statement, and it was never promoted externally as such, but Helping Old People Eat (and the ensuing acronym HOPE) struck a chord with an ever-increasing number within the company and went on to tip the Pru toward a much clearer strategic vision, even beyond Wood's tenure as leader.

The New Zealand police had a great SUSS-line for nearly 100 years: *"To work with the community to maintain the peace"*. Then, in the 1990s, consultants were brought in to replace this motto with a more professional-sounding mission statement. They came up with this:

> To contribute to the provision of a safe and secure environment where people may go about their lawful business unhindered and which is conducive to the enhancement of the quality of life and economic performance.

After ten years of bemusement and disquiet, it was a senior sergeant who advocated moving back to the future by reverting to a simple statement "Safer communities together". Senior management within the Force had the vision to promote this idea. Not only does it connect the organization to a proud tradition, offer a clear view of who the key stakeholders are for the future (community groups), and clearly distil a strategy into three words, it's a lot easier to paint on the side of a police car!

Four words for HOPE, three words for SCT . . . can it be done in less than three words? J.M. Dru's book *Disruption* (1996) advocates leaders reducing strategies to single words. While one route to value innovation might be to think of the adjective that you might add to a conventional product or service, Dru challenges us to think the verb that best captures the organization's desired distinctiveness. Dru says that the best brands are easy to associate with singular verbs: Apple opposes, IBM solves, Virgin enlightens, Sony dreams.

The simplicity of SUSS-lines gives them clarity and purpose. SUSS-lines must strike right to the point, delivering a message which is memorable and easily understood. And rather than being overly intellectual, they should inspire action. As the Roman politician Cato reminds us, "When Cicero spoke, people marvelled. When Caesar spoke, people marched". But also, and importantly, because simple statements tend to be brief and evocative rather than prescriptive, they leave space for people to work within them and grow into them, interpreting them differently for new times, new situations and different personalities. The 'unifying' element of distilling or sussing means articulating a view of what innovation and entrepreneurial activity should be broadly aimed at achieving or improving which works across different scenarios and perspectives.

And yet, a leader in this context should be more than a receptacle for everybody else's views. As with the 'linking' to key external stakeholders in the previous element, 'sussing' requires us to prioritise selectively. In theatre rehearsals, we observe directors either holding a distorting mirror up to the actors—appearing to endorse their suggestions whilst turning them into something else—or bouncing the suggestion back to them. The reflection is a critical one, questioning the bases and assumptions through which decisions are made. This demonstrates a key function of leadership that enables innovation and entrepreneurship—sussing out the values and capabilities of other people's values and capabilities in order to better articulate them. Neither Mark Wood nor the police sergeant invented their SUSS-lines: all the elements were there already; they simply articulated them. Like a good surfer, they picked out a naturally occurring wave and rode it.

Articulating a unifying vision for the New Zealand police force involved distilling not only the present priorities but also drawing on the past. Hewlett-Packard's SUSS-line works in a similar way. Recognising that they couldn't win an all-out price war, Hewlett-Packard saw the need to distil what set them apart. The phrase they came up with, 'the rules of the garage', drew together the individualistic pioneering spirit of the company's founders, Bill Hewlett and Dave Packard, toiling away in their little inventor's shed in Palo Alto and the company's subsequent history of significant innovation. Like Apple, IBM, Virgin and Sony, they managed to boil this all down to one underlying verb: 'Invention' and have subsequently ensured that wherever one sees the HP symbol, it stands upon the word 'Invent'.

While it may not be possible to suss every organization's strategy into a word, brevity is certainly the aim. A simple word or phrase is usually more inclusive, adaptable and unifying than a lengthy mission statement. Having this as an aim also encourages leaders to be strategic by focussing on what's important. Seth Godin (2009; see also Godin, 2002) outlines the problem thus: "If you can't explain your strategic position in eight words or less, then you don't have one". But Samuel Goldwyn probably said it better a long time ago: "If you can't write down your movie idea on the back of a business card then you ain't got a movie".

### 3. Promote Good Ideas From Anywhere in the Organization to Others Who Can Help Them Grow

Having discussed how leaders of innovation and entrepreneurship provide benefits by interacting externally to link those who are innovating within an organization to people and networks beyond it and by sussing or distilling the key mantras or mission that define a purpose toward which innovation and entrepreneurial behaviour can be directed, a third dimension that leadership can provide is to interact between different levels of an organization to promote and spread good ideas to others within the organization who can help them develop.

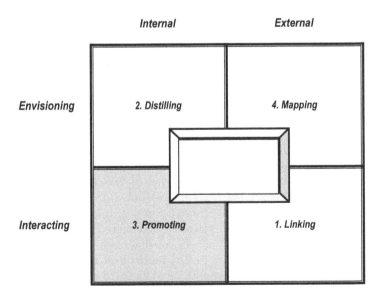

*Figure 5.7* Leading as promoting

Adapted from Bilton and Cummings (2010). Used with permission from the authors.

*Promoting* from below depends on the other dimensions we have discussed already. Linking with external stakeholders and 'sussing' the internal vision provides a context for promoting ideas from within. Many ideas may appear promising, but it is hard to define which of these are best suited to a particular organization unless these other two dimensions are also being put to use. Conversely both sussing and linking are both supported by interacting with people and promoting ideas.

Beyond this, there are three values and norms, or three T's, that can help enable good leadership of innovation and entrepreneurship by promoting good ideas that might not otherwise receive sponsorship:

- **Trust**—people must believe that their thinking will be treated with respect and that due credit will be given as their innovative and entrepreneurial ideas come to fruition.
- **Teamwork**—trust leads to teamwork, in that a good idea freely given up by an individual (or group) can then be knocked around and developed by others. This also entails that all parties have an ability to switch between leading and supporting (following) as the situation demands.
- The **'traverse'**—trust and teamwork will be enhanced if people can see some pathways to the top and recognise some ideas which have filtered up to the highest levels. They are less likely to put effort into developing and sharing new ideas if they can't see how good ideas can climb within the company.

One of the biggest obstacles to these conditions in large companies is that those in formal leadership positions are hardly seen. The age of e-mail and virtual communication often gives senior leaders an illusion of connection, without other people in their organization actually feeling their presence. In Jack Welch's old-fashioned words: to inspire trust and "rally the team, you need to see, hear and feel the team, and they need a regular dose of the real you". But it is still true that without an actual feeling of connection, it is difficult for ideas to traverse the organization, because there is not the trust or teamwork to nurture them.

These three norms and values are common in team sports and in the arts. In arts organizations, for example, leadership functions typically traverse the company, rather than being invested in single individuals. The individualistic culture and project-based nature of creative enterprise means that fixed roles and functions are shared, exchanged or combined—in theatre, there are directors who act, actors and designers who direct, writers who do both. This overlap and exchange between roles allows different types of leaders at different levels of the organization to delegate to each other's strengths. From the outside, it is sometimes difficult to tell who is leading and who is following. Without a fixed hierarchy and without identifiable leaders taking control, leadership comes from unexpected places—a deputy director or head of department might be driving key decisions as much as the nominal leader.

Sadly, in our experience, this 3T environment, with its absence of visible hierarchies or strong charismatic leaders, has prompted suggestions that arts organizations are suffering from a leadership 'crisis'. External bodies have subsequently sought to professionalise the arts by bringing in management consultants and executives from other industries to create more business-like structures. Unfortunately, though, parachuting in 'business' trouble-shooters in this way has generally done more harm than good. In the UK arts sector, changes in leadership driven by external stakeholders (the board of the Royal Opera House, the BBC governors) have led to appointed leaders having to battle internal suspicions (and dwindling trust and teamwork) before they can even begin to address the external challenges. In a situation where conventional businesses might have learned from a leadership model in the arts which effectively promotes ideas from within, the imposition of a model in the other direction has only exacerbated the mutually destructive animosity between 'creatives' and 'suits' (Bilton & Cummings, 2010). A 'crisis in arts leadership' can become a self-fulfilling prophecy.

A major difference, however, between most arts or sporting organization and many conventional businesses is size. It's a lot easier for trust, a sense of team and the possibility of traversing to flow in a smaller arts organization, where people know each other and have a singular set of values. The leader of an organization of any scale, however, cannot lead innovation and entrepreneurship from the top or the front. They lack the expert knowledge and likely the unique design point of view to do so. They must instead seek to lead from the middle, attempt to suss out and connect with the culture of the organization, act as a link person between key people external to the organization and people inside it and be able to identify and promote promising ideas that are developing within the organization.

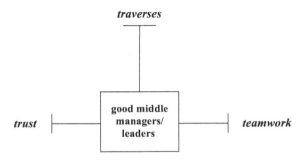

*Figure 5.8* The three T's of leading innovation and entrepreneurship from the middle by promoting from below

This is why we would add one final crucial part to successful leading by promotion: investing in developing and retaining good middle managers. Much maligned in the past two decades, a really good middle manager plays an essential role in communicating broader visions and political realities downwards and helping to develop and promote good ideas from below. As odd as it may sound, there may be nobody as important in leading innovation and entrepreneurial activity in an organization as a good middle manager.

### 4. Mapping a Way Forward

Whereas 'sussing' distils the internal values and raison d'etre of the organization to simple statements, our second envisioning dimension of leadership which enables innovation and entrepreneurship is about mapping a pathway that connects this internal focus to external realities, opportunities and threats. 'Mapping' is comparable to the chalkboard used by coaches to translate a simple objective into a more detailed game plan. Coaches, managers and players stand outside the action, using graphical tools to communicate how they see the play unfolding and to demonstrate which moves may be the most effective. TV sports commentators often draw on interactive screens to demonstrate this 'eye of God' perspective. White boards, flip charts, freeze frames from TV footage, play books, game cards are all useful vehicles for conveying positions and dynamics on a contested space over

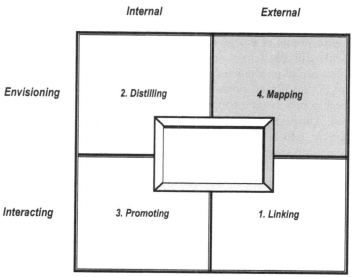

*Figure 5.9* Leading as mapping

Adapted from Bilton & Cummings (2010). Used with permission from the authors.

time. In effect, mapping is about strategy, but not strategic management in the way that this is traditionally developed and communicated in most organizations: the dreaded strategy-away-days, paralysing over-analysis, and 120-page reports printed out and filed on top-shelves of bookcases or filing cabinets never to be looked at again. And as we have already noted, matters of strategy help provide boundaries within which innovation and entrepreneurial activities take place.

A recent survey asked executives which areas of strategy required greater emphasis. The most common response, according to 79 per cent of respondents, was the need to "more effectively communicate their strategy internally" (Hunter & O'Shannasy, 2007). Another Harvard Business School study found that on average, 95 per cent of employees across a wide range of organizations could not articulate their company's strategy (Kaplan & Norton, 2005).

One of the biggest problems in this regard is that leaders generally capture and communicate strategy in a strategic planning document packed with text and numbers. Graphics tend to be used to communicate technical data, but not to map out ideas or a pathway forward. Consequently, many strategies fail to encourage innovation not because they are poorly planned or implemented without enthusiasm, but because they are poorly expressed. Those in the organization are not sure what their leaders envision, so any innovation or entrepreneurship is stymied by uncertainty or developed in an uncoordinated or ill-directed way. This leads to much frustration and wasted effort.

Strategies are hardly ever communicated through effective pictures or maps in business: but if leaders can do this, it can help provide the middle way we have been describing in this chapter: between providing innovators and entrepreneurs a degree of confidence in the overall direction being sought while still allowing scope for people and groups to think differently within these broad parameters.

Rethinking the development and communication of strategy as part of the leadership process is a topic that requires a chapter of its own to cover it (at least). And so that is what we do in the next chapter. Having outlined three ways in which leaders can facilitate more effective innovation and entrepreneurship from the middle: linking internal and external stakeholders; sussing or distilling the essence of what the organization is about; and promoting good ideas from anywhere—particularly parts of an organization which often don't get the attention from leaders that they deserve; a fourth, developing and promoting the mapping of strategies, gets a chapter all its own.

We have, however, explored leadership that enables innovation and entrepreneurship with sufficient depth such that Table 5.1 below offers a summary of our thinking as it relates back to our framework for theory building.

*Table 5.1* Leadership for innovation and entrepreneurship: a summary

| Component | Key issues and ideas |
| --- | --- |
| Challenges | General context of ambiguity, complexity and paradox. |
| | How to lead innovation and entrepreneurship when the leader does not personally have the cutting edge knowledge that drives these things. |
| | Innovation is powered by discipline and free thinking AND entrepreneurial activity stems from dilettante wandering and focussing on clear goals. |
| | Leadership for innovation and entrepreneurship require neither too little nor too much encouragement and direction setting. |
| Purpose of leadership | Centring the organization's focus and direction and, simultaneously, ensuring sufficient latitude and support exists for the creativity that drives innovation and entrepreneurship to flourish. |
| Values and norms | Humility      Value diversity of perspective<br>Respect for freedom      Encourage debate<br>Collaboration      Trust<br>Innovation      Teamwork<br>Entrepreneurship      Open pathways to the top of the<br>Risk taking      organization (traverse) |
| Domains | Moving across all levels of the organization—from the bottom, to see the latest interactions and development, to the top to understand what is possible, and to the middle to manage the interactions between innovations bubbling up and the funding to promote them flowing down. |
| | Moving inside and outside the organization, to understand internal capabilities and external opportunities and threats. |
| | Draws on the 'gut' (intuition) and other bodily senses. |
| Leader | Is located in the 'middle' of the organization—is neither distant nor superior. |
| | Is 'in tune' with the values that people share within the organization. |
| | Broad experience, but may lack the latest expert knowledge: needs to be humble and collaborative enough to the follow the leads of others and work, often behind the scenes, to coordinate these efforts. |
| | Can cope with ambiguity, complexity and paradox. |
| | Links the outside with the inside of the organization. |
| | Provides clear and simple guiding messages. |
| | Promotes good idea from anywhere. |
| | Maps a way forward. |
| Follower | Highly intelligent, has expert knowledge and a unique point of view that needs to be nurtured and encouraged. |
| | Generally does not like being told what to do and dislikes phonies. |
| | May be the 'creative genius' or the entrepreneur. |
| | May be a collaborative team member. |
| | Will engage in questioning and debate. |
| Leader-follower relationship | Trust |
| | Respect |
| | Co-operative |
| | Ability and willingness to challenge ideas |

We now turn to explore our ideas on how we may revitalise strategic leadership.

## References

Amabile, T. M. (1998). How to kill creativity. *Harvard Business Review*, (September), 77–87.

Amabile, T. A., and M. Khaire. (2008). *Creativity and the role of the leader*. Boston: Harvard Business School Publishing.

Angwin, D., & Cummings, S. (2011). *The strategy pathfinder: Core concepts and live cases*. Chichester, UK: Wiley.

Aurelius, M. (1945). Meditations. In I. Edman (Ed.), *Marcus Aurelius and his times: The transition from Paganism to Christianity* (pp. 11–133). New York: Walter J. Black Publishers.

Badaracco, J. L. (2002). *Leading quietly: An unorthodox guide to doing the right thing*. Boston, MA: Harvard Business School Press.

Bilton, C., & Cummings, S. (2010). *Creative strategy: Reconnecting business and innovation*. Chichester, UK: Wiley.

Burns, J. M. (1978). *Leadership*. New York: Harper Row.

Byham, W. C. (2009). Start networking right away (even if you hate it). *Harvard Business Review*, 87(1), (January), 22–22.

Collins, J. C. (2001). *Good to great: Why some companies make the leap . . . and others don't*. New York, NY: Harper Business.

Collins, J. C., & Porras, J. I. (2005). *Built to last: Successful habits of visionary companies*. London: Random House.

Cummings, S., & Angwin, D. (2015). *Strategy builder: How to create and communicate more effective strategies*. Chichester, UK: Wiley.

Cummings, S. (2002). *Recreating strategy*. London: Sage.

De Geus, A. (1997). *The living company*. Boston, MA: Harvard Business School Press.

Dru, J. M. (1996). *Disruption: Overturning conventions and shaking up the marketplace*. New York: Wiley.

Drucker, P. (1994). *Innovation and entrepreneurship*. New York: Harper & Row.

Galton, F. (1907). Vox populi. *Nature*, 75, (March 7), 450–451.

Gershon, M. D. (1998). *The second brain: The scientific basis of gut instinct*. New York: Harper Collins.

Gigerenzer, G. (2007). *Gut feelings: The intelligence of the unconscious*. London/New York: Penguin Books.

Gladwell, M. (2000). *The tipping point: How little things can make a big difference*. London: Little, Brown.

Gladwell, M. (2005). *Blink: The power of thinking without thinking*. London: Allen Lane.

Godin, S. (2002). *Survival is not enough: Zooming evolution and the future of your company*. London: Simon & Schuster.

Godin, S. (2009). *Purple cow: Transform your business by being remarkable new edition*. New York: Portfolio.

Hunter, P., & O'Shannasy, T. (2007). Contemporary strategic management practice in Australia: 'Back to the Future' in the 2000s. *Singapore Management Review*, 29(2), 21–36.

Jackson, B., & Parry, K. (2011). *A very short, fairly interesting and reasonably cheap book about studying leadership* (2nd ed.). London, UK: Sage.

Kaplan, R. S., & Norton, D. P. (2005). The office of strategy management. *Harvard Business Review*, 83(10), 72–81.

Lafely, A. G. (2009). What only the CEO can do. *Harvard Business Review*, (May), 54–62.

McGuiness Institute (2016). Improving strategy stewardship in the public service. September, 2016. Retrieved from http://strategynz.info/2015-government-department-strategies-index-presentation/.

Mendelow, A. (1991). Environmental scanning: The impact of the stakeholder concept. In the *Proceedings of the second international conference on information systems* (pp. 407–418). Cambridge, MA: Cambridge Univeristy Press.

Peters, T. J. (1990). *Thriving on chaos*. Harper and Row: New York.

Reicher, S., Haslam, A., & Platow, M. (2007). The new psychology of leadership. *Scientific American Mind*, 18(4), (August/September), 22–29.

Surowiecki, J. (2005). *The wisdom of crowds: Why the many are smarter than the few and how collective wisdom shapes business, economies, societies, and nations*. New York: Anchor Books.

Tichy, N. M., & Bennis, W. (2007). *Judgment: How winning leaders make great calls*. New York: Portfolio.

Tidd, J., & Bessant, J. (2009). *Managing Innovation: Integrating technological, market and organizational change* (4th ed.). Oxford: John Wiley & Sons.

Uzzi, B., & Dunlap, S. (2005). How to build your network. *Harvard Business Review*, 83(12), (December), 53–60.

Weber, M. (1947). In H. H. Gerth (Ed.), *From Max Weber: Essays in sociology: Translated, edited and with an introduction by HH Gerth and C. Wright Mills*. New York: Kegan Paul.

Weisberg, R. (2006). *Creativity: Understanding innovation in problem solving, science, invention and the arts*. Hoboken, NJ: John Wiley and Sons.

# 6  *Leading in* Strategy

Stories make pictures, pictures make connections, connections help you to see complexity more simply, and to remember.

Kathryn Berkett

## Introduction

There are two recent developments in thinking about strategic management that support and help us explore further the idea that 'mapping' is an important task for leaders of innovation and entrepreneurship in organizations (which is where the last chapter left off). These developments are that good leaders of strategy should be good storytellers and that good leaders of strategy should be good at developing, using and promoting good visuals that help communicate strategy. These things are important because a strategy is only as good as its implementation; a strategy must be implemented by many in an organization, not just a few, and it is hard for many to implement a strategy if they do not understand it.

This brings us quickly to the heart of the challenge that inspires this chapter, one that relates to the many contextual paradoxes upon which this book is founded. This is that a good leader of strategy today must, on the one hand, provide a clarity of direction that enables people to operate in a unified way. On the other hand, they also need to avoid providing so much prescriptive detail as to inhibit people from seizing or creating new opportunities that were not, and perhaps could not have, been anticipated when the strategy was developed. Stories and pictures are ideal vehicles for conveying a sense of strategy without a deadening prescription. Stories make pictures, pictures inspire stories and both enable connections to be understood and make it possible to see how new ones could be formed, moving forward.

A good example of these dual channels, radio and pictures, working together in this regard to map and sell a new strategic direction is one often told by Ben Rich, Chief Executive of Lockheed's legendary Skunk Works programme. Rich could never get the Pentagon generals whom he relied upon for sponsorship to grasp the completely revolutionary nature of the Stealth aircraft until he took a ball bearing (with the same radar profile as the Stealth) to a meeting, rolled it across the table to them and said, "Here's your airplane!". Rich knew he 'had them' when a general caught the ball, held it in his hand and looked up at him (Rich & Janus, 1996).

Another example, often relayed in strategy courses, to describe the communicative value of a simple strategy framework—even though we understand that the world is more complex than, say, a two-by-two matrix—goes as follows:

> The young lieutenant of a Hungarian detachment in the Alps sent a reconnaissance unit into the icy wilderness. It began to snow immediately, and unexpectedly continued to snow for two days. The unit did not return. The lieutenant feared that he had dispatched his own people to death. However, on the third day the unit came back. Where had they been? How had they made their way?
> 'Yes', they said. 'We considered ourselves lost and waited for the end. We did not have any maps, compasses or other equipment with which to ascertain their position or a probable route out. But then one of us found an old tattered map in a seldom used pocket. That calmed us down. The map did not seem to quite fit the terrain but eventually we discovered our bearings. We followed the map down the mountain and after a few wrong turns eventually found our way'.
> The lieutenant borrowed the map and had a good look at it. 'This isn't a map of the Alps', he said. 'It's a map of the Pyrenees'.

This story is apocryphal: some says it is true, others not (Weick, 1987; Cummings & Wilson, 2003). But like the first example from Skunk Works, it conveys something to which most can relate. Even if that image is not fully representative, even if it is just a metaphor, even if it may even not be the correct image, it can provide the confidence in others to move on, see connections, recalibrate and then use their own judgement to move on again.

All creativity requires shuttling between defining problems and positing solutions, redefining problems and refining solutions. Stories and pictures help people imagine solutions so that they can create—so they don't just get bogged down in defining problems.

## Storytelling and Strategy

In 1991, David Boje (1991) wrote an article that was published in *Administrative Science Quarterly* called "The storytelling organization: A study of story performance in an office-supply firm". It was revolutionary for its time, exploring how the everyday stories that passed between workers were not as inconsequential or un-strategic as business researchers may have assumed. (It also seems, in hindsight, to have prefigured the now-famous television series *The Office* which followed it a decade later).

David Barry and Michael Elmes, former colleagues and good friends of ours, took this idea further and applied it specifically to rethinking what was important in strategy in "Strategy retold: Toward a narrative view of strategic discourse", an article published in the *Academy of Management Review* (Barry & Elmes, 1997). They explored strategic management as a form of fiction, discussed the problems strategists faced in making strategic discourse both credible and novel and considered how the use of strategic narratives may play a critical part in this and how ideas could become even more important within the "virtual" organizations of the future.

While the concept of strategists as storytellers seemed unusual and even far-fetched in the early 1990s, by the 2000s, the idea gathered support and became more widespread. Books such as *Storytelling in Organizations: Facts, Fictions, and Fantasies* (Gabriel, 2000), *The leader's guide to storytelling: Mastering the art and discipline of business narrative* (Denning, 2005) and Boje's own *Storytelling organizations* (2008) popularised the notion.

And the concept has now been explored in the academic leadership literature too, where titles such as *To thine own self be true: The effects of enactment and life storytelling on perceived leader authenticity* (Weischer, Weibler & Petersen, 2013), *Constructing leadership by storytelling-the meaning of trust and narratives* (Auvinen, Aaltio & Blomqvist, 2013) and *Who is leading, leader or story? The power of stories to lead* (Sintonen & Auvinen, 2013) have made this a common theme among leadership researchers in the 2010s.

While this is important stuff in combination with visualising strategy, the idea of a leader of strategy as a storyteller covers ground that we trod in the previous chapter, when exploring how leaders like Mark Wood used stories to capture the essence of what an organization was about. What hasn't been covered yet to any great extent in the leadership literature, and what we focus on now for most of the remainder of the chapter, is the value of leaders visualising the development and communication of strategy. Treating this as a key practice for effective strategic leadership, we examine in more detail the kinds of behaviours, attributes, norms and values of leaders and followers that are involved in adopting this approach.

## Visualisation and Strategy

> Leaders often think complexity means complicated. A key leadership task is finding a way to simplify complexity rather than presenting situations in a complicated way.
>
> Shaun Coffey

A recent edition of *Fortune* magazine profiling Alan Mulally (*Fortune*, May 25, 2009) did something considered unusual. The journalist was so surprised and impressed by CEO Mulally's *drawing* of Ford's strategy, scribbled with his own hand in preparing for the interview, he asked if they could reproduce it in the magazine. It was a vivid illustration of Ford's challenge,

Mulally's vision and the need to communicate this effectively to all stake-holders. As Mulally says in the article, and on the drawing, "communicate, communicate, communicate. . . . Everyone has to know the plan". It is a vivid illustration of the power of a simple, personal graphic for communicating strategy.

This *Fortune* article is reminiscent of a classic *Business Horizons* article by Karl Weick (1983) entitled "Misconceptions about Managerial Productivity". In it, Weick outlines how stochastic practices like medicine or management or being a mechanic are different from many other fields of knowledge, in that effective practice is not about thinking before or separate from action, but acting and thinking in unison. "Medicinal diagnosticians", he outlines (1983, p. 48), "do not follow the sequence: observe symptom, make diagnosis, prescribe treatment. Instead they . . . observe symptom, prescribe treatment, make diagnosis. They can diagnose . . . only after they see how [the disease] responds to treatment, not before". Outlining the formula "How can I know what I think until I see what I say?", Weick (1983, p. 49) writes of how the action of developing drawings and maps creates meaning, animates debate, and facilitates shared diagnoses and action in organizations. They are prototype models that enable various treatment scenarios to be thought through or tested out. "The world of the manager is senseless until [someone] produces some action that can be inspected . . . you can't make sense of a situation until you have something tangible to interpret". Given that an organization is of a scale far larger than a human body or a motorcycle, graphical representations are powerful animating objects that can be interpreted in this regard.

Mulally's drawing, and revisiting Weick's article, illustrate a perennial business problem and a solution that still remains largely untapped. How can executives communicate a complex message, the strategy of the firm, to a wide variety of stakeholders, so that the message is understood and remembered? What methods are there for communicating strategy effectively and what can executives do to improve the way they currently communicate? As the examples above suggest (and the practice of many managers who perhaps used to doodle 'back of an envelope ideas' a lot more frequently would reinforce), individualised graphics can be a powerful communication mechanism and aid to strategic thought. However, in the 30 years since Weick's *Business Horizons* paper, the question of *how* to do this effectively has received little explicit attention.

Outside of the leadership and management literature, cognitive scientists have understood that people can receive and understand complexity far more readily if it is presented graphically, rather than textually. People have better recall of pictures and printed words receive less 'processing attention' (Foos & Goolkasian, 2005). Educational psychologists, since Piaget and Brunner first explored these ideas over 80 years ago, have understood that the best way to learn, and retain what we learn, is to build understanding through combining three elements.

The first element is the *concrete* or 'hands-on' doing of tasks. The second is *pictorial or graphical* aids to help conceptualise. The third is associating these things with abstract representative symbols: *language and numbers* (Anghileri, 2005). Without the basis provided by the first two elements, learning through language and numbers alone is not particularly effective. Click on any guide or manual, for anything from a television set to a bicycle, and think about how hard it would be to act upon if there were no pictures alongside the text and numbers.

Research also suggests that the biggest concern that managers have with regard to strategy is how they can communicate it effectively. A recent survey asked executives what were the areas of strategy requiring greater strength or emphasis. At the top of the list for 79 per cent of respondents was the need to more effectively communicate their strategy internally (Hunter & O'Shannasy, 2007).

Recent research has shown how PowerPoint slides can help to advance the kind of things that Weick posited as important: the cartographic rendering of boundaries and distinctions, the collaboration that comes from discussing an image projected before ones' eyes (Kaplan, 2011). However, PowerPoint slides are often bounded by the decisions made by the programmers that designed the generic package and are difficult for the individuals to whom they are being projected to re-interpret and manipulate. We might borrow Mathew Crawford's (2009) argument from *Shop Class for the Soul* to suggest that, more often than not, PowerPoints are indicative of a culture that can no longer lift the lid and tinker with or adapt the fundamental workings of an object.

In keeping, company strategies are generally captured in, and communicated by, documents and generic PowerPoints packed with text and numbers, or with graphics that are hard to follow or relate to. While people do often learn about strategy by enacting it on a day-to-day basis (the first element of understanding), business strategy is hardly ever communicated through effective pictures or graphics (the second element). It should not be a surprise, therefore, that many people in most organizations are not sure what to *do* to enact a company's particular strategy, or that they have default a view of what to do that may be quite different from other people in the organization. Without good individualised graphics, they lack the proper foundation for learning, remembering and acting.

Curiously, useful graphical aids to help communicate complexity are commonplace in other stochastic fields of endeavor. For instance, sports commentators often draw on interactive screens to demonstrate to their TV audiences how football strategies work out. Coaches, managers and players make extensive use of graphical tools for immediate communication of how they see the play unfolding and to demonstrate what moves may be the most effective. Drawing on white boards, flip charts, freeze frames from TV footage, play books, game cards are all useful vehicles for conveying positions and dynamics on a contested space over time. In military practice, the graphic is also critical. It is important to train people in as many 'concrete' situations as possible to simulate 'live' scenarios (first element), and it is also important to express strategy through verbal and written commands (third element), going forward. But these two strategic strands are effectively joined by pictorial representation of the situation at hand and map making and map-reading are crucial parts of one's training. And graphical communication is key and well developed in medicine, architecture, design and so on.

Conventionally, individualised pictures have seldom been used in the development, leadership and presentation of an organization's strategy. Subsequently, leaders lack an appreciation of that second pictorial element of understanding critical for communicating, learning and understanding. Consequently, many strategies fail not because they are poorly planned or implemented without enthusiasm, but because they are poorly expressed. Putting these various ideas together, then, we propose that a revitalised form of strategic leadership would have as a core purpose *the building of engagement in the strategic development of an organization and mapping out a path for the future*, this being enabled by stories and pictures.

## The Visualizing Strategy Story So Far

> I am a great lover of these processes of division and generalization, they help me to speak and think.
>
> Plato

## Picturing Strategy in the Management Literature

Since Weick's (1983) article, academic writers have nibbled around the edges of this idea of visualizing strategy. Academic discussion on the value of presenting strategy using pictures in addition to text can be traced to the early 1990s, where it was noted that "managers have long recognized the importance of map-like products" (Fiol & Huff, 1992, p. 273) and that "maps used as [management] tools [would become] increasingly important in an uncertain world that requires managerial judgement" (Fiol & Huff, 1992, p. 273). The benefits of using map-like pictures to enhance strategy communication was listed as including their ability to help managers make sense of complexity, focus attention and trigger memories, signal priorities and supply missing information, simplify and aid the communication of complex ideas and divorce ideas from specific speakers—making them more accessible to debate and modification (Huff, 1990; Fiol & Huff, 1992).

The frameworks most associated with communicating strategy graphically, Kaplan and Norton's Strategy Map, and the related notion of the Balanced Scorecard, also emerged in the early 90s. Kaplan and Norton (2005) argued that the current, lengthy and text-laden forms of communicating strategy were not effective (e.g., "Our research reveals that, on average, 95% of a company's employees are unaware of, or do not understand, its strategy", p. 72). And that the Scorecard's and Strategy Map's visual 'comprehensive snapshots' would "help organizations view strategies in a comprehensive, integrated and systematic way", expose thinking and "gaps in strategies that would enable [. . .] early corrective actions" (Kaplan & Norton, 2000, p. 60). They would enable strategy to be 'bottled' "so that everyone could share it" (Kaplan & Norton, 1996, p. 40), thereby 'motivating' (and even 'obligating') 'breakthrough improvements' (Kaplan & Norton, 1993, p. 4).

While Kaplan and Norton have done much to publicise the problem of a lack of clear communication and, as a result, effective leadership in strategy, the application of their frameworks has generally led to visualisations that are at once blandly generic and overly complicated (just do a Google image search of 'strategy maps' to see).

Henry Mintzberg flirted with the idea in the late 1990s. In *Organigraphs: Drawing how Companies Really Work* (Mintzberg & Van der Heyden, 1999), Mintzberg and his co-author claimed that the generic triangular hierarchy of boxes and lines that we call organization charts are now 'irrelevant'. 'Organigraphs' (subjective 'mind-maps' containing any number of different shapes that symbolise and 'convey meaning') are where it's at, and leaders must now "create a customized picture of their company".

Mintzberg argues that organigraphs do not eliminate boxes altogether, but they add other elements into them, such as networks, hubs and other shapes that reflect how a particular place works and interacts with its environment. "Organigraphs are more than just pictures", they explain, "they are also maps. They provide an overview of a company's territory— its mountains, rivers, and towns, and the roads that connect them". The organigraphs depicted in Mintzberg and Van der Heyden's article illustrate how companies do not operate like a typical value chains or other generic strategy frameworks, but in unique configurations of resources and relationships. "Seeing such relationships illustrated can help a company understand the need for different managerial mind-sets throughout the organization", Mintzberg and Van der Heyden explained.

In the 2000s, Kim and Mauborgne (2002, p. 77) provided renewed impetus for seeing strategy in pictures in addition to words by stating that "building [a strategy] process AROUND A PICTURE yields much better results". And more recent works have continued to advocate the use of drawing, drawings and pictures in strategy development and communication, using approaches such as the 'business model canvas' (Osterwalder & Pigneur, 2010; Meyer, Höllerer, Jancsary & Van Leeuwen, 2013; de Salas & Huxley, 2014).

And it has been claimed, that strategic management, more than any other business discipline, lends itself to the use of frameworks. Michael Porter, developer of many of the most popular picture-plus-words strategy frameworks, in looking back at 30 years of strategic management research, articulated the value of frameworks to the field as related to their ability to help "highlight omitted variables, the diversity of competitive situations, the range of actual strategic choices, and the extent to which important parameters are not fixed but continually in flux" (1991, p. 98). "Frameworks", Porter went on to explain "identify the relevant variables and the questions which the user must [then] answer in order to develop [their own] conclusions". And in recent times, others have begun to explore the cognitive benefits that using graphical strategy frameworks can provide to people in organizations, exploring in more depth the added value that managers may achieve from using well-known frameworks in a strategy development process (Wright, Paroutis & Blettner, 2013; Jarzabkowski & Kaplan, 2015).

However, in the 1990s many academics claimed that using generic strategy frameworks led to a dumbing-down. Ralph Stacey (1990) claimed that a new world of complexity meant that conventional strategy frameworks are 'trite', 'flimsy' and 'redundant'. A paper by David Knights (1992) described Michael Porter's much used strategy framework, the Generic Strategy Matrix, a typical modernist positioning grid, as a classic example of the "myth of progress that underlies the demand for stable and positive management knowledge". Knights claims that despite the fact that Porter's model is too simple to reflect the reality for managers they continue to cling to it. Furthermore, says Knights, it detracts from giving attention to 'subjectivity' by "disciplining modern management regimes into emulating it".

But perhaps it really depends on how conventional strategy images and frameworks are used. The past five years have witnessed the proliferation of visualisation companies in all parts of the globe, with names like Visory, the Karl Weick inspired SeeWhatYouMean, MapTheMInd, Rizoomes and XPlane (Ong, 2016). And what these companies are doing seems to actually be helping organizations give much more attention to subjectivities, while still using some of the familiar graphical shapes of business frameworks. Recent books like *Business Model Generation* (Osterwalder & Pigneur, 2010) encourage leaders to draw their own strategies, as do many other books (e.g., Cummings & Angwin, 2015; Kalbach, 2016) which form part of what publishers are calling their 'visualisation' series of titles.

It seems that simplistic generic frameworks can provide a useful simple, shared language for dividing and thinking and speaking in individualised ways: that these images of strategy are being used, combined and customised in a positively post-modern way. However, like much that is 'new' in management, these developments lag a long way behind ideas in social theory, philosophy and the arts, from which we might learn much. By the 1970s, cultural commentators were already beginning to write of the exhaustion of the 'modernist' worldview and a re-appreciation of pre-modern subjectivity. Modernism's reductionist approach to searching for the underlying functional laws of all things, combined with the relentless quest for 'the new', had led from non-representational impressionist art to cubism (the distillation of objects into their essential boxes and lines) to abstractionism, and on to the 'white canvas' as the encapsulation of all things—an encapsulation that no individual could relate to. In architecture, it had led to the international style, the same building everywhere based on the universal maxims of essentialism, functionality and efficiency, no matter the local context. In modern music, from atonality to noise to absolute silence.

Jean-Francois Lyotard expressed these developments as 'Postmodernity' in 1979. "The ground-zero of contemporary culture", Lyotard (1984—the year the English translation of Lyotard's *Postmodernity* was published) claimed, "must be eclecticism". Five years before business guru Theodore Levitt was proclaiming that globalisation, best practice and advances in communications technology were bringing us ever closer to homogenised universal products and services, Lyotard was arguing otherwise. The same information technology was actually leading, he claimed, to a greater global appreciation of local difference. This enabled individuals to move beyond the quest for keeping up with singular international styles and develop their own particular identities through the establishment of webs of relationships between different things. In post-modernity, Lyotard (1984) wrote:

> One is free to listen to reggae, watch a Western, eat Macdonald's for lunch and local cuisine for dinner, wear Paris perfume in Tokyo and retro clothes in Hong Kong.

In keeping, people became increasingly incredulous toward 'meta-narratives'—universal maxims or criteria over and above particular instances (e.g., Science, Communism, Capitalism) that claimed to capture the essence of things through averages and general laws and tell individuals what norms they must follow. Post-modernity sees the re-appreciation or embracing of particular paths and many different views and playful combinations of styles taken from different traditions and time zones according to individual or local preferences. Obviously, in this book, our whole approach of offering localist, possibly eclectic, approaches to revitalise leadership in a multiplicity of ways is itself deeply informed by the ethos of post-modernism.

While the 'shapes' of the modern industrial era were the triangular hierarchy, the tree and the linear causal line of production, we appear now to be witnessing individualised nodal constellations crisscrossing these and other forms. At the time Lyotard was writing about the 'Postmodern Condition', Giles Deleuze and Felix Guattari (1988) might be seen to anticipate these developments in their arguments against the "trees, roots, and radicles" upon which modern 'arborescent culture' was based. While they did not seek to dismiss the standard "trees that people had growing in their heads" for classifying things, they advocated more chaotic "underground stems, aerial roots, adventitious growths and rhizomes" as alternative images. They subsequently favoured "nomadology" as an approach to knowledge: individual wandering and eclectic combinations or networks of elements, rather than one common path toward greater objectivity. This alternative 'shape' is apparent in the cities in which many of us now live. According to geographer David Harvey (1990), the post-modern city is:

> A labyrinth, honeycombed with such diverse networks of social interaction oriented to such diverse goals that the encyclopaedia becomes a maniacal scrapbook filled with colourful entries which have no determining rational or economic scheme.

Post-modernism, therefore, should not be thought of as the death of globalisation, the dismissal of modern forms, nor indeed the banishment of leadership with authority, but as the paradoxical networking of global and local, general and individual, for specific purposes. Bernard Cova (1996) subsequently describes post-modernism as a series of paradoxes and a breaking down of either/or distinctions:

* Fragmentation *with* globalisation;
* Heterogeneity *with* uniformity;
* Passive consumption *with* active customisation;
* Individualism *with* tribalism;
* Old *with* new.

Thinking of an example of a post-modern visualisation in this regard might lead us to a quite old, non-representative piece of graphic design that has been remade and individualised many thousands of times: Harry Beck's London Underground map. Here, geographic representation is eschewed for one man's diagram. It may not be rational in an objective representational sense, but it does not claim to be. Everybody knows that the distances between lines and stations are not 'factual'. However, Beck's map is memorable and open to nomadology, individual customisation or montage. Indeed, as Beck said, the map "must be thought of as a living and changing thing, with schematic 'manipulation' and spare part osteopathy going on all the time" (Garland, 1994). Subsequently, anyone who has lived in or visited London will find their own lives being understood, networked and communicated in relation to particular parts of it. The map is not reality, but its symbols have become language and people interact with it to schematise their lives in ways that are useful to them in making decisions and taking particular courses. Beck's original map is still the basis of the London Underground map to this day and the basis of most of the world's metro transport maps.

Paradoxically, simple, open, non-representative visualisations images like the tube map (or a value chain or other old strategic management shapes, if they are understood as similarly non-representative, malleable to personal imprinting and customisation) help us outline our individuality in these labyrinthine post-modern times. Borrowing from Plato's premodern perspective, such "processes of division and generalization help us to speak and think". Seeing images of strategy thus, rather than as objective representations of how the world really is, we could argue that they can be used in individualised ways to actually enhance subjective mapping. Contrary to the views of Knights and Stacey described above, we might suggest here that a simple strategic image that people can take and adapt have in fact never been more useful than they are in these increasingly complex times.

While academics like Stacey and Knights were right in saying that conventional strategy frameworks are 'trite' and 'flimsy' and that leading strategy much more than just deploying these things without thinking about the context, the call to make such images 'redundant' may be a case of throwing out the baby with the bath-water. While things are more complex than a two-by-two matrix, good strategies often come from the interaction between local individuals and such images. As with the Hungarian army example or the tube map, these images need not represent the world all in one. Their divisions and generalisations animate and orient people; they provide a shared language. They act as sounding boards and points of convergence—even if people chose to disagree with them and debate why. So long as we recognise them as such, there is no need for belittling—strategic thinking is the richer for them.

David Harvey's (1990) *The Condition of Postmodernity,\* begins with this quotation from Jonathan Raban's (1974) *Soft City*, a novel about a London life:

> For better or for worse the city invites you to remake it, to consolidate it into a shape you can live in. Decide who you are, and the city will again assume a fixed form around you. Decide what it is, and your own identity will be revealed, like a map fixed by triangulation.

There may be no better expression of the worth of exploring different strategic images in the post-modern manner described here, seeing which ones may be particularly useful to connect with, which ones help people to triangulate or begin mapping their own particular concerns. The onus is, first and foremost, on individuals to know themselves and their particular companies. Leaders who understand this can resourcefully use many different frameworks to good purpose. Do that and they will develop a further understanding of their own and other companies and be able to use more frameworks to greater effect. And so on, with the people involved becoming more insightful and resourceful.

## Picturing Strategy in Practice

While this post-modern theorisation of how leaders can stitch together singular unique images and stories in order to develop and communicate strategy, may be new, the practice of developing such images (although rare) is not a recent phenomenon. Perhaps one the earliest, and certainly one of the most interesting, is this picture (Image 6.2 below) of the Disney Company's operations drawn in 1957 (by Walt Disney himself). It depicts, in the best way Disney knew, how the various creative outputs of the organization drew from and fed into one another as a system (you can see it by searching "Disney strategy map 1957").

Our first observation of executives using visual imagery to convey a strategy occurred when an executive from Komatsu drew his company's strategy from the previous decade for one of us (Steve) in the United Kingdom in the late 1990s by adapting a familiar strategy framework: the Generic Strategy Matrix. Outlining a typical strategy framework contrasting market share against quality, he drew a big circle to show that Komatsu's main rival, Caterpillar, dominated the industry with the biggest market share and highest perceived quality. This was acting as a barrier against Eastern competitors like Komatsu. However, Komatsu's strategy, which had focussed on low-cost segments (which he drew as a circle to the left of the Caterpillar circle), was to break this perception. Komatsu would seek to invest heavily in R&D to target particular high-quality niches as a way to showcase their technological prowess (he drew smaller circles with Ks in them underneath the Caterpillar circle to represent this). They would then seek to deploy different product ranges to *encircle* and nibble away at Caterpillar's business on *two* fronts: cost, translated into lower prices, but also quality (he depicted this with arrows directed toward 'nibble marks' on Caterpillar circle from Komatsu's circles below and left). This simple graphic, and a few brief words, made Komatsu's strategy as clear as a bell:

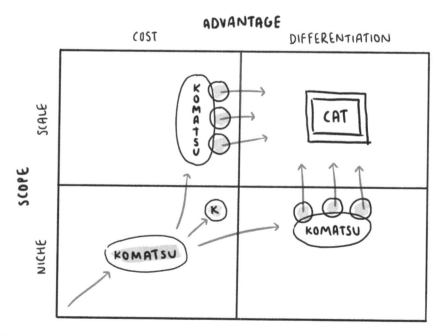

*Image 6.1* Komatsu's strategy, late 1989/1990s

Adapted from Cummings and Angwin (2015). Used with permission from the authors.

The picture below (Image 6.2) conveys the strategic identity and competitive advantage of the company concerned, a bookstore chain called Ottakar's, better than any words could on their own. Faced with increasing competition from large, multi-national book-chains, booksellers wanted to maintain and build local loyalty among book lovers in each of the individual communities that their stores had grown up in and were attuned to. As an illustration of this, staff from each store where invited to draw their own individual locator maps for their web-pages, replete with local landmarks, bookish references and other quirks. Each was different. Each conveyed a particular love of books and a belonging to their local community.

The next figure (Image 6.3) shows another good practice example: multi-national supermarket giant Tesco's strategy steering wheel. The strong red segment draws the eye to the top left with the primary focus on the customer. The eye is then steered around the circle from left to right, the top to bottom around back to relate all of the other segments back to the customer perspective. The eye is also drawn to the cool blue in the centre showing how everything leads to Tesco's mission and motto: 'every little helps'. The eye is then able to walk in and out of the circle from macro to micro and back. The shape, colours and simplicity (six basic zones) add up to a very memorable image.

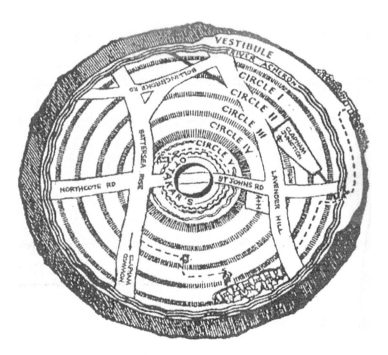

*Image 6.2* Ottakar's strategic identity

From Cummings and Angwin (2015). Used with permission from the authors.

*Image 6.3* Tesco's strategy steering wheel

From Cummings and Angwin (2015). Used with permission from the authors.

When Rob Fyfe became CEO of Air New Zealand in the early 2000s he wanted a wider range of employees and other stakeholders to feel connected to the company's emerging strategy. He and a team from across all aspects and levels of the organization tried to get to the heart of what their strategy was about by distilling the strategy into a few lines and then used doodles and drawings to sketch out the details. The inclusion of common office objects and stains made it less daunting and more intimate than a normal strategic planning document: as if you were sitting at a desk or coffee table with Fyfe as he is taking you through it (see Image 6.4 below).

What is it that these effective envisioning maps share? They are simple. They are engaging. They could be manipulated and changed to grow with newly promoted ideas. And, they appear unique and particular to the leadership teams that have developed them. Unlike a lot of vision statement or strategic plans, they are personal.

But also they enable envisioning the relationship between the micro and the macro, the big picture and the detail. They connect an internal core strategy or SUSS-line with a wider set of perspectives and stakeholders, mapping out the behaviours which will translate that idea into action. This a particularly important aspect of strategic mapping—and strategic leadership. Indeed, the process of strategic mapping is a key behaviour or practice that contributes to effective strategic leadership. As Edward Tufte explains, people respond to this macro/micro effect: "We love to [be able to] see the

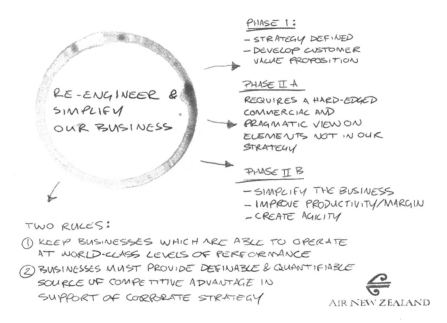

PHASE 1:
- STRATEGY DEFINED
- DEVELOP CUSTOMER
  VALUE PROPOSITION

PHASE II A
REQUIRES A HARD-EDGED
COMMERCIAL AND
PRAGMATIC VIEW ON
ELEMENTS NOT IN OUR
STRATEGY

PHASE II B
- SIMPLIFY THE BUSINESS
- IMPROVE PRODUCTIVITY/MARGIN
- CREATE AGILITY

RE-ENGINEER &
SIMPLIFY
OUR BUSINESS

TWO RULES:
① KEEP BUSINESSES WHICH ARE ABLE TO OPERATE
  AT WORLD-CLASS LEVELS OF PERFORMANCE
② BUSINESSES MUST PROVIDE DEFINABLE & QUANTIFIABLE
  SOURCE OF COMPETITIVE ADVANTAGE IN
  SUPPORT OF CORPORATE STRATEGY

AIR NEW ZEALAND

*Image 6.4* Air New Zealand's strategy, early 2000s

From Cummings and Angwin (2015). Used with permission from the authors.

big picture *and* personalize the data". Any device that enables this is thus extremely engaging (Google Maps, for example).

Because incorporating too much detail can turn people off or paralyse them, strategic mapping should focus on just the few dimensions necessary to aid decision making in a particular arena. Certainly, while three dimensions may enable us to better represent reality, we find it much better to work with a two-dimensional map or graphic. And, within two dimensions, a useful general rule is to aim for no more than seven colours, no more than seven directions or seven value categories and not to introduce too many different shapes. By simplifying complexity in this way, we contribute to the ability to see both the micro and macro, to see a particular detail that may relate specifically to a particular part of the system while seeing the system as a whole. We can move in and out of focus, on a vertical plane—like a zoom-lens: much like Harry Beck's London Underground map.

A good strategic leadership visualisation invites such interactions. Beck's tube map invites us to trace our route with our fingers, to share our perspectives on it with our travelling companions, to annotate it with additions, reminders and doodles particular to individual aims and goals. And as with any map, once we have added to it physically we (and our team of co-customisers in the middle of organization) have a greater mental connection with it.

*The Present and the Future of Leading Strategy Through*
*Visualisation (and Storytelling)*

By the end of 2015, a few major organizations were starting to visually express strategy in individualised ways. From a sample of the companies listed on the Fortune 100 list, One Hundred Best Places to work, and 50 Most Respected Companies lists—a total, due to duplication across the lists, of approximately 180 companies—five companies communicated their strategy with a visual. This is up from one the same list in 2011 (Ong, 2016). The six companies are Proctor & Gamble 2011; Caterpillar 2015; Home Depot 2015; Medical Scripts 2015; Proctor & Gamble 2015; and Unilever 2015 (you can see all six in the @strategybuild twitter feed). What is particularly interesting is their post-modern presentation. They take elements familiar to modern management thinking or frameworks and play with or circumvent these images in new ways. Caterpillar and Home Depot's pictures take the conventionally modern triangular shape of an organization and, in Caterpillar's case wrap three key stakeholders around it. For Home Depot, however, the triangle is adapted using a familiar metaphor relevant to what the company does (i.e., it comes with a story that helps people make connections that help them remember it): a three-legged stool.

The next two examples, a picture from Proctor & Gamble's website in 2011 (shown below in Image 6.5), and the representation of Medical Scripts strategy from 2015, customise the familiar shape of strategic management's most popular graphical framework, Michael Porter's (1985) 'Value Chain'. A framework which depicts how value is added in a production process and directed to meet customer needs.

**P&G Growth Strategy:** *Touching and improving more consumers' lives in more parts of the world more completely*

WHERE TO PLAY:

1. Grow leading, global brands and core categories

2. Build business with underserved and unserved consumers

3. Continue to grow and develop faster-growing, structurally attractive businesses with global leadership potential

HOW TO WIN:

1. Drive Core P&G Strengths in consumer understanding, brand building, innovation and go to market

2. Simplify, Scale and Execute for competitive advantage

3. Lead change to win with consumers and customers

*Image 6.5* Proctor & Gamble, 2011

From Cummings and Angwin (2015). Used with permission from the authors.

The final examples are from P&G in 2015 and Unilever. P&G is very reminiscent of the McKinsey Seven-S model, which is designed to depict six expressions of an organization's culture build around its shared or core values. Unilever's is designed in keeping with the idea of a virtuous circle. Both relate to concepts of systems thinking with the whole being greater than the sum of the parts.

We have presented the visualisations of strategy above not because we think they should be copied, but to inspire others by giving some idea of how a simple visualisation of strategy might look. Indeed, at the heart of leading strategy through stories and visualisation is the notion of resolving paradoxes, such as aiming for individual expression and shared meaning, global understanding and local appreciation, by taking context seriously and reflecting the particular context in which one leads. While the pictures we have represented here may have worked for the organizations they were developed for at the time they were developed, they would not work for other organizations in different contexts.

Consequently, there is no best practice model here. Designing a strategy by visualizing strategy is, by nature, abductive—it is about leading by imagining the future in a post-modern way, rather than developing generalisations through a modernist inductive/deductive logic that distils the past into a general average. As Seth Godin (2003) wrote, "You can't be remarkable by following someone else who's remarkable. . . . The thing that all great companies have in common is that they have nothing in common".

Bilton and Cummings developed a similar critique of the tendency to chase best practice in management and leadership, leading to homogenisation in industries (and declining competitiveness and average margins), in the book *Creative Strategy* (2010). In that discussion, they developed a framework to help lead by moving beyond best practice that may also be useful here (see below).

They identified four alternative mindsets to best practice by creating a matrix that crossed orientation to innovation: creation or discovery; and our understanding about how we best learn: either through observing empirically or feeling intuitively. These practices deliberately reconfigure the relationship between leader and follower while simultaneously removing the requirement for leaders to be hold all the answers. The first three alternative mindsets for leading strategy are:

- focussing on sharing, discussing and developing an understanding '*worst practices*'—because we learn more from ours and other failures than we learn from success.
- focussing on promoting and debating '*good practices*' (an idea borrowed from IBM, of all companies. IBM started to discourage staff from talking of 'best practice' because it implies that there is only one best way that cannot be surpassed, which encourages complacency);

- a leadership focus on identifying particular *'promising practices'* that may already exist within your organization rather than seeking to import in ideas via management consultants or other intermediaries.

Together, thinking through these three mindsets, can lead to a team developing a better understanding of 'next practice', what they (and only they—due to their unique context) can do 'next'—rather than simply adopting what was determined, in the past, to be best practice.

Getting to the middle of this matrix, and leading strategy by discussing the worst visualisations of strategy—a words and numbers-based tome of a strategy report of 110+ pages perhaps, or those complicated diagrams found when imaging searching for strategy maps—and looking at and debating which elements of good practice strategy visualisation might be worth adopting and adapting for a particular enterprise are recommended steps.

Doing this can enable strategy leaders to work, from the middle, with their team to focus on developing *'next practice'*: their particular visual expression of a strategy. And perhaps some stories that they and others explain, support it and connect this image to that their context.

Taking context seriously in leadership means just that: it means that someone cannot be a remarkable leader by following other remarkable

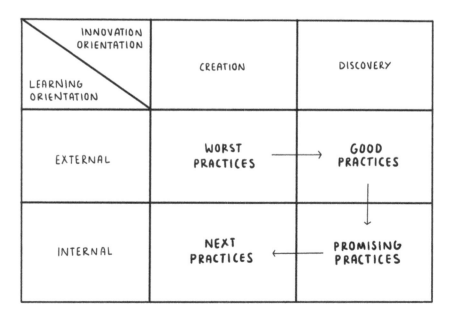

*Diagram 6.1* The next practice matrix (Bilton & Cummings, 2010)

Reproduced with the permission of the authors.

leaders, be that one leader in particular or some notional average of their characteristics or behaviours. This arises when leaders trust in their own virtues (as Marcus Aurelius advised in the previous chapter) and are guided by their own context. If we accept that contexts are different there can no longer be one-best-way to lead. Perhaps this is what the term 'authentic leadership' should mean?

Table 6.1 below connects our account of strategy leadership with our framework for contextualised theorising. In our next chapter, attention turns to leadership in the context of organizational governance, where oversight of the strategic inventiveness advocated here takes place.

*Table 6.1* Strategy leadership: a summary

| Component | Key issues and ideas |
| --- | --- |
| Challenges | How can a leader effectively involve organization members in strategy development and facilitate the effective communication in world where people still seek certainty, despite an increased need to be agile? |
| Purpose of leadership | Building engagement in the strategic development of an organization and mapping out a path for the future. |
| Values and norms | Inclusivity, Innovation, Integration |
| Domains | Internally within the organization at multiple levels and at interfaces between the organization and external stakeholders. |
| Leader | Must be able to encapsulate what the organization stands for, map a clear course forward and be able to convey these things in good stories and visualisations. |
| Follower | Often strategy is something that is seen to happen to followers rather than something they are a part of. In new contexts, organization members and stakeholders must feel engaged in the organization's future in order to partake in strategy development and implementation and suggest new opportunities and potential developments as they come into view. |
| Leader-follower relationship | As with Innovation and Entrepreneurship, strategy in this kind of context needs to be mapped out from the middle, or heart, of the organization. Consequently, leaders and others must work together to create and communicate strategy and to coordinate the adaptation of that strategy and the environment develops. |

# References

Anghileri, J. (2005). *Children's mathematical thinking in the primary years.* New York: Continuum International Publishing.

Auvinen, T., Aaltio, I., & Blomqvist, K. (2013). Constructing leadership by storytelling-the meaning of trust and narratives. *Leadership & Organization Development Journal,* 34(6), 496–514.

Barry, D., & Elmes, M. (1997). Strategy retold: Toward a narrative view of strategic discourse. *Academy of Management Review,* 22(2), 429–452.

Bilton, C., & Cummings, S. (2010). *Creative strategy: Reconnecting business and innovation.* Oxford: Wiley.

Boje, D. M. (1991). The storytelling organization: A study of story performance in an office-supply firm, vol. 45. *Administrative Science Quarterly,* 106–126.

Boje, D. M. (2008). *Storytelling organizations.* London: Sage.

Cova, B. (1996). The postmodern explained to managers: Implications for marketing. *Business Horizons,* 39(6), 15–23.

Crawford, M. (2009). *Shop class for the soul.* New York: Penguin.

Cummings, S., & Angwin, D. (2015). *Strategy builder: How to create and communicate more effective strategies.* Oxford, UK: Wiley.

Cummings, S., & Wilson, D. (Eds.). (2003). *Images of strategy.* Oxford, UK: Blackwell.

de Salas, K., & Huxley, C. (2014). Enhancing visualisation to communicate and execute strategy: Strategy-to-process maps. *Journal of Strategy and Management,* 7(2), 109–126.

Deleuze, G., & Guattari, F. (1988). *MilleFigureaux: Capitalism and schizophrenia.* London: Althone.

Denning, S. (2005). *The leader's guide to storytelling: Mastering the art and discipline of business narrative.* John Wiley & Sons: Chichester, UK.

Fiol, C. M., & Huff, A. S. (1992). Maps for managers: Where are we? Where do we go from here? *Journal of Management Studies,* 29(3), 267–285.

Foos P. W., & Goolkasian, P. (2005). Presentation format effects in working memory: The role of attention. *Memory & Cognition,* 33, 499–513.

Gabriel, Y. (2000). *Storytelling in organizations: Facts, fictions, and fantasies.* Oxford, UK: Oxford University Press.

Garland, K. (1994). *Mr Beck's underground map.* London: Capital Transport Publishing.

Godin, S. (2003). *Purple cow: Transform your business by being remarkable.* London: Penguin.

Harvey, D. (1990). *The condition of postmodernity.* Oxford: Blackwell.

Huff, A. S. (1990). *Mapping strategic thought.* Chichester, UK: John Wiley & Sons.

Hunter, P., & O'Shannasy, T. (2007). Contemporary strategic management practice in Australia: 'Back to the Future' in the 2000s. *Singapore Management Review,* 29(2), 21–36.

Jarzabkowski, P., & Kaplan, S. (2015). Strategy tools in use: A framework for understanding "technologies of rationality" in practice. *Strategic Management Journal,* 36(4), 537–558.

Kalbach, J. (2016). *Mapping experiences: A complete guide to creating value through journeys, blueprints, and diagrams.* New York: O'Reiley.

Kaplan, R. S. (2011). Strategy and powerpoint: An inquiry into the epistemic culture and machinery of strategy making. *Organization Science,* 22(2), 320–346.

Kaplan, R. S., & Norton, D. P. (1993). Putting the balanced scorecard to work. *Harvard Business Review,* 71(5), 134–140.

Kaplan, R. S., & Norton, D. P. (1996). *The balanced scorecard: Translating strategy into action.* Cambridge, MA: Harvard Business Press.

Kaplan, R. S., & Norton, D. P. (2000). Having trouble with your strategy? Then map it: Focusing your organization on strategy with the balanced scorecard. *Harvard Business Review*, 78, (September–October), 49–59.

Kaplan, R. S., & Norton, D. P. (2005). The Office of strategy management. *Harvard Business Review*, 83, (October), 72–81.

Kim, W. C., & Mauborgne, R. (2002). Charting your company's future. *Harvard Business Review*, 80(6), 76–83, 153.

Knights, D. (1992). Changing spaces: The disruptive impact of a new epistemological location for the study of management. *Academy of Management Review*, 17(3), 514–536.

Lyotard, J.-F. (1984). *The postmodern condition: A report on knowledge.* Manchester: Manchester University Press.

Meyer, R. E., Höllerer, M. A., Jancsary, D., & Van Leeuwen, T. (2013). The visual dimension in organizing, organization, and organization research: Core ideas, current developments, and promising avenues. *Academy of Management Annals*, 7(1), 489–555.

Mintzberg, H., & Van der Heyden, L. (1999). Organigraphs: Drawing how companies really work. *Harvard Business Review*, (September/October), 87–94.

Mulally, A. (2009). Fixing up Ford. *Fortune*, (May 25), 41–47.

Ong, C. (2016). *Facilitators and inhibitors to visualizing information in organisational practice.* Unpublished Master's Thesis. Victoria University of Wellington, New Zealand.

Osterwalder, A., & Pigneur, Y. (2010). *Business model generation: A handbook for visionaries, game changers, and challengers.* Oxford: John Wiley & Sons.

Porter, M. E. (1985). Competitive advantage: creating and sustaining superior performance. New York: Free Press.

Raban, J. (1974). *Soft city.* London: Fontana.

Rich, B., & Janus, L. (1996). *Skunk works: A personal memoir of my years at lockheed.* San Francisco, CA: Back Bay Books.

Sintonen, T., & Auvinen, T. (2013). Who is leading, leader or story? The power of stories to lead. *Tamara: Journal for Critical Organization Inquiry*, 8(2), 95–109.

Stacey, R. (1990). *Dynamic strategic management for the 1990s.* London: Kogan Page.

Weick, K. (1983). Misconceptions about managerial productivity. *Business Horizons*, 26(4), 47–52.

Weick, K. (1987). Substitutes for strategy. In D. Teece (Ed.), *The competitive challenge: Strategies for industrial innovation and renewal* (pp. 211–233). New York: Ballinger.

Weischer, A. E., Weibler, J., & Petersen, M. (2013). "To thine own self be true": The effects of enactment and life storytelling on perceived leader authenticity. *The Leadership Quarterly*, 24(4), 477–495.

Wright, R. P., Paroutis, S. E., & Blettner, D. P. (2013). How useful are the strategic tools we teach in business schools?. *Journal of Management Studies*, 50(1), 92–125.

# 7   *Leading in* Governance

## Introduction

The fields of *leadership* and *corporate governance* have, in their own rights, become the focus of significant recent interest for academics and business practitioners alike. Often addressing similar phenomena, research efforts rarely interact or engage with each other, existing in a state of 'splendid isolation'. This is the source of great surprise and more than a little consternation on the part of senior executives we interact with, whose complex and urgent reality precludes the luxury of such a clean and simple demarcation. Indeed, leadership in the governance context must of necessity bridge in practice what is often distant and at odds in theory. Responding to this, in this chapter, we *selectively* draw from research in both the governance and leadership literatures to highlight ideas we believe have particular value in our effort to formulate a new approach that theorises the practice of leading in governance. Our understanding of the strategic challenges which boards face relies on the analysis offered in the previous chapter; however, we shift the lens here by focussing on the context of governance and how leadership can usefully take form in that context. This chapter expands and builds upon an earlier argument that was initially advanced by Erakovic and Jackson (2012).

Part of the reason for the distance that exists between knowledge of 'leadership' and of 'governance' is the fact that each research field draws upon quite disparate disciplinary roots for their guidance and inspiration: corporate governance is primarily rooted in accounting and commercial law, leadership in the disciplines of psychology and, to a lesser extent, sociology and political science. Another reason is that the corporate governance and leadership researcher communities tend to take on quite different worldviews or 'frames' when they study organizations. The former tend to foreground a 'structural frame', which privileges policies and procedures, whereas the latter tend to foreground a 'human resources frame', which privileges people and their interrelationships (Bolman & Deal, 2003). Whatever the causes for this estrangement, the net effect is that researchers in these two fields have not actively considered their respective theoretical frameworks, as well as their empirical insights, from which each could learn. This has, arguably, resulted in too little attention to the value that leadership can bring to effective governance and too little understanding of the nature of governance for its implications for leadership theory and practice.

Our effort here contributes to long overdue and much needed work to integrate and cross-fertilise research efforts between corporate governance and leadership. Their strengths and weaknesses mutually complement each other: leadership has traditionally been strong in casting light on significant informal, interpersonal dynamic processes within organizations, but has tended to confine its attention to the middle and lower ranks of the organization, at the exclusion of senior executives and boards, and could be generally accused of being legally naïve. Corporate governance scholars, on the other hand, have developed a sophisticated legal understanding of the organization and have considerable experience working at its upper echelons. They have, however, tended to be hamstrung by a pre-occupation with formal, static and impersonal theoretical models. We believe that there is much to be gained by creating a theoretical rapprochement between the two fields, enabling fresh insights to inform 'governing leadership', that is, leadership undertaken in the corporate governance setting.

Corporate governance provides the organizational framework within which leadership is enacted. It sets the stage for leadership at the top of the organization and has an indirect but significant impact upon leadership processes at other levels within the organization. Yet, while corporate governance provides a structure for the relationships among core stakeholders (e.g., shareholders, boards and managers), it is leadership practices which provide the motivation and impetus to make corporate governance effective in the achievement of the organization's purpose and goals (Davies, 2006). In this respect, we argue *the purpose of governing leadership is to 'energise' governance efforts to go beyond matters of conformance to address issues of performance and opportunity, so as to 'add value' to the organization.* In advancing this purpose, good governance can serve to sustain good leadership.

The transition of board member roles from 'organizational controllers and monitors' to 'organizational leaders' has been welcomed as a positive development by many corporate governance commentators. Organizational stakeholders expect from their governors (i.e. directors) to represent and respond—not just dictate results and define problems or command solutions. These expectations, which closely resemble leadership virtues, demonstrate a radical movement from orthodox components of governance (e.g., finance, strategy, facilities) to deeper and potentially more powerful facets of governance (e.g., values, beliefs, mission, agendas) (Chait, Ryan & Taylor, 2005). 'Discovering' governance as a leadership activity, that is, seeing governance as a multidimensional practice, can enhance stakeholders' trust and commitment to the organization. Moreover, it can serve to improve the effectiveness of governors (Huse, 2007). These shifts in orientation provide an important backdrop for how we conceptualise leadership in the context of governance.

One feature that leadership and governance have in common is their elusive nature when it comes to deciding on a common definition that can explain their scope and intent. It is arguable, though, that leadership holds a clear edge over governance in terms of its ambiguity and lack of agreement (Bryman, Collinson, Grint, Jackson & Uhl-Bien, 2011)! For the purposes of this chapter, we define leadership as "an influence relationship among leaders and followers who intend real changes that reflect their mutual purposes" (Rost, 1993, p. 10) and corporate governance as "the process whereby people in power direct, monitor and lead corporations, and thereby either create, modify or destroy the structures and systems under which they operate" (McGregor, 2000, p. 11).

In laying out our approach to governing leadership, we highlight three key dimensions to its practice: team leadership on the board, the chair's leadership of the board and strategic leadership by the board. We identify ideas that help flesh out the processes and practices in each dimension that enable and reflect the kind of leadership approach we think is needed. We conclude the chapter by raising a number of pertinent research questions that can be profitably researched by taking both a 'leadership in governance' and a 'governance in leadership' perspective.

## Recent Developments in Corporate Governance Research—and Their Implications for Leadership in Governance

The traditional corpus of governance research has tended to emphasise a static, one-dimensional view of corporate governance that narrowly emphasises the central importance of developing a normative approach, rather than a more expansive, dynamic and thickly descriptive approach to its subject (for criticism of the agency theory and traditional governance framework, see Finkelstein & Mooney, 2003; Grandori, 2000; Huse, 2005; Johnson, Daily & Ellstrand, 1996 among others).

Unable to make a meaningful and useful connection between the abstract, rarified nature of much of the corporate governance research and the reality of their day-to-day experience, many practitioners we encounter have turned away and largely ignored it. Consequently, there is a general feeling that corporate governance research has failed to harness its full potential in terms of its scope and practitioner impact (Filatotchev & Boyd, 2009). This is all the more remarkable and lamentable given the widespread media attention that issues related to corporate governance now receive, as well as the urgency with which regulators are viewing these issues. Part of the reason for this has been the field's preoccupation with agency theory as a conceptual framework (Daily, Dalton & Cannella, 2003; van Ees, Gabrielsson & Huse, 2009). Another factor is the ambiguous evidence that has been accumulated, which has failed to adequately identify and problematise which governance variables actually influence corporate performance. As Grandori (2004, p. 1) has stressed, "there is a diffuse dissatisfaction with the prevailing conceptualizations of governance".

Some researchers, however, have discovered new ways of conceptualising governance by breaking away from the theoretical frameworks that have historically dominated the field, and have applied new approaches (e.g., contingency, behavioural and evolutionary) in an effort to generate some fresh understanding of the complexities inherent to governance processes (see, for example, Aguilera, Filatotchev, Gospel & Jackson, 2008; Filatotchev, Toms, & Wright, 2006; Van Ees, et al., 2009). In one such shift, researchers have moved beyond 'either/or' thinking. This involves embracing a paradoxical approach to governance, focussed on the importance of the dynamic balance between control and collaboration approaches in governance (Sundaramurthy & Lewis, 2003). A control approach protects a corporation from self-serving behaviour and reduces goal conflict, while a collaborative approach encourages co-operation between board and management and fosters trust and goal alignment. Acceptance, understanding and management of control-collaboration tensions promote learning and improve governance (Sundaramurthy & Lewis, 2003). A contingency lens suggests the leadership capability to contend with such paradoxes is a basic requirement.

An 'evolutionary' understanding of governance challenges is also relevant in our view (e.g., Boeker & Karichalil, 2002; Filatotchev & Wright, 2005; Lynall, Golden & Hillman, 2003). This means conceptualising governance as a dynamic system which evolves throughout the organizational life-cycle. Governance practices change and develop as an organization progresses throughout different stages, from start up to maturity and even to decline. Each stage is characterised by a different configuration of resources, 'dominant' organizational actors and specific internal and external relationships, which may influence the evolution of the governance structure. Hence, from a leadership perspective, the capability to understand the varying needs of the organization as it 'evolves' over time is crucial to ensure the leadership response is 'in tune' with the organization's needs.

A focus on board behaviour (Huse, 2005) is a further key dimension. The idea of looking into the 'black box' of board behaviour is innovative and challenging for researchers, as they have rarely had the opportunity to directly witness and observe the processes of board meetings. It is remarkable and of great concern that Gabrielsson and Huse (2004) have found that less than one out of eight articles in the leading journals discusses actual board behaviour (Huse, 2005). In formulating an account of leadership in the context of governance, however, paying attention to the actual behaviour of the board, as a collective entity and of its individual members, constitutes an important point of focus.

The fundamental principles of behavioural theory assumes that the purpose of the board is to add value to the corporation by aiding it, not in the sense of maintaining control over it, but through communication and collaboration, "engaging in collective processes of search and discovery" (van Ees et al., 2009, p. 308). The traditional monitoring role of the board, however, has left little room for building mechanisms of trust within organizations (Caldwell & Karri, 2005). Legislation may serve a purpose in realigning the intentions of directors and executives "straying from the path of good governance" (Kocourek, Burger & Birchard, 2003, p. 6), but good governance in the real sense will only occur when the individuals concerned consciously *choose* to govern well. In the situation where the governance is reduced to a check-list exercise, the potential for leadership is lost; there is no space for leadership to express itself through discernment, discussion and good decision making.

We believe that the primary purpose of the board is to provide leadership even as it simultaneously provides governance. In terms of governance, this can be usefully conceptualised as comprising three modes, which intersect with leadership: (1) the fiduciary mode, whereby boards are concerned primarily with the stewardship of tangible assets, (2) the strategic mode, whereby boards create a strategic partnership with management and (3) the generative mode, whereby boards provide a less recognised but critical source of leadership for the organization (Chait et al., 2005). When trustees (or board members) operate in all three of these modes, the board achieves a state of 'governance as leadership' (Chait et al., 2005).

The essence of the generative mode is to move beyond the boundaries of "performance and conformance functions" of the board (Tricker, 1994) and to look towards the future. It is in this mode that leadership is most likely to be able to develop. It is fundamentally collaborative and relational, and it occurs in the interactions between directors, the CEO and other executives. Each actor is vital to the governance process, as each has its own views to offer in developing a comprehensive, multi-dimensional picture of the organization's future. In this way, the board's focus moves away from "aggregating different interests towards sharing the commitment to develop the company" (Christensen & Westenholz, 1999, p. 274).

This position complements an emerging perspective in governance research, according to which governance structures and processes develop interdependently within distinctive organizational contexts. Four major drivers, though which the board of directors can actively promote leadership processes throughout the organization, have been identified (Erakovic, Jackson & Kudumula, 2011). These are: a co-operative spirit on the board; organizational knowledge-sharing systems established by the board; employee empowerment; and the power of the collective will (or the absence of a single leader).

Our contribution, to extend these existing understandings of governing leadership, is framed by a focus on three important dimensions in which governance and leadership come together to a greater or lesser extent in any organization: team leadership on the board; the chair's leadership of the board; and strategic leadership by the board. Our discussion below of the challenges, roles and responsibilities involved in each of these three dimensions draws out the leadership behaviours, attributes, norms and values that each demands, pursuant to overall purpose we proposed earlier for governing leadership. Figure 7.1 below visualises these three dimensions and how they sit within the intersection of leadership and governance.

## Team Leadership on the Board

Boards occupy a central role at the intersection between governance and leadership processes. However, the extent to which this is actually recognised, let alone actively fostered and capitalised upon, varies from company to company, depending upon the expectations that are traditionally placed upon the board and the philosophies of those who sit on the board, most notably the chair and CEO, but not confined to them. Forbes and Milliken (1999) describe boards of directors as being typically "large, elite and episodic decision making groups that face complex tasks pertaining to strategic-issue processing" (p. 492). This view is underpinned by the traditional view of boards as being the "brain and soul of the organisation" (Pearce & Zahra, 1991, p. 136). Effective boards should, therefore, amount to more than a summation of individual contributions. Moreover, the interpersonal dynamics of different individuals working together in a board-level environment can either genuinely add or detract from value form the organization.

Why then, are boards often criticised as being ineffective? Chait et al. (2005) identify three main problems that are invariably associated with poor board performance. First, a board may be a dysfunctional group in which strong self-interest, divergent personalities, conflicting interests and

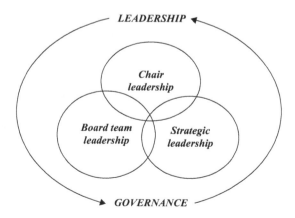

*Figure 7.1* Governing leadership

communication barriers prevent collaboration and effective deliberation. Second, the board may become disengaged and not show any intention of being engaged with each other or the organization they govern. Third, despite good intentions, members may not be sufficiently informed about their role or the organization. The last of these reasons is cited as being the most common. Moreover, research has shown that the limited competencies and lack of awareness at the board may put constraints on their decision-making capabilities and cause organizational inefficiencies (van Ees et al., 2009). In contrast, by exhibiting team leadership, a board's purpose can be solidified and the diverse talents sitting around the board table can be fully drawn upon to identify and move on genuine value-creating strategies.

There are two extant streams of research in the context of board leadership (Huse, Gabrielsson & Minichilli, 2009). The first looks at the boardroom dynamics or actual board behaviour. Developing trust between the board members and having open and honest interactions within the board and with the CEO are considered important pre-conditions for effective governance (Holloway and van Rhy, 2005). Further, although directors are elected or appointed to the board because of their individual skills and knowledge, they work as a group (Huse, 2007). In a group, people work with each other and the final outcome is the result of their joint efforts. Therefore, they are dependent on each other. Through their relationships, directors develop a specific boardroom culture (Leblanc & Gillies, 2005) which, to provide for an effective board's functioning, needs to balance trust and distrust (Nooteboom, 1996), closeness and distance, dependence and interdependence (Huse, 1994), as well as consensus and conflict in the boardroom. Many authors (e.g., Barratt & Korac-Kakabadse, 2002; Gautier, 2002; Huse, 2007) argue that more research is required within the context of the boardroom to understand what can be changed to encourage talented individuals and executives to thrive in the board environment. Gray (2007) points out that the overemphasis upon structural aspects of governance has lulled shareholders into "a false sense of security . . . and has led many boards to ignore the less visible, but more important cultural and procedural aspects of governance" (p. 61). While these challenges remain, developing trust, open communication and the capacity to work collaboratively clearly emerge as important behaviours and norms for governing leadership.

The second stream of research draws attention to the board as a value-creating team. The concept of 'adding value' is broad and incorporates matters such as improving board interrelationships to enable more healthy and robust discussion and utilising board members' strengths to create a well-balanced team. Adding value is closely related to the purpose of the board, to the performance function and to effective organizational leadership. Knowledgeable members on the board and a skilled and competent team leader contribute to value creation (Carver & Oliver, 2002; Kaufman

& Englander, 2005). Directors, therefore, should behave as team members, both within the boardroom and in relationship with management, and they need to have experience and resources strategically important to the organization (Carver & Oliver, 2002; Kaufman & Englander, 2005). By including strategic information that different board members possess, boards enhance their decision-making abilities. Such boards are capable of assisting the company to create and sustain competitive advantage (Carver & Oliver, 2002). The gains that such boards produce arise from co-operation. Consequently, then, board members should be expected to develop and even model the same level of teamwork that they expect of their senior management team and their front line production or sales teams.

To perform as a team, members of the board need to be able to acquire, absorb and understand strategic information, to communicate the information among themselves and with the senior management team, to influence the strategic orientation of the company and to communicate their decisions and major changes with other inside and outside stakeholders. If we consider the above activities as part of the influence process which facilitates the performance of the board, we can see that they all illuminate various aspects of leadership such as group processes, power relations, personality or competence qualities. More specifically, these activities are the components of what is described as transformational leadership. According to this approach to leadership, "the leader [is] someone who defines organizational reality through the articulation of a vision, and the generation of strategies to realize that vision" (Jackson & Parry, 2008, p. 28). It has been shown that transformational leadership supports team effectiveness (Jung & Sosik, 2002), individual performance (Jung & Avolio, 2000) and entrepreneurial behaviour. The kind of transformational leadership we envisage here is not about individualistic, heroic efforts. Rather, it is about the collective capability and will of the board to go beyond the status quo and imagine, in conjunction with other key stakeholders such as senior management, a better future for the organization and to craft strategies to deliver that better future.

## The Chair's Leadership of the Board

There is widespread acceptance among those who examine board leadership dynamics that the role of the chairperson is central and critical (Carter & Lorsch, 2004; Huse, 2009; Leblanc, 2005; McNulty, Pettigrew, Jobome & Morris, 2011). A value-creating board member, the chair must carry out a number of tasks: he or she should seek to build trustful relationships among board members and with the CEO; support the board members to become effective team members by motivating and providing them with all of the information they might need; encourage open communications within and outside the boardroom; facilitate robust discussions at the meetings; and actively develop and refine governance structures and processes (Huse, 2009). To be able to perform these tasks in support of an effective board, the chair needs to be enthusiastic, highly capable in managing processes, possess high levels of integrity and be highly respected and thorough in preparing meetings. To fulfil these requirements requires an authentic commitment to the organization and to the work required to contribute effectively as chair.

An important function of a chair's leadership role is mediating the relationship between the board and the CEO (Gabrielsson, Huse & Minichilli, 2007; Roberts & Stiles, 1999). Two leadership concepts that are particularly useful in this discussion are transactional leadership and co-leadership. Transactional leadership characterises the traditional foundation for board-CEO relationships (Bass & Avolio, 1990). The essence of this relationship is distilled in a formal contractual agreement between the board and CEO. At this point, transactional leadership intersect with agency theory assumptions on relations between principals and agents. For example, the transactional leadership factor of 'contingent rewards' (conformity with performance targets) is related to outcome-based contracts in the principle-agent research (Eisenhardt, 1989). An outcome-based contract motivates the agent (CEO) to behave in co-alignment with the principal's (board) preferences. In the situation where board members perform controlling and monitoring roles in the organization, the CEO (and other managers) will avoid risk-taking behaviour and will not engage into radical advancement of the organization. The board/chair's transactional leadership style does not empower the CEO to promote change. Rather, the CEO is encouraged to mobilise resources to achieve clearly defined short-term goals and to improve existing organizational capabilities. This type of board-chair leadership is likely to result in organizational exploitation rather than exploration (March, 1995). Exploitation promotes those governance practices and forms that facilitate elaboration of existing strategies and the preservation of current organizational legitimacy (Kraatz & Block, 2008). Balancing exploitation (short-term goals, improvements of existing capabilities and resources, repetition, systematic reasoning, coordinating activities, monitoring) and exploration (long-term vision, development of new strategies, risk-taking behaviour, mentoring, creativity) is an important aspect of the board-chair-CEO relationship, which can have important consequences for organizational survival.

Co-leadership is a further aspect of the chair's leadership that we see as desirable. First coined by Heenan and Bennis (1999), 'co-leadership' is defined as two leaders in vertically contiguous positions who share the responsibilities of leadership. They describe co-leaders as "truly exceptional deputies—extremely talented men and women, often more capable than their more highly acclaimed superiors" (Heenan & Bennis, 1999, p. 6). Heenan and Bennis observe that "we continue to be mesmerized by celebrity and preoccupied with being No. 1". However, this tendency overvalues the contribution of the chair or CEO and simultaneously depreciates the contributions of subordinates. "The genius of our age is truly collaborative", they write, "the shrewd leaders of the future are those who recognize the significance of creating alliances with others whose fates are correlated with their own" (Heenan & Bennis, 1999, p. viii). When it comes to leadership an old cliché may well ring true: "two heads are better than one".

Although co-leadership has yet to undergo rigorous analysis, several scholars suggest that it improves leadership effectiveness (Alvarez & Svejenova, 2005; Heenan & Bennis, 1999; O'Toole, Galbraith & Lawler, 2002; Sally, 2002). Upper Echelons Theory, as conceived by Hambrick and Mason (1984), provides us with some insight into why this might be. This theory suggests that leadership is an important ingredient of organizational performance; however, the complexity of organizations makes it improbable that one leader alone will be able to exert great influence over all members of the organization. A formal co-leadership (i.e. co-CEO, co-chair, co-director) structure can help to make this more likely, but these remain the notable exception rather than the rule.

In addition, Hambrick (1989) argues that strategic leadership occurs in an environment embedded in ambiguity, complexity, and information overload. An important responsibility of top-level organizational leaders is enabling the organization to adapt to this complex environment (Boal & Hooijberg, 2000). The skills required to successfully negotiate this increasingly complex environment are extensive and may be too broad to be possessed by one leader (Alvarez & Svejenova, 2005; Storey, 2005). Collaboration at the senior leadership level improves the success of the strategic organizational partnership (Huxham & Vangen, 2000), allowing top corporate managers adequate attention for different aspects of the leadership tasks, including day-to-day operational activities and long-term strategy (Bass, 1990). It also gives the organization an opportunity to continue, even when one of the top leaders leaves the organization.

## Strategic Leadership by the Board

Organizations are complex entities, each having its own life cycle, decision-making processes, embedded ways of functioning and different needs at different times. In order to be responsive to the continually evolving needs of the organization, governance structures need to follow flexible patterns of tasks and structures (Pye, 2002). Once board members understand the organizational context and their purpose, the hope is that they may conceive ways in which they can individually and collectively contribute to adding value to the organization. The board's contribution to strategy-making is an important value-adding activity and something that is genuinely considered to be the purest demonstration of the board's leadership role. Although this is widely recognised within the management literature and in conventional governance practice, the nature of and extent to which the board should be actively involved in shaping strategy is still highly controversial and hotly debated within the corporate governance literature (Pugliese et al., 2009).

For a long time, a directorship has been conceived of by many corporate governance theorists as a one-dimensional job that entails control and monitoring. While many notable high-performing companies have compellingly demonstrated the role of the board as strategy makers, the prevailing view remains unchanged, namely that board members are still not utilised anywhere near as much as they could and should be as strategy shapers (Chait et al., 2005; Lorsch & MacIver, 1989). Board members' job design tends to be too restricting or inadequately defined. Moreover, the time they devote to board business is insufficient. The net result of being shut out of the strategy formulation process (in other than a token, rubber-stamping way) is that many board members end up becoming disillusioned and ineffectual because they believe they are not able to add real value to the organization.

Having investigated not-for-profit boards, Chait et al. (2005) assert that many boards are ineffective because board members are dissatisfied with their role and are only formally engaged in the organization's affairs. Researchers and practitioners argue that it is of vital importance for any organization to have an active and engaged board. We do not have to be convinced of the importance of this when we talk about employee engagement levels, so why should this, then, not be the case for board members too? A number of studies (e.g., Carpenter & Westphal, 2001; Carter & Lorsch, 2004; Johnson et al., 1996; McNulty & Pettigrew, 1999; Pettigrew & McNulty, 1995; Ravasi & Zattoni, 2006; Zahra & Filatotchev, 2004) have indeed revealed that increased involvement on the part of directors in strategy formulation, strategic decision making and strategic restructuring leads to higher levels of firm performance, especially in the situation of environmental uncertainty (Geletkanycz & Hambrick, 1997). Furthermore, numerous empirical investigations provide the evidence of board involvement in various strategies, such as innovation strategy, R&D strategies, internationalisation and strategic change (for an overview of the studies refer to Pugliese et al., 2009).

Taking a 'leadership' perspective as regards these challenges, the board can and should provide active support to management in strategy formulation and implementation (Huse, 2007). Directors are appointed by shareholders to protect their interest and to work in the best interests of the company. There is a growing demand by increasingly active shareholders for directors' to play an active rather than a passive role in guiding a company's future development (Sullivan & Kelly, 2008). By drawing upon their external knowledge and expertise, the board members are in an excellent position to advise management on important strategic issues for the company to face and to provide them with the access to external resources that management would otherwise not be able to have. Through these activities, directors support and empower management and contribute to the company's strategic competitive advantage. The comprehensiveness of this role is especially emphasised in smaller organizations on their transitional stages (Zahra & Filatotchev, 2004). The 'how to' of this strategic leadership contribution can be informed by the approach outlined in the previous chapter, which is equally as applicable to board members as to senior management.

## Conclusion

Having sound leadership and governance processes are vital to the long-term health and vitality of any organization. However, there is an insufficient understanding of how these processes should best be maintained and properly balanced and what roles senior managers and board members should play in orchestrating and participating in them. The board's role in not only promoting good governance within the organization but also good leadership is finally being recognised by some scholars (Heracleous, 1999), but significant theoretical and empirical research is still missing. Reflecting on the various debates about leadership and governance, we have proposed that the purpose of governing leadership is to energise governance efforts to go beyond matters of conformance to address issues of performance and opportunity, so as to 'add value' to the organization. This purpose, we think, speaks to the enabling potential of leadership but without decrying the grounding that governing leadership has in attending to the requirements of good governance.

We have shown that progress has already been made in bringing leadership and governance perspectives together by a number of scholars but this effort has been isolated and unsystematic. And, drawing on various strands of research we have highlighted key ideas that can be called on in developing a theorisation of leadership in the context of governance. Specifically, to advance on existing efforts which have highlighted the paradoxes involved in governance, the evolutionary characteristics of organizations and behavioural aspects of board effectiveness, we identified three important dimensions of governing leadership: team leadership on the board; the chair's leadership of the board; and strategic leadership by the board. For each of these, we have highlighted some key challenges and explored the kinds of attributes, behaviours, values and norms that contribute to the enactment of effective governing leadership.

The following two tables summarise our ideas. The first outlines key linkages between related governance and leadership concepts and relevant research streams. The second summarises our theorisation of governing leadership using the theory-building framework that guides this book.

*Table 7.1* Key conceptual linkages between leadership and governance

| Intersecting processes | Main concepts | | Research streams |
| --- | --- | --- | --- |
| | Governance | Leadership | |
| Team leadership of the board | Team production model Boardroom culture Collective decision making Board composition Board working style | Group processes Power relations Personalities Competence qualities Shared transformational leadership | Actual board behaviour (Huse, 2005, 2007; van Ees et al., 2009); Collective leadership (Burns, 1978; Bass, 1998 Locke, 2003); Leaderless work-groups (Barker, 1993) |
| Chair leadership on the board | Directors' roles Governance processes and structures Chair-CEO relationship | Facilitation Relationship building Motivation Trust Transactional leadership Collaboration | Authentic Leadership (Avolio & Gardner, 2005); Transactional Leadership (Bass & Avolio, 1990); Co-leadership (Heenan & Bennis, 1999); Board Leadership (Leblanc, 2005; McNulty et al., 2011) |
| Strategic leadership by the board | Board roles Board effectiveness Board involvement Stewardship Accountability | Empowerment Leadership style | Board and value creation (Huse, 2009); Board involvement in strategy (McNulty & Pettigrew, 1999; Hendry & Kiel, 2004) |

In the interests of encouraging others to join us and those scholars who have already begun to actively engage in and experiment with a 'governing leadership' perspective, we have identified the following list of research questions that is by no means exhaustive but demonstrates the range and scope of work that needs to be undertaken:

- What can the governance field learn from the leadership field and vice versa?
- How might we begin to creatively conceptualise the integration of governance with leadership processes within the contemporary organization? How do these relate to management processes?
- To what extent *are* and *should* boards be responsible for providing and promoting creative and innovative leadership within the organization?

*Table 7.2* Governing leadership: a summary

| Component | Key issues and ideas |
|---|---|
| Challenges | Balancing conformance and performance |
| | Determining an appropriate organizational strategy |
| | Ensuring effective stewardship |
| | Contending with internal board dynamics; board-management dynamics; board-shareholder dynamics |
| | Lack of knowledge/understanding about role or the organization |
| | Balancing trust and distrust; closeness and distance; dependence and interdependence; consensus and conflict |
| | How to 'add value' through harnessing the collective capability of board members to create and sustain competitive advantage |
| | Governing leadership has three dimensions: team leadership on the board; the chair's leadership of the board; strategic leadership by the board |
| Purpose of leadership | To energise governance efforts to go beyond matters of conformance to address issues of performance and opportunity, so as to 'add value' to the organization. |
| Values and norms | Discernment |
| | Teamwork |
| | Foster knowledge sharing and support others to fulfil their role |
| | Empower employees |
| | Enable the collective will |
| | Build trustful relationships |
| | Encourage open communication and robust discussion |
| Domains | Internally within the organization, mainly with senior management and externally with other key stakeholder |
| Leader | defines organizational reality through the articulation of a vision, and the generation of strategies to realise that vision |
| | Collaborative |
| | Strategic |
| | Develops trusting relationships; is open and honest |
| | Chair has the role of ensuring board processes are robust, transparent and well organised; co-leads with the CEO |
| | Absorb, understand, communicate strategic information and decisions |
| | Influence the strategic direction by balancing 'exploitation' of existing capabilities with 'exploration' of the new |
| Follower | Is often simultaneously a leader (e.g., senior management)—may be a co-leader |
| Leader-follower relationship | Trust, openness and honesty |
| | Collaboration |
| | Generative |
| | Transformative, not transactional |

- How do leadership and governance processes interplay within different strategic and institutional contexts?
- What can be done to promote a more energetic engagement between governance and leadership processes? To what extent should and can these be kept separate? Does the unstable environment provide a specific milieu for such an engagement?
- Do environments with unstable structural characteristics and those with unique historical and cultural developments require specific combinations of governance structures and leadership styles?
- Who leads governance? Who governs leadership? What come first?
- What is the connection between the board effectiveness and board leadership style?
- How does teamwork in the boardroom 'work'? Are leaderless boards really leaderless?
- What are the roles of boards in uncertain environments?
- How does a democratised governance structure shift the locus of leadership within organizations?
- What influence can a board have upon fostering leadership throughout the organization?
- How can leadership development and governance development activities be productively integrated?

By way of guidance, we would like to close the chapter by highlighting two important implications for future research. First, we propose integrative research efforts in investigating leadership and governance. We perceive these two are integral part of the governance discussions as we cannot see how directors can operate without providing leadership to the organizations that they are appointed to guard, support and advise. In this analysis, as in any other governance analysis, the importance of contextual factors needs to be taken into consideration. Roles of directors, relationships between the board and management and chair and the CEO are different in different legal systems of governance, and in different stages of organizational life cycle and in companies with different ownership structures. These factors should definitely shape future discussions on leadership and governance. Therefore, international comparative studies and longitudinal studies investigating the changing nature of directors' (leadership) roles over time may contribute to a better understanding of effective governance forms and practices.

Second, the conceptual integration of leadership and governance highlights the need for multi-theoretical approaches. Governance researchers have already emphasised the importance of multi-theoretical and multi-disciplinary research in governance (e.g., Cornforth, 2003; Huse, 2005; Tricker, 2000; Zahra & Pearce, 1989) and the limitations of single perspective approach (agency theory, in particular) in understanding complex phenomenon such as governance (Nicholson & Kiel, 2004). In a similar fashion, leadership researchers have also begun to build the case for multi-theoretical and multi-disciplinary research (Grint, 2005; Jackson & Parry, 2008: Avolio, Walumbwa & Weber, 2009). Indeed, there are interesting parallels between the two fields in terms of the predominance of one theoretical perspective over the past 20 years—transformational leadership has tended to shade out nascent theoretical perspectives in much the same way that agency theory has in the corporate governance field.

Simply by taking the time to become familiar with the key theoretical debates and methodological traditions within each reach community's field, we can begin to open up to other research possibilities in particular the very real possibility of working together in joint research projects and initiatives. This is a step that will no doubt be welcomed by research sponsors as well as practitioners, who are on a daily basis trying to trade off and bring together critical leadership and governance processes within the organizations they lead *and* govern.

# References

Aguilera, R. V., Filatotchev, I., Gospel, H., & Jackson, G. (2008). An organizational approach to comparative corporate governance: Costs, contingencies, and complementarities. *Organization Science*, 19(3), 475–492.

Alvarez, J. L., & Svejenova, S. (2005). *Sharing executive power: Roles and relationships at the top*. Cambridge, UK: Cambridge University Press.

Avolio, B. J., & Gardner, W. L. (2005). Authentic leadership development: Getting to the root of positive forms of leadership. *The Leadership Quarterly*, 16, 315–338.

Avolio, B. J., Walumbwa, F. O., & Weber, T. J. (2009). Leadership: Current theories, research, and future directions. *Annual Review of Psychology*, 60, 421–449.

Barker, J.R. (1993). Tightening the iron cage: Concertive control in self-managing teams. *Administrative Science Quarterly*, 38 (3), 408–37.

Barratt, R., & Korac-Kakabadse, N. (2002). Developing reflexive corporate leadership. *Corporate Governance: An International Review*, 2(3), 32–36.

Bass, B. M. (1990). From transactional to transformational leadership: Learning to share the vision. *Organizational Dynamics*, 18(3), 19–36.

Bass, B. M. (1998). *Transformational leadership: Industrial, military and educational impact*. Mahwah, NJ: Lawrence Erlbaum.

Bass, B. M., & Avolio, B. J. (1990b). Training and development of trans-formational leadership: Looking to 1992 and beyond. *European Journal of Industrial Training*, 14, 21–27.

Boal, K. B., & Hooijberg, R. (2000). Strategic leadership research: Moving on. *Leadership Quarterly*, 11, 515–549.

Boeker, W., & Karichalil, R. (2002). Entrepreneurial transitions: Factors influencing founder departure. *Academy of Management Journal*, 45(4), 818–826.

Bolman, L. G., & Deal, T. E. (2003). *Reframing organizations: Artistry, choice, and leadership*. San Francisco, CA: John Wiley & Sons.

Bryman, A., Collinson, D. Grint, K., Jackson, B., & Uhl-Bien, M. (Eds.). (2011). *Sage handbook of leadership*. London: Sage.

Burns, J. M. (1978). *Leadership*. New York: Harper & Row.

Caldwell, C., & Karri, R. (2005). Organizational governance and ethical systems: A covenantal approach to building trust. *Journal of Business Ethics*, 58(1–3), 249–259.

Carpenter, M. A., & Westphal, J. D. (2001). The strategic context of external network ties: Examining the impact of director appointments on board involvement in strategic decision making. *Academy of Management Journal*, 44, 639–661.

Carter, C. B., & Lorsch, J. W. (2004). *Back to the drawing board: Designing corporate boards for a complex world*. Boston, MA: Harvard Business School Press.

Carver, J., & Oliver, C. (2002). *Corporate boards that create value: Governing company performance from the boardroom*. San Francisco, CA: Jossey-Bass.

Chait, R. P., Ryan, W. P., & Taylor, B. E. (2005). *Governance as leadership: Reframing the work of nonprofit boards*. New Jersey: John Wiley & Sons.

Christensen, S., & Westenholz, A. (1999). Boards of directors as strategists in an enacted world: The Danish case. *Journal of Management and Governance*, 3, 261–286.

Cornforth, C. (2003). Introduction: The changing context of governance: Emerging issues and paradoxes. In C. Cornforth (Ed.), *The governance of public and nonprofit organizations: What do boards do?* (pp. 1–20). London, UK: Routledge.

Daily, C. M., Dalton, D. R., & Cannella, A. A. (2003). Corporate governance: Decades of dialogue and data. *Academy of Management Review*, 28(3), 371–382.

Davies, A. (2006). *Best practice in corporate governance: Building reputation and sustainable success*. Aldershot, UK: Gower.

Eisenhardt, K. M. (1989). Agency theory: An assessment and review. *Academy of Management Review*, 14(1), 57–74.

Erakovic, L. & Jackson, B. (2012). 'Promoting leadership in governance and governance in leadership' in Davila, A., Elvira, M., Ramirez, J. and Zapata-Cantu, L. (Eds). *Understanding Organizations in Complex, Emergent and Uncertain Environments*. Basingstoke, UK: Palgrave. pp 68-83.

Erakovic, L., Jackson, B., & Kudumula, S. (2011). Leadership and governance in the professional context: The case of an architectural firm. Paper prepared for the 27th EGOS Colloquium in Gothenburg, Sweden, July.

Filatotchev, I., & Boyd, B. K. (2009). Taking stock of corporate governance research while looking to the future. *Corporate Governance: An International Review*, 17(3), 257–265.

Filatotchev, I., Toms, S., & Wright, M. (2006). The firm's strategic dynamics and corporate governance life-cycle. *International Journal of Managerial Finance*, 2, 256–279.

Filatotchev, I., & Wright, M. (Eds.). (2005). *The life cycle of corporate governance: Corporate governance in the new global economy*. Cheltenham, UK: Edward Elgar.

Finkelstein, S., & Mooney, A. (2003). Not the usual suspects: How to use board processes to make boards better. *Academy of Management Executive*, 17(2), 101–113.

Forbes, D., & Milliken, F. (1999). Cognition and corporate governance: Understanding boards of directors as strategic decision-making groups. *Academy of Management Review*, 24(3), 489–505.

Gabrielsson, J., & Huse, M. (2004). Context, behaviour and evolution: Challenges in research on boards and governance. *International Studies of Management and Organisation*, 34(2), 11–36.

Gabrielsson, J., Huse, M., & Minichilli, A. (2007). Understanding the leadership role of the board chairperson through a team production approach. *International Journal of Leadership Studies*, 3(1), 21–39.

Gautier, A. (2002). Men behaving badly: Getting it right in the boardroom. *New Zealand Management*, 49(4), 26–32.

Geletkanycz, M. A., & Hambrick, D. C. (1997). The external ties of top executives: Implications for strategic choice and performance. *Administrative Science Quarterly*, 42, 654–681.

Grandori, A. (2000). Conjectures for a new research agenda on governance. *Journal of Management and Governance*, 4(1–2), 1–9.

Grandori, A. (2004). Introduction. In A. Grandori (Ed.), *Corporate governance and firm organization: Microfoundations and structural forms.* Oxford, UK: Oxford University Press, 1-30.

Gray, J. (2007). Myths and reality. *Canadian Business*, 80(16/17), 60–63.

Grint, K. (2005). *Leadership: Limits and possibilities.* London: Palgrave.

Hambrick, D. C. (1989). Guest editor's introduction: Putting top managers back in the strategy picture. *Strategic Management Journal*, 10 (Summer), 5–15.

Hambrick, D. C., & Mason, P. A. (1984). Upper echelons: The organization as a reflection of its top managers. *Academy of Management Review*, 9(2), 193–206.

Heenan, D. A., & Bennis, W. G. (1999). *Co-leadership, the power of great partnership.* New York, NY: John Wiley & Sons.

Hendry, K., & Kiel, G. (2004). The role of the board in firm strategy: Integrating agency and organisational control perspectives. *Corporate Governance*, 12(4), 500–520.

Heracleous, L. Th. (1999). The board of directors as leaders of the organisation. *Corporate Governance: An International Review*, 7(3), 256–265.

Holloway, D. A., & van Rhyn, D. (2005). Effective corporate governance reform and organisational pluralism: Reframing culture, leadership and followership. *Corporate Governance: Does Any Size Fit? Advances in Public Interest Accounting*, 11, 303–328.

Huse, M. (1994). Board-management relations in small firms: The paradox of simultaneous independence and interdependence. *Small Business Economics*, 6(1), 55–72.

Huse, M. (2005). Accountability and creating accountability: A framework for exploring behavioural perspectives of corporate governance. *British Journal of Management*, 16(S1), S65–S79.

Huse, M. (2007). *Boards, governance and value creation: The human side of corporate governance.* Cambridge, MA: Cambridge University Press.

Huse, M. (Ed.). (2009). *The value creating board: Corporate governance and organizational behaviour.* New York, NY: Routledge.

Huse, M., Gabrielsson, J., & Minichilli, A. (2009). How board contribute to value creation. In M. Huse (Ed.), *The value creating board: Corporate governance and organizational behaviour* (pp. 523–532). New York, NY: Routledge.

Huxham, C., & Vangen, S. (2000). Leadership in the shaping and implementation of collaboration agendas: How things happen in a (not quite) joined-up world. *Academy of Management Journal*, 43(6), 1154–1175.

Jackson, B., & Parry, K. (2008). *A very short, fairly interesting and reasonably cheap book about studying leadership.* London, UK: Sage Publications.

Johnson, J. L., Daily, C. M., & Ellstrand, A. E. (1996). Boards of directors: A review and research agenda. *Journal of Management*, 22(3), 409–438.

Jung, D., & Avolio, B. (2000). Opening the black box: An experimental investigation of the mediating effects of trust and value congruence on transformational and transactional leadership. *Journal of Organizational Behavior*, 21, 949–964.

Jung, D., & Sosik, J. (2002). Transformational leadership in work group: The role of empowerment, cohesiveness, and collective efficacy on perceived group performance. *Small Group Research*, 33, 313–336.

Kaufman, A., & Englander, E. (2005). A team production model of corporate governance. *Academy of Management Executive*, 19(3), 9–22.

Kocourek, P. F., Burger, C., & Birchard, B. (2003). Corporate governance: Hard facts about soft behaviors. *Strategy + Business*, 30, 1–12. Retrieved from http://strategy-business.com.

Kraatz, M. S., & Block, E. S. (2008). Organizational implications of institutional pluralism. In R. Greenwood, C. Oliver, K. Sahlin-Andersson, & R. Suddaby (Eds.), *The handbook of organizational institutionalism* (pp. 243–275). Thousand Oaks, CA: Sage.

Leblanc, R. (2005). Assessing board leadership. *Corporate Governance: An International Review*, 13, 654–666.

Leblanc, R., & Gillies, J. (2005). *Inside the boardroom: How boards really work and the coming revolution in corporate governance*. Mississauga, ONT: John Wiley & Sons.

Locke, E. A. (2003). Leadership: Starting at the top, in C. L. Pearce and J. A. Conger (eds), *Shared leadership: Reframing the hows and whys of leadership*. Thousand Oaks, CA: Sage, 271–84.

Lorsch, J. W., & MacIver, E. A. (1989). *Pawns or potentates: The reality of America's corporate boards*. Boston, MA: Harvard Business School Press.

Lynall, M. D., Golden, B. R., & Hillman, A. (2003). Board composition from adolescence to maturity: Multitheoretic view. *Academy of Management Review*, 28(3), 416–432.

McGregor, L. (2000). *The human face of corporate governance*. New York, NY: Palgrave.

McNulty, T., & Pettigrew, A. (1999). Strategists on the board. *Organization Studies*, 20(1), 47–74.

McNulty, T., Pettigrew, A., Jobome, G., & Morris, C. (2011). The role, power and influence of company chairs. *Journal of Management and Governance*, 15(1), 91–121.

March, J. (1995). Disposable organizations and the rigidities of imagination. *Organization*, 2(3/4), 427–440.

Nicholson, G. J., & Kiel, G. C. C. (2004). A framework for diagnosing board effectiveness. *Corporate Governance: An International Review*, 12(4), 442–460.

Nooteboom, B. (1996). Trust, opportunism, and governance: A process and control model. *Organization Studies*, 17(6), 985–1011.

O'Toole, J., Galbraith, J., & Lawler, E. E. (2002). When two (or more) heads are better than one: The promises and the pitfalls of shared leadership. *California Management Review*, 44, 65–83.

Pearce, J., & Zahra, S. (1991). The relative power of CEOs and boards of directors: Associations with corporate performance. *Strategic Management Journal*, 12(2), 135–153.

Pettigrew, A., & McNulty, T. (1995). Power and influence in and around the boardroom. *Human Relations*, 48(8), 845–873.

Pugliese, A., Bezemer, P., Zattoni, A., Huse, M., Van den Bosch, F. A. J., & Volberda, H. W. (2009). Board of directors' contribution to strategy: A literature review and research agenda. *Corporate Governance: An International Review*, 17(3), 292–306.

Pye, A. (2002). Corporate directing: Governing, strategising and leading in action. *Corporate Governance: An International Review*, 10(3), 153–163.

Ravasi, D., & Zattoni, A. (2006). Exploring the political side of board involvement in strategy: A study of mixed-ownership institutions. *Journal of Management Studies*, 43(8), 1671–1702.

Roberts, J., & Stiles, P. (1999). The relationship between chairmen and chief executives: Competitive or complementary roles? *Long Range Planning*, 32(1), 36–48.

Rost, J. C. (1993). *Leadership for the twenty-first century*. Westport, CT: Praeger.

Sally, D. (2002). Co-leadership: Lessons from the Republican Rome. *California Management Review*, 44, 65–83.

Storey, J. (2005). What next for strategic-level leadership? *Leadership*, 1(10), 89–104.

Sullivan, B., & Kelly, M. (2008). Activists in the boardroom. *Corporate Board*, (July/August), 10–14.

Sundaramurthy, C., & Lewis, M. (2003). A control and collaboration: Paradoxes of governance. *Academy of Management Review*, 28(3), 397–415.

Tricker, R. I. (1994). *International corporate governance: Text, readings and cases*. New Jersey: Prentice Hall.

Tricker, R. I. (2000). Editorial: Corporate governance: The subject whose time has come. *Corporate Governance: An International Review*, 8(4), 289–296.

van Ees, H., Gabrielsson, J., & Huse, M. (2009). Toward a behavioural theory of boards and corporate governance. *Corporate Governance: An International Review*, 17(3), 307–319.

Zahra, S., & Filatotchev, I. (2004). Governance of the entrepreneurial threshold firm: A knowledge-based perspective. *Journal of Management Studies*, 41(5), 885–897.

# 8 Revitalising or Revolutionising?
## Leadership Scholarship

## Introduction

The preceding five chapters have illustrated how a deep engagement with context-specific issues, needs and challenges offers a new basis for forming theorisations that are tailor-made to guide practice in different contexts. Using the theory-building framework set out in Chapter 2, we have explored the organizational contexts of supervisory management, human resource management, innovation and entrepreneurship, strategy and governance, identifying how each has different implications for leadership theory and practice. Attention has gone to the specific challenges that are of particular salience to each of these contexts. We have proposed a particular purpose for leadership in each. We have highlighted values and norms, along with the boundaries, or domains, of leadership action that we normatively argue are relevant to leadership in these different settings. We have also explored the attributes, behaviours, rights, roles and responsibilities of leaders and followers in these different contexts and the kind of leader-follower relationship the balance of the analysis implies.

In this chapter, our focus shifts to the context of this very endeavour—that of leadership scholarship. We turn our theory-building framework back on ourselves, to explore, firstly, the challenges which impede the further development of the leadership studies field. We then use this analysis to formulate a statement of purpose intended to guide those who want to make a leadership contribution to leadership studies. We consider the values and norms that we think have most salience to leadership in this context, as well as the domains of leadership in leadership studies, before turning to consider the attributes, behaviours, roles, rights and responsibilities that leaders and followers in leadership studies might benefit from and the kind of relationship that is implied as a consequence. The propositions here will likely seem provocative to some; however, we make no apologies for advocating that leadership scholars ought themselves to practice leadership and have their practice informed by theory.

## Challenges in Leadership Studies

Amongst the multiplicity of theories, perspectives and methodologies that scholars bring to the production of leadership knowledge, there are many research problems that warrant further investigation. Those matters are not our primary concern here. Rather, our interest is the state or characteristics of the field overall and the kinds of challenges we believe it is facing, matters that impede the extent to which leadership studies is an intellectually vibrant community offering insightful and provocative knowledge for the world of leadership practice. As you may recall, in Chapter 1, we identified a number of concerns with the 'leadership science' approach which dominates leadership studies. We reiterate those concerns here, however our analysis now proceeds by deploying our theory-building model, as we seek to outline what leadership in leadership studies might entail.

A very significant challenge with this field of inquiry, then, is that much of the knowledge produced is so modest in scope and, simultaneously, often so abstracted in its conception of phenomena as precisely defined 'variables', that its translation to the world of practice remains highly unlikely (Alvesson, 1996; Tourish, 2015). The growing influence of critical approaches to leadership (Collinson, 2011), which we also explored in Chapter 1, is often motivated in part by such concerns.

We suggest a *typical* example of this concern is a recent study in which the authors report finding "support for the presence of change oriented leadership having a direct effect on firm performance". They further identify that "firms with change oriented CEO's that embody obsessive passion do not benefit from higher firm performance" while "CEOs with harmonious passion strengthen [the] relationship between change-oriented leadership and firm performance" (Sirén, Patel & Wincent, 2016, p. 653). No doubt this study meets all the requirements for a respectable, credible piece of research, and we do not single it out as somehow especially egregious or problematic. However, drawing a connection between 'change oriented CEO's' and 'firm performance' is something practitioners and market analysts already do every day, so no contribution to practice seems likely to arise from this, while the invention of a distinction between 'obsessive' and 'harmonious' passion also seems unlikely to translate into knowledge of practical value. We suggest studies and findings of this character meet the Tourish test of 'sterile preoccupations' and 'unrelenting triviality' (2015, pp. 137–138), as do so many other studies in our field today.

While we have noted earlier that we accept the value of such 'normal science' efforts to incrementally expand a field of knowledge, the sheer dominance of work of this nature, especially amongst those adhering to the 'leadership science' paradigm, is problematic. Closely related challenges include an excessive, fetishised concern with methodological rigour at the expense of relevance and a lack of attention to bold, difficult or controversial questions (Alvesson, 1996; Spoelstra, Butler & Delaney, 2016; Wilson, 2016). Basic assumptions and established traditions are questioned far too infrequently (Hunter, Bedell-Avers & Mumford, 2007; Wilson, 2016). Overall, one might venture to say that far too much passive following of conventional thinking is occurring within leadership studies and that there is far too little leadership aiming to shake up the status quo, confront difficult problems and offer genuinely novel approaches. Incrementalism has its place in the research process. However, when it dominates the field to the extent which it now does in this field, the result is insufficient thought leadership and an excess of subservient followership. The situation makes for a lot of deadly dull prose and, more importantly, fails to connect with the urgent and serious challenges facing leadership practice, such as those we have identified throughout this book.

The manner in which the 'leadership science' paradigm routinely ignores the challenges posed to it by interpretive, social constructionist and/or critical perspectives can also be taken to indicate an excess of passive following, as scholars adopt and then maintain narrow foci of attention, rather than ranging more broadly. Surely, Burns's (1978) proposition, that conflict is a key aspect of leadership which fosters personal, organizational and societal development, is widely known, yet in avoiding the conflict that exists between 'leadership science' and alternatives to it, the productive potential of what we might learn from each other is being missed. The compartmentalisation of the field into divergent camps which, by and large, simply do not engage with each other is highly problematic. When the field's so-called leading journal shows so little interest or regard for the value of alternative perspectives and approaches (Spoelstra et al., 2016), it is little wonder that other fora more welcoming of diverse perspectives have emerged. When the methodological and epistemological drawbridges go up to the extent that is now evident in *The Leadership Quarterly* (Spoelstra et al., 2016), scholars who hold genuine and deeply considered reservations with the 'leadership science' paradigm find their work is excluded and marginalised. This, we think, is at odds with the kind of scholarly leadership that should be role modelled in leadership studies.

A further concern is the functionalist orientation which dominates leadership studies, a frame of thinking which routinely forecloses consideration of non-instrumental, socio-political, aesthetic, embodied and philosophical concerns that enable a stepping away from an obsessive concern to enhance workplace performance (Alvesson & Deetz, 2000; Parker, 2002). We think what is at stake in workplace leadership, for example, is so much more interesting than questions of how manager-leaders influence worker-followers to work harder and longer, yet this narrowly instrumental, performative focus is nigh on hegemonic in leadership studies, and has been for some time (Alvesson, 1996; Wilson, 2016). This orientation may have the wider effect of inhibiting a greater focus on values and questions of higher purpose by practitioners, directing their attention to the performative effects and organizational benefits that can accrue, rather than the human benefits that better leadership may offer and the human challenges it entails (Ciulla, 2004).

The ideological character of much leadership scholarship, in which the presence of a heroic leader is simply assumed from the outset to be desirable and potent, is of considerable concern (Alvesson & Kärreman, 2015, Spoelstra, 2013). Other sources of influence, such as market conditions, legislation, policy, strategy and culture, are routinely ignored in leadership studies, as if a leader's 'agency' were somehow free from the influence of matters of 'structure' (Giddens, 1984; Wilson, 2016). The problematic inclination toward 'adjective leadership' theorising is linked to this, where one personal quality of leaders is singled out and deemed so important as to warrant it forming the basis of a theory. These factors result in an over-emphasis on the leader's qualities and impact at the expense of any understanding of the contribution of followers or the influence of context, implying, too, that 'leadership', or at least our understanding of it, can be reduced to one key personal attribute or one key process (Alvesson, 1996; Wilson, 2016). This reductionist tendency, we argue, is starkly at odds with the multi-faceted character of the leadership phenomenon and how it may be understood (Grint, 2000; Ladkin, 2010; Sinclair, 2007); and therefore serves practitioners poorly, implying they simply need to adopt a particular formula and all will be well. Advancing simplistic, formulaic approaches to what is a complex world of practice fails to connect deeply with the challenges involved, rendering such scholarship of little real value.

The dominance of psychology, as the underpinning disciplinary training and orientation of many involved in leadership studies (Gardner, Lowe, Moss, Mahoney & Cogliser, 2010), may well be an important contributor to these various concerns. This is not to say psychology does not have important contributions to make to our understanding of leadership. But so too do philosophy, history, sociology and the arts and humanities, for example, yet only a small proportion of organizational leadership studies call on these traditions (Gardner et al., 2010). Compounding this, is the important institutional driver of the quantitative predilections of (mostly) US-based journals, along with the graduate education opportunities for aspiring leadership scholars in the US, many of whom are functionalist, 'scientific' and psychology-dominated in orientation (Tourish, 2015; Wilson, 2016). A broader church of leadership scholarship needs to be built, one that welcomes and embraces the true diversity of those with an interest in leadership.

What all the above goes to suggest, then, is that leadership studies as a field is well overdue for an intellectual revolution to shake it up. This substantial shift should be driven by levels of reflexivity amongst leadership scholars that have not traditionally been encouraged. To this end, we should be regularly asking such qestions as:

- is my study merely following an established line of inquiry?;
- what real world challenges does my work contribute to addressing?;
- what non-instrumental human benefits may come from my work?;
- what ethics and politics inform my work?;
- what disciplinary lens can I add to my core orientation, enabling me to engage more richly with the phenomena of leadership?; and
- what can I learn from those who disagree most strongly with me about the assumptions and limits of my preferred paradigm?

These and related questions challenge us as scholars to go beyond incrementalism, to resist careerist pressures, to question orthodoxy and to seek out how we mightt each make a more powerful leadership contribution. Addressing these questions means taking risks and being courageous -- just as we exhort leadership practitioners, so we need to exhort ourselves.

This will mean we need to bring greater imagination into the research process. It means collaborating with others whose ideas challenge our own, in the hope that the constructive conflict gives rise to new understandings, just as Burns advocated (1978). If doing all this invokes self-doubt and perhaps even fear, then this likely brings scholars closer to the space in which reflexive leaders operate (Ford, Harding & Learmonth, 2008); thereby guding us to practice what we preach. To the extent that we can learn through *first-hand experience* that leadership practice is often filled with uncertainty and a sense of danger (Grint, 2000; Sinclair, 2007), this will likely improve our ability to develop theories that recognise the complex nature of leadership and to offer leadership education and development that enables deep learning and positive change.

The challenges that we and other commentators argue face leadership studies are ones that affect all scholars working in the field. Irrespective of our individual paradigmatic stance, favoured theories and methods and research focus, we *all* have a stake in trying to address these issues. Working on our own leadership first, then, inspiring others could—and we believe should—revolutionise leadership studies.

## Purpose in a Revolutionised Leadership Studies

The analysis presented above provides something by way of a roadmap for the challenges that leadership in leadership studies (LiLS) is faced with, pointing toward both the kinds of *ends* or results which LILS needs to seek to achieve and the kinds of *means* that might be most conducive for so doing. However, our theory-building model asks us to develop a specific statement of purpose for leadership in a given context, one that goes beyond our general statement of purpose for leadership that we offered in Chapter 2, namely *'enabling the achievement of shared goals, via means that are consistent with shared values'*. The question of the purpose of leadership also directs us to think about the kinds of ends or results for which leadership is called into being and, we think, to contemplate the kinds of means to be deemed intsrtumentally, ethically and aesthetically acceptable in striving to secure the desired ends.

In thinking about the purpose of LiLS, then, we think the wider context of academia, in particular its collegial and scholarly traditions, values and norms, as well as the emergence in recent decades of institutional forces and practices which erode these, are also important to consider. The normative expectations of the academy include important matters such as the fearless pursuit of knowledge; the importance of open debate and dialogue amongst scholars; the expectation of methodical, unbiased and transparent data collection, analysis and reporting; the nurturing of future scholars; and the expectation that scholarly knowledge serves humanity as a whole (see, for example, Academy of Management Code of Ethics, 2006). However, considerable concern has been raised about the increasing influence of managerialism and careerism in academia, as well as the adverse effects of audit regimes and journal rankings on scholarship and collegiality (e.g., Dearlove, 1997; Khurana, 2007; Willmott, 2011).

We believe LiLS should be informed by these matters, cleaving to the best of the collegial and scholarly traditions, values and norms and countering those forces and practices which seek to erode them, whilst also taking account of the particular challenges facing leadership studies. As a consequence, we propose the following statement of purpose for LiLS: *enabling the advancement of leadership knowledge that goes beyond instrumental concerns to provide genuine insight and benefit to all, by adhering to the best of the collegial and scholarly traditions, values and norms of academia.*

In considering this statement of purpose, we note how this kind of leadership contribution is one that is open to all, hence it encourages participation and aligns with distributed, shared, and pluralistic accounts of leadership (Denis, Langley & Sergi, 2012; Gronn, 2000; Pearce & Sims, 2000). The statement also speaks to the kinds of leadership practice and process that are envisaged, that which goes beyond instrumentalism, seeks to benefit all and adheres to academic values. Conceptualising LiLS in practice and process terms connects with a wider suite of theories that adopt a similar basis for thinking about leadership, both within and beyond the 'leadership science' paradigm (Jackson & Parry, 2011). Its grounding in various normative concerns also means ethical considerations are placed at the 'heart' of this approach, consistent with Ciulla's guidance (1995). For all these reasons, we hope, then, that the proposed statement of purpose is one that leadership scholars will recognise as of direct salience to leadership studies.

Advancing this purpose is something to which all leadership scholars could and, we argue, should contribute. Despite the divergent and often incommensurate perspectives that are prevalent in the field, this statement of purpose could serve as a uniting factor for the revolution we are calling for, implying an avoidance of blood-letting in the process (for a start, this would be inconsistent with the best of collegial and scholarly traditions, norms and values!) and instead encouraging a shared sense of community that carries us beyond that which otherwise divides us. Every act which is consistent with this purpose, whether large or modest in its impact, can be understood as contributing to it, as scholarly endeavours are not lived as a grand design, but from moment to moment. At each moment of one's scholarly practice, there exists the potential to move beyond what is already thought and already known, in pursuit of knowledge that can provide insight and benefit to all. In orienting one's scholarly pursuits to going beyond merely instrumental concerns in advancing leadership knowledge, seeking to benefit all and adhering to the best of the collegial and scholarly traditions, norms and values of academia, this leadership contribution can become part of the daily lived experience of all leadership scholars, a collective and cumulative shift in energy and focus that could indeed revolutionise leadership studies.

## Values and Norms for Leadership in Leadership Studies

Turning now to the next key question which our framework for theory building requires of us, we focus on exploring *what values and norms ought to guide and constrain leadership in this setting?* By this stage in the theory-building process certain matters, namely the challenges of salience to leadership in this context and the purpose we have proposed for it, are now to be taken as 'givens' as we advance the theorisation.

The preceding discussion, then, makes evident that the values and norms accepted by academia more broadly are important for guiding ethically appropriate leadership in leadership studies. These influences imply, too, that LiLS ought not be directive in orientation, nor can it simply assume that 'followers' have some developmental gap which a leadership contribution needs to address. Nuturing future scholars, an important value and norm of the academy, does imply a more experienced scholar providing advice and guidance to one with less experience. Nonetheless, we think the influence of the best of the traditions, norms and values of the academy also means there is strongly implied egalitarian and communitarian mindset that shapes LiLS and that a concern with community building is an important value and norm for LiLS.

Turning back to the challenges we identified as facing leadership studies, and which informed the purpose statement for LiLS; addressing these matters also implies certain values and norms are important to the practice of leadership in leadership studies. Valuing constructive conflict and a willingness to listen to those with whom one disagrees is vital. Valuing bold or difficult questions, novelty of thought and a focus on the serious, substantive issues facing practitioners are all important to a LiLS that can enable positive change in our field. Developing connections between otherwise divergent perspectives and approaches, to aid in breaking down silos within the field, could be an especially useful norm for guiding LiLS at this stage of its history. As our review of the field in Chapter 1 showed, leadership studies in the past did deploy this kind of multi-disciplinary approach, and it is only in the modern era that a more uni-disciplinary approach has come to dominate.

We hope the connections we have made in this book, between leadership knowledge and knowledge about supervisory management, human resource management, innovation and entrepreneurship, strategy and governance, offers an example of the kind of bridge-building efforts that we think need to be adopted as a key value. A wider concern with human well-being, beyond merely instrumental concerns, is also implied if LiLS is to help in the revolution we have advocated is needed. As part of all this, a norm of reflexivity needs to be encouraged, in which leadership scholars seeking to make a leadership contribution recognise that, in trying to work on or in the field, they must simultaneously reflect on how they go about this. Doing this, we think, suggests humility is a further key value that should inform LiLS.

## Domains of Leadership Activity

The next aspect of our model to be addressed requires us to consider: *upon which parts of our lives and in what ways ought LiLS be permitted to act?* These questions are intended to demand further consideration of the boundaries intended to be placed on leadership action, to further ensure its ethical grounding. LiLS, as envisaged here, is primarily concerned with advancing scholarly contributions and with fostering the intellectual vibrancy and capability of the scholarly community; hence its prime focus is located in the public, professional domain of scholarly work. These efforts, however, should not be located only within the setting of the lecture hall or campus staff club: active engagement as a public intellectual is an important domain for LiLS.

Beyond this, given we have also noted the importance of reflexivity to inform LiLS, this implies that work on the self, not merely the external object of one's inquiry, also forms part of the domain of LiLS. And, in the context of the collegiality which we have indicated is a key value for LiLS, this reflexive effort could readily be undertaken in collaboration with others, thus crossing into the interpersonal domain. In such instances, the values and norms identified earlier can act as guides for action as to what constitutes an appropriate leadership contribution in the personal domain of a fellow scholar.

## Leader Personal Attributes, Behaviours, Rights, Responsibilities and Role

Thus far, our exploration of leadership in leadership studies has addressed the 'outer layer' of our theory-building model (see Diagram 2.2). We have considered the challenges which, we argue, face those involved in leadership studies, identified a purpose in light of those issues and its location within the wider academy, and discussed the values and norms which we propose ought to inform leadership in this context. We have also identified the domains of life in which LiLS operates: the public, professional work of one's scholarly inquiries; the self, as part of a reflexive effort to examine one's own leadership contribution; and the personal domain of other scholars, as part of a collaborative reflexive engagement. Given all these matters, attention now turns to the question of *what are the personal attributes, behaviours, rights, responsibilities and role of the leaders in leadership studies?* In considering this, our analysis draws out what is implied by the preceding discussion as to the expectations held here of leaders in leadership studies.

What should be immediately clear is that the approach taken here does not imply that holding a formal position need form part of LiLS; hence, there is no need to discuss the role, rights and responsibilities of leaders in leadership studies. This means the focus goes to personal attributes and behaviours. From the preceding analysis, a reflexive stance as regards one's leadership efforts is clearly a key issue. We identified earlier some important questions that could form part of this reflexive practice (see page __). To this, we add that contemplation about the nature and focus of one's leadership contribution is also needed, so that answers can be formed to questions of 'how', 'where', 'with whom', 'on what topics', 'relying on what assumptions and values' and 'for what ends' the leadership contribution is to be enacted. Thoughtful reflection on the self, in particular its intellectual strengths and predilections and its habitual ways of engaging with others and managing itself, is a further element of this reflexive practice. Engaging in these reflexive behaviours aids in fostering a mindful leadership approach that plays to one's personal strengths. This means, too, that 'being the best I can be', according to our own individual character, situation and ability, is a vital aspect of leadership in leadership studies.

Other important attributes and behaviours which we suggest will support a constructive approach to leadership in leadership studies comprise an habitual questioning of basic assumptions and established findings, and engagement with those who hold different views, so as to learn from them and spark up constructive conflict, a la Burns (1978). Attentiveness to the serious challenges facing the world of leadership practice, helping to shape a research agenda that generates substantive and not merely instrumental contributions, can also inform the 'public intellectual' contribution which we see as a vital component of leadership in leadership studies. Engagement with diverse traditions and disciplines beyond one's core orientation will enable an inclusive leadership approach, and one which continuously seeks to 'go beyond' current boundaries. These behaviours provide a potential antidote to the problems of reductionist theorising and methodological fetishism discussed earlier. A concern to foster the strength of one's community through encouraging the development of others constitutes a further leadership contribution.

From the above analysis, the overall picture that emerges is that to engage in LiLS entails nothing more than being a mindful, intellectually curious and rigorous scholar, aiming to make a substantive contribution to the betterment of humanity and striving to work in accordance with the best traditions, values and norms of the academy. It relies in large measure on behaviours that we would expect to be instilled through our training and socialisation as scholars, supported by whatever intellectual capacities with which nature has endowed each of us. LiLS as described here, then, could simply be part of the normal expectations that leadership scholars have of themselves and other members of this community. Adopting the behaviours discussed here, however, will aid in overcoming the excessive amount of passive following of conventional thinking which currently plagues the field. No permission is needed to take on this leadership contribution. It is, quite simply, a matter of seizing the opportunities that are before each of us: Carpe Diem!

## Follower Personal Attributes, Behaviours, Rights, Responsibilities and Role

In light of the analysis we have presented in this chapter, there is no requirement to identify follower roles, responsibilities and related rights as part of our approach to LiLS. Focus thus turns to the attributes and behaviours involved in the practice of followership in leadership studies. And, what should be evident is that the kind of approach we seek here is that which challenges and engages in debate with those offering a leadership contribution. The contribution quite properly involves active support of leaders' efforts, in seeking to strengthen and extend a line of inquiry. However, questioning what has been proposed is also vital.

The nature of knowledge production, in which each new study should offer something new to our understanding, suggests that 'leading' and 'following' may be especially fluid states in this context. A junior scholar may 'lead the field' via the questions they ask, the methods they use or the findings their study gives rise to. Yet simultaneously, as we engage with and learn from the work of others, as we cite their work approvingly or otherwise, we follow the pathway they have helped shape. Notably, then, the follower behaviours we advocate can result in a reversal, or switching, of the leader/follower position: in identifying limitations in what has been proposed (by someone enacting a leadership contribution) and how it can be improved upon, the follower thereby steps into making a leadership contribution.

To the extent that scholars are continuously engaged in this kind of interaction with the work of others, we may understand that followership, like leadership, is a normal part of scholarly work. The emphasis we place on our conception, however, is that critical questioning of established positions and common assumptions, going beyond a merely instrumental orientation, reaching across disciplinary and paradigmatic boundaries and forging a strong connection with the serious issues facing the world of practice are all key expectations. Engaging in these behaviours will aid in the revolution we advocate is needed, helping us to shift the field to become one where concerns about 'sterile preoccupations' and 'unrelenting triviality' can no longer be put forward as valid criticisms (Tourish, 2015, pp. 137–138).

## The Leader-Follower Relationship

The focus and purpose of the leader-follower relationship here turns on contributing to the overall purpose of LiLS, namely *enabling the advancement of leadership knowledge that goes beyond instrumental concerns to provide genuine insight and benefit to all, by adhering to the best of the collegial and scholarly traditions, values and norms of academia*. This clearly indicates that attention goes to scholarly concerns in this relationship. Further, given we propose that leadership scholars should understand themselves as needing to offer *both* leadership and followership contributions as part of their membership of this community, focus must also be placed on mutual support to enable these contributions.

The fluid nature of 'leading' and 'following' in leadership studies discussed above means the relationship is not typically one grounded in clearly defined roles and responsibilities. This, we think, means mutual respect and collegiality are central features. It also means that the deference often accorded to esteemed professors needs to be treated with some caution, insofar as it could result in a 'fixing' of the leader-follower relationship in ways we think are at odds with the purpose of LiLS. Those involved in the development of emerging scholars, and in leadership education and development, must be especially mindful of 'handing over' leadership opportunities and taking on a followership role in order to strengthen the overall leadership capability of the field.

Shared reflexivity is also indicated as a focal point of the leader-follower relationship here, drawing on the reflexive practices identified earlier. This in turn implies high levels of trust are needed and, again, that collegial ways of interacting, rather than unequal power relations, should be important features of this relationship. This reflexive, trusting, collegial relationship serves to foster the inclination and skill to question convention and orthodoxy. In bringing the self of the leader and follower into focus, recognising the sheer fluidity of these states, reflexive examination of the *first-hand* experience of leadership and followership can act as a source of inspiration, helping scholars go beyond instrumental concerns to examine the wider human dimensions of the leadership phenomenon. A shared experience of inquiry, discovery and personal and professional development, in which flipping between leading and following is understood as both normal and desirable, thus characterises the kind of leader-follower relationship that will best serve to advance the leadership studies field.

Table 8.1 provides a summary of our model for LiLS.

*Table 8.1* Leadership in leadership studies: a summary

| Component | Key issues and ideas |
|---|---|
| Challenges | A sharp divide exists between theory and practice: the field is plagued by research grounded in 'sterile preoccupations' resulting in findings that are marked by 'unrelenting triviality' (Tourish, 2015, pp. 137–138). |
| | 'Normal science' incrementalism dominates, but more questioning of dominant paradigms and a greater focus on real world challenges and bold, difficult and controversial questions is needed. |
| | Methodological fetishism prevails, meaning the concern for rigor crowds out a focus on relevance. |
| | There is insufficient dialogue and constructive conflict occurring between the 'leadership science paradigm' and alternative perspectives. |
| | Functionalist, instrumental and performative concerns dominate, but a wider orientation is needed. |
| | Much leadership knowledge is ideological in character, reinforcing the status of 'heroic leaders', assuming a surfeit of 'agency' and lacking attention to issues of 'structure'. |
| | 'Adjective leadership' facilitates reductionist tendencies and formulaic approaches. |
| | A psychological lens dominates leadership research. |
| | There is a need for reflexivity amongst leadership scholars, asking questions of our research approach. |
| | There is too much passive following of conventional thinking and too little leadership that seeks to shake up the status quo, confront difficult challenges and offer genuinely novel approaches. |
| Purpose of leadership | Enabling the advancement of leadership knowledge that goes beyond instrumental concerns to provide genuine insight and benefit to all, by adhering to the best of the collegial and scholarly traditions, values and norms of academia. |
| Values and norms | Collegial and scholarly traditions, values and norms of the academy. |
| | Foster future scholars and contribute to community building. |
| | Egalitarian and non-directive leadership approach. |
| | Value constructive conflict and willingness to listen to competing views. |
| | Value bold, difficult questions, novelty of though and a focus on the serious, substantive issues facing practitioners. |
| | Seek out connections between divergent perspectives and approaches. |
| | Concern with human well-being. |
| | Reflexivity as to one's own scholarly practice. |
| | Humility as to one's own limitations. |
| Domains | Public, professional domain of scholarly work. |
| | Public intellectual domain. |
| | Intrapersonal domain—reflexive work on the self. |
| | Interpersonal domain—collaborative reflexive work with peers. |

*(Continued)*

*Table 8.1* (Continued)

| Component | Key issues and ideas |
|---|---|
| Leader | Not a formal role with rights and responsibilities; contribution open to all; normal part of one's scholarly contribution. |
| | Reflexive practitioner, aware of one's intellectual, intrapersonal and interpersonal strengths, predilections and habits, seeking to 'be the best I can be'. |
| | Critically questions established positions and common assumptions. |
| | Reaches across paradigmatic and disciplinary boundaries. |
| | Goes beyond a merely instrumental orientation. |
| | Forges a strong connection with real-world issues. |
| | Seeks to foster others' development and the community. |
| | Adheres to the best of the traditions, norms and values of the academy. |
| Follower | Not a formal role with rights and responsibilities; normal part of one's scholarly contribution. |
| | Challenges and engages with those offering a leadership contribution; provides support and seeks to strengthen what leaders have offered. |
| | Steps into the leadership role whenever possible. |
| | Follows by learning from others. |
| Leader-follower relationship | Scholarly focus, to advance the purpose of LiLS. |
| | Leading and following are interchangeable states, and scholars are expected to make both kinds of contribution. |
| | Mutual support, trust, respect, collegiality. |
| | Shared reflexivity and shared experience of inquiry, discovery and personal and professional development. |

## Conclusion

In this book, our aim has been to explain why leadership theory and practice needs to be revitalised and to demonstrate how this can be done. Our core proposition is that because leadership arises in, and to be effective must respond to, a given context, that theory-building efforts should likewise pay heed to the contexts in which practice arises, seeking to offer advice that is attends to the issues salient to that context. This approach constitutes a localist alternative to the universalist hegemony that is generally advocated within leadership studies; indeed, in this chapter, we have argued that leadership studies is itself facing a crisis of leadership, one which warrants a tailored response.

Our theory-building model comprises seven main areas of focus, each of which may be called on in relation to a specific context, to help inform what may constitute a relevant approach for that context. These issues are:

* the challenges that leadership will encounter and must address;
* the purpose of leadership;

- the values and norms that should inform leadership;
- the domains, or boundaries, of leadership;
- leaders' desired personal attributes, behaviours, rights, responsibilities and role;
- followers' desired personal attributes, behaviours, rights, responsibilities and role;
- the leader-follower relationship, in particular its purpose, focus and boundaries.

Over the course of the book, we have sought to demonstrate the fertility of examining these issues in different contexts, through our proposals for revitalised approaches to leading in the contexts of supervisory management, human resource management, innovation and entrepreneurship, strategy, governance and, finally, leadership scholarship. We have demonstrated different ways in which the model can be deployed, through methodically working from the outer to the inner circles, and through a more dynamic process of drawing in its different elements in grappling with the nature of effective leadership in a given context.

The various formulations we have developed are, of course, still one step removed from the unique settings an actual practitioner will encounter and are, hence, heuristic rather than prescriptive in orientation. However, our theory-building approach still brings us much closer to the messy realities of practice then conventional, univeralist or abstracted theorising can achieve. The formulations offered also enable ready adaptation to better fit the needs of a specific setting, while the model itself can clearly be applied to examine many other contexts, something we certainly hope will happen.

Our assumption in this book has been that leadership is not easy or straightforward, hence efforts to theorise leadership should fully connect with and relate to its complex nature. Our approach does not lend itself to a neat and tidy two-by-two boxed diagram, as is so commonly advanced in our discipline. We have offered direct critique of many of the most influential ideas and conventions in our field of study, building the case as to why it needs to be revitalised. In trying to embrace the challenges of leading in different contexts and by paying heed to their particular demands, we have sought to demonstrate how leadership theory and practice can be revitalised. Looking ahead, our hope is that others will now take up the agenda and approach advocated and exemplified here in order to revitalise leadership theory and practice in as many contexts as possible. Lead or follow on!

# References

Academy of Management (2006). Code of ethics. *Academy of Management Website, AOM.org*. Retrieved from http://aom.org/uploadedFiles/About_AOM/Governance/AOM_Code_of_Ethics.pdf.

Alvesson, M. (1996). Leadership studies: From procedure and abstraction to reflexivity and situation. *The Leadership Quarterly*, 7(4), 455–485.

Alvesson, M., & Deetz, S. A. (2000). *Doing critical management research*. London: Sage.

Alvesson, M., & Kärreman, D. (2015). Intellectual failure and ideological success in organization studies: The case of transformational leadership. *Journal of Management Inquiry*, 25(2), 139–152.

Burns, J. M. (1978). *Leadership*. New York: Harper & Row.

Ciulla, J. B. (1995). Leadership ethics: Mapping the terrain. *Business Ethics Quarterly*, 5(1), 5–28.

Ciulla, J. B. (Ed.). (2004). *Ethics, the heart of leadership* (2nd ed.). Westport, CT: Praeger.

Collinson, D. (2011). Critical leadership studies. In A. Bryman, D. Collinson, K. Grint, B. Jackson, & M. Uhl-Bien (Eds.), *The Sage handbook of leadership* (pp. 181–194). London: Sage.

Dearlove, J. (1997). The academic labour process: From collegiality and professionalism to managerialism and proletarianisation? *Higher Education Review*, 30(1), 56–74.

Denis, J.-L., Langley, A., & Sergi, V. (2012). Leadership in the plural. *The Academy of Management Annals*, 6(1), 211–283.

Ford, J., Harding, N., & Learmonth, M. (2008). *Leadership as identity: Constructions and deconstructions*. Basingstoke: Palgrave Macmillan.

Gardner, W. L., Lowe, K. B., Moss, T. W., Mahoney, K. T., & Cogliser, C. C. (2010). Scholarly leadership of the study of leadership: A review of The Leadership Quarterly's second decade, 2000–2009. *The Leadership Quarterly*, 21(6), 922–958.

Giddens, A. (1984). *The constitution of society: Outline of the theory of structuration*. Los Angeles, CA: University of California Press.

Grint, K. (2000). *The arts of leadership*. Oxford: Oxford University Press.

Gronn, P. (2000). Distributed properties: A new architecture for leadership. *Educational Management Administration and Leadership*, 28, 317–338.

Hunter, S. T., Bedell-Avers, K. E., & Mumford, M. D. (2007). The typical leadership study: Assumptions, implications, and potential remedies. *The Leadership Quarterly*, 18(5), 435–446.

Jackson, B., & Parry, K. (2011). *A very short, fairly interesting and reasonably cheap book about studying leadership* (2nd ed.). London, UK: Sage.

Khurana, R. (2007). *From higher aims to hired hands: The social transformation of American business schools and the unfulfilled promise of management education*. Princeton, NJ: Princeton University Press.

Ladkin, D. (2010). *Rethinking leadership: A new look at old leadership questions*. Cheltenham, UK: Edward Elgar.

Parker, M. (2002). *Against management: Organization in the age of managerialism*. Oxford: Polity.

Pearce, C. L., & Sims, H. P. (2000). Shared leadership: Toward a multi-level theory of leadership. In M. Beyerlein (Ed.), *Advances in interdisciplinary studies of work teams* (Vol. 7, pp. 115–139). London: Emerald.

Sinclair, A. (2007). *Leadership for the disillusioned: Moving beyond myths and heroes to leading that liberates*. Crows Nest, NSW: Allen & Unwin.

Sirén, C., Patel, P. C., & Wincent, J. (2016). How do harmonious passion and obsessive passion moderate the influence of a CEO's change-oriented leadership on company performance? *The Leadership Quarterly*, 27(4), 653–670.

Spoelstra, S. (2013). Leadership studies: Out of business. In J. Lemmergaard & S. M. Muhr (Eds.), *Critical perspectives on leadership: Emotion, toxicity and dysfunction* (pp. 171–182). Cheltenham, UK: Edward Elgar.

Spoelstra, S., Butler, N., & Delaney, H. (2016). Never let an academic crisis go to waste: Leadership studies in the wake of journal retractions. *Leadership*, 12(4), 383–397.

Tourish, D. (2015). Some announcements, reaffirming the critical ethos of leadership, and what we look for in submissions. *Leadership*, 11(2), 135–141.

Willmott, H. (2011). Journal list fetishism and the perversion of scholarship: Reactivity and the ABS list. *Organization*, 18(4), 429–442.

Wilson, S. (2016). *Thinking differently about leadership: A critical history of leadership studies*. Cheltenham, UK: Edward Elgar.

# Index